Johnston and Robson Mill History
New Hope Creek
(Orange Co., N.C.)

Stewart Dunaway

Johnston and Robson Mill History

Version 3 – August 16, 2010

© All rights reserved 2010

ISBN – 978-0-557-12754-2

WWW.LULU.COM/sedunaway

Table of Contents

Introduction 6
    THE JOHNSTON FAMILY OF ORANGE COUNTY. 7
        Hillsboro Exodus 12
    JOHNSTON/ROBSON MILL - TIME-LINE 13
    MILL OPERATION TIME LINE 13
    LOCATIONS 14

The Mill Story Begins - 1793 21
    MILL SITE 22
    MILL BUILDING 23
        Wheel Well 27
    MILL RACE 31
        Millwright Commentary 39
    DAM 40
    HOUSE SITE 46
    HOME OR AN ORDINARY? 57

George Johnston Sells Mill to William and Edward Robson - 1811 61
    ROBSON FAMILY 61
        1783-1859 61
        1860 – 1870 (Civil War) 62
        1870-1880 62
        1880-19xx 62
        Edward Robson (mystery man) 64
        Robson Family Tree 65
        Robson Family Cemetery 66
        Slaves 69

George Johnston Erects a Saw Mill on New Hope - 1820 73
    SEARCH FOR THE SAW MILL 76

William Robson vs. George Johnston Law Suit - 1823 81
    JOHNSTON – RUFFIN LETTER - 1823 97
    ROBSON APPEALS - 1823 103
    FINAL JUDGMENT OF THE APPEAL - 1825 104

George Johnston Sells land – 1821 to 1826 105
    GEORGE JOHNSTON LAND INFORMATION 106

William Robson and - New Hope Land – 1825-1833 108
    WILLIAM ROBSON GIVES THE ESTATE TO HIS SONS – 1862-1867 108

    William Robson Land Information 108
    Mill Site Transition to Duke Forest 110
        Robson to Sharp and Tate (1873) *110*
        Sharp & Tate to Robert M. Dickson (1913) *110*
        Dickson to Erwin Cotton Mill Corp (1925) *111*
        Erwin Cotton Mill Corp. *112*

Key Locations 114
    Mason Spring 114
    Babs Branch 119
    Adjacent Land 126

Turkey Farm Road Mill Survey (Charles W. Johnston Mill) 128
    The Mill Remnants 130
        Dam...... .... *135*
    Mill Foundation 142
    Mill Race 144
    Other Features 146
    Aerial Images – Transition (1938, 1955, 1975, 2003) 150

Modern and other Johnston Land Transactions 154
    Miscellaneous Deed Tables 155

Deed Transcripts 157
    Modern Deed Info 170

Plats related to the Deed Transcripts 171
    Caswell Grant, to Blackwood to Johnston 171
    Plat 3/73 174
    Plat 5/472 174
    Plat 5/472 175
    Plat 10/65 176
    Plat 6/156 177
    Plat 5/488 178
    Plat Book – 3/37 - 1940 179
    Plat Book - 83/145 181
    Plat Book – 83/166 182
    Allen Plat (Land grant) on New Hope Creek 185
    Courtney Plat (New Hope Creek) 186
        Courtney Survey – and plat *189*
    Richard Caswell Deed – Plat 192
    William Blackwood – Granville Grant – Buffalo Creek – 1754 195
    William Blackwood – Granville Grant – Haw River - 1754 198

CHARLES JOHNSTON – LAND GRANT..201

Appendix A – Johnston Family Cemetery..**204**

Appendix B – George Johnston Estate Papers...**208**

Charles Johnston Response – 1833..*209*

George M. Johnston Responds - 1834..*212*

Thomas Johnston Responds..*217*

Deposition of Andrew Burns...*225*

Deposition of Alexander Gattis..*226*

Deposition of Archibald Brockwell...*228*

Deposition of Daniel Booker..*231*

Deposition of Joseph Kirkland..*232*

Deposition of Thomas D. Watt...*234*

Deposition of William Duskin..*236*

Appendix C – Charles W. Johnston Estate Papers..**239**

References and Notes **251**

REFERENCES 252

Index..**253**

Introduction

In my efforts to transcribe records in the North Carolina Archives (Raleigh), I found mill petitions filed (by county) under miscellaneous. Without going into a very lengthy review of why there were petitions, let me simply state that it was a requirement to petition the County courts to dam up a river for a mill. This was required in order to prevent interactions of mills on the same river, as well as the surrounding landowners when the mill pond was formed, from the dam. In fact, the 2 acre mill pond was an early form of imminent domain. If you owned land on both sides of a river, then no need to condemn the land, however, a petition still had to be filed. If the land was not owned on the other side, then the other owner (across the stream) had his land condemned (based on a court hearing), and he received payment from the mill owner (fair market value of the land). These petitions establish the general date (year) in which a mill was established. The mill owner had one year in which to erect a mill upon filing a petition. It is even possible they forgo the erection based on numerous reasons, so the petition does not guarantee the mill was established. As time moved forward, and the population increased, mills increased in quantity as well. This would ultimately lead to confrontations between mill owners, and land owners. Flooding is the primary problem, when the mill owner increases the dam height. This caused law suits to be filed. These legal matters were included in the mill petition files. It was this exact issue that prompted my research into this mill seat. George Johnston Sr., and his son George Jr. were sued by William Robson.

Today, two mills on New Hope Creek are identified by two differing names, that being, Johnston's Mill, and Robson's Mill. One mill is preserved (Land Conservatory) to the west of Turkey Farm Road, called the "Old Johnston Mill". The Duke Forest mill is called (today) the "Robson Mill". The deed records are easy to follow for the "Robson Mill", which was the old George Johnston Mill of 1793 (confused yet?), which Johnston would sell to William Robson (1811). As history moves forward, William Robson would pass the mill, and surrounding land on to his son J.W. Robson. Let's take a look at what the remnants have to show us in the 21st century about these two sites.

This book is written in chronological order. I think this is the best way to follow the history in order to learn which mill came from whom.

Special thanks to Charles "Chuck" W. Johnston taking the time to visit with me (June 2009), and share family information. Chuck is a direct descendant of the Johnston family, residing in Durham. The family still owns some land from the original New Hope Plantation.

Thanks to David Southern (Orange Co. Historian expert) who continued to assist, when possible. Also thanks to the very kind, and supportive personal at Duke Forest (Judson, and Marissa).

Stewart

The Johnston Family of Orange County.

This book was not written to provide detailed genealogy information. However, in order to understand who owned the mill site, and their descendants, some basic genealogy is necessary. It is interesting the name George was used for many years, and then Charles became the most common given name. As anyone who deals in genealogy will know, having four George Johnston's around, can add to confusion over who is who! The book, *The Gentle Johnstons and their Kin* by Henry Poellnitz Johnston was my source (Orange Co. Public Library, and NC State Genealogy Library). I will refer to this book as the "Johnston Family Book".

Here is a very rudimental family tree. This book will focus on George Sr., George M. (Jr.), and then follow Charles W. II, and Charles W. III, then ending with James Martin Johnston.

- Charles Wilson Johnston (b. 1725 – d. 1789)
- Martha Blackwood (b. 1754, D. 1790)
    - George Johnston (b. 2/20/1762, d. 11/4/1830)
    - Mary Mulholland
        - Martha (Married Gray Huckabee)
        - Charles Wilson b.1798 (married Lydia Cabe)
            - Charles Wilson b.1839, d.1916 (married Agnes)
                - Samuel Cabe (1877-1917)
                - Charles Hughes (1882-1929)
                - Joseph Henry (1889-1918 WWI death)
                - James Martin (wills the home estate, and Mill on Turkey Farm Rd)
                - John Thomas (unmarried)
            - John Cabe (1833-1856)
            - Thomas
            - George Wilson (1823-1828)
        - George M. Johnston (married Elizabeth Bond – Gov. Thomas Burke relative)
            - George Doherty Johnston (AL)
                - George Burke Johnston (AL – inherits Gov. Burkes pocket watch)
        - Thomas M. Johnston b.1802 (marries Eliz Ann Moore)
        - Mary Jane b.1803 (marries William Duskin)
        - Elizabeth b.1805 (marries Thomas King)
        - Sarah Bowman b. 1807 (marries James Sloan)

According to the Johnston family book, these early pioneers landed, and settled in the Hawfields. However, it gets rather difficult to follow where in this massive area of the Hawfields they resided in. In fact, reading their history book it really makes it sound like New Hope is the eastern edge of the Hawfields, although I don't agree. Never the less, the Orange County history begins with Charles Johnston, and his first son, George

Johnston Sr, as I will entitle him. He is the owner of the early mill on New Hope Creek. Before leaving Hawfield, it should be noted there are a few land transactions by a George Johnston in the Hawfield area. This is NOT the George Johnston (married to the Blackwood family) but the "second" George Johnston that was alive, and residing in the Hawfiled community (married to McNair).

According to the Johnston Family book, Charles Wilson Johnston, and his wife Martha Blackwood move to the New Hope area – leaving the Hawfield locale. In addition, this book states that George Johnston (who I refer to as George Sr.) was born in a house named – Green Hill. This infers that Green Hill was not built by George Sr., but by his dad (Charles W.). George Sr., was the only boy born to Charles. W., and Martha Blackwood, and inherits all the land of Charles. Charles W. Johnston's will (Orange County Will Book – B, pg.74-77) June 9, 1789 states that *"all my real estate that I now own…"* goes to him. Everything else is to his daughters, via son-in-laws. It is assumed Charles dies in this same year (1789). His burial location is unknown.

Thanks to some newspaper articles (Chuck Johnston visit) I was able to understand the "homestead" or home sites better. There are two home sites. One home site was a log cabin at the corner of Whitfield road, and SR #86, which was removed during the construction of I-40. This was Charles W. Johnston's home site, and could date into the 175x-178x era. This house (pictured here on the left) was known as the "Red House" which was painted red for many years.

Old Johnstone Home North Of Chapel Hill

> **Estate Papers – A possible treasure chest**
>
> *In the NC State Archives, filed by each county, are a number of boxes that contain original estate papers. These papers are filed during deaths, where estates need to be settled via legal proceedings. Some estates are contested by siblings or other relatives. Here is where land can be subdivided or other legal discussions can take place. George Johnston's estate papers will provide insight to so much of his last days, and how the land gets divided I HIGHLY RECOMMEND THE READER GOES TO APPENDIX B and read this section before reading on!*

The second house was located off of Turkey Farm Road, just north of Whitfield Rd. It was called "Green Hill" (pictured below). This is the home site where the "George Johnston Family" cemetery resided, until it was removed. In one newspaper (assume Chapel Hill Newspaper – article was written by Robbie Hooker – no date) article it stated, *"…Miss Hattie Blackwood, historian of the New Hope Church, a royal grant was made to Charles Johnston in 1756. His son, George, born in 1762 built the house that is not standing. He passed the home place on to his son, Charles Wilson, when he died in 1830. The house was thus apparently built sometime in the decades immediately preceding 1800. A. L. Honeycutt Jr., Restoration Specialist with the Department of Archives and History in Raleigh, has inspected the house on three occasions and pinpoints the date in the third quarter century…"* The article continued by saying they had no idea when George Johnston came to this particular area. However, based on deed research, we now have the time-frame (1784). My guess would be that, Green Hill home was built 1784-1799. The sign, outside the new location of Green Hill states circa 1750. I do not agree. Maybe the old log cabin was built in 1750 era, but certainly not Green Hill.

Based on another newspaper article (penciled date on the copy was 12/3/67), the house was to be moved, due to a recent purchase of the land for a commercial business called Fiber Industries. The house was bought by Mr. Coman, and was relocated to land on the corner of SR #70, and Lawrence Drive. It was in this time period (1966-67) in which the family cemetery was moved to New Hope Church cemetery.

George states in a letter to Judge Ruffin, that he fought in the Revolutionary War. In their family history book it states that George served under Gen Greene. Yet, that is rather broad, but possibly true, in that, Gen Greene commanded the Southern Campaign, which covered the time-period from, 1780-1783. George did not file a pension. George starts to buy land in the 1780's where this land adjoins his relatives land, William Blackwood. This will be the core land holdings of the general New Hope area.

George gives his land to his kids, before he dies. George M., and his brother Charles M., will be the main land holders, and will keep the home estate in the Johnston family for many more generations. In fact, Charles M. Johnston's son, Charles W. will keep the home estate, and then his son, James M. will finally pass it on to the 20th century.

Below is the 1938 aerial image of the Plantation (Green Hill) west of Turkey Farm Road.

Below, is a 1955 aerial photograph of the Charles Johnston plantation where the house "Green Hill" resided, before being relocated.

Hillsboro Exodus

It is an amazing story of the exodus of Hillsborough residents to the state of Alabama. It warrants a history book unto itself. I was aware of this transition via my research of Gov. Thomas Burke. His daughter (never married) moved to Perry Co., Alabama in the 1830's. It seemed as if everyone in town was told, "come on down". This now includes (in my research) some of the Johnston family members, and their relatives.

Gov Burke dies (early on in his life), his wife remarried; a Rev. War soldier, George Dougherty. George knew Thomas Burke. George Dougherty, and Mary Wilson Burke (widow) have two girls. George too, dies prematurely. These two girls marry David Yarborough, and George Bond. Bond's daughter (Elizabeth) marries George M. Johnston. THEY move to Alabama. There are MANY families that uproot, and move to Perry County, and other counties in Alabama. I read a number of letters from the Johnston's (Johnston family history book) which discuss all their friends in Perry County, and how it was like old home. Land was cheap, weather fine, and the outlook on their investments, and making money was outstanding.

Gray Huckabee, who married George Johnston's eldest daughter, moved to Perry Co, and died there in 1877. Thomas M. Johnston moved to Greensboro (AL) along with George M. in the 1832-34 time periods. Thomas M. Johnston dies in Hale Co. AL in 1869.

Some historians think the mass exodus was over slavery issues. In all the letters I have read (1820-1840 time periods - Burke, Johnston, Bond, Yarborough etc.) I have not seen this discussion, or any "sour" view of Hillsboro. All I read were the great opportunities this part of Alabama provided (primarily inexpensive land).

The Johnston family in Alabama inherits a number of very old articles from Gov. Thomas Burke that I would not have imagined. In one list it stated an old valuable family photo album, stamp/crest of Burke, and Burkes "gold Revolutionary pocket watch"(Amazing).

The Johnston's, which remain in Orange County, continue to reside in the same area. It is interesting to note that in the Will of Charles W. Johnston (dated 1912) he stated, 1.5 acre of land was preserved for the burial of the colored, and if they didn't use it, then the burial ground would revert back to the children. This cemetery is located about 25 yards north of Whitfield Road where the power line easement crosses (north side).

Note: Complete history of Governor Thomas Burke can be found in the only book written about this great man's life (*The Complete History of Thomas Burke*) by this author.

Johnston/Robson Mill - Time-line

1784 – George Johnston Sr. buys two pieces of land from John Young (457 acres) on New Hope Creek

1792 – George Johnston Sr. buys another tract of land on New Hope (520 acres) from David Meredith.

1793 – George petitions for erecting a mill on New Hope Creek

1795-1797 – George continues to amass New Hope Creek land from Allen, Courtney, Blackwood and NC Land grants. (over 1000 acres).

1811 – George sells his grist and merchant mill to Robson with 143 acres of surrounding land.

1820 – January 15/17, George Johnston started erecting a saw mill on New Hope.

1820 – May 20, William Robson buys 2 acres (1.5a) of land from William Blackwood.

1823 – Robson sues George Johnston (Johnston's "saw mill" becomes the issue) flooding Robson's 1.5 acres.

1825 – George Johnston Sr./Jr. – Not guilty. Robson looses his appeal.

1830 – George Johnston Sr. Dies (Nov 4) – Age 68

1831 – George M. Johnston marries Elizabeth Bond (related to Gov. Thomas Burke inherits his pocket watch)

1842 – John Robson – son of William dies (June 28).

1862 – William Robson sells the mill and land to his son J. W. Robson

1863 – William Robson sells more New Hope land to his son (300 acres)

1867 – William Robson sells his last holding to his son on New Hope (281 acres)

1871 – April 4, William Robson dies – age 88.

1872 – February 7, Ann Robson – Wife of William Robson dies – age 77.

1873 – J. W. Robson sells the **12 acre mill site** tract to Robert H. Sharp and John L. Tate.

1874 – Robert H. Sharp sells his half interest in the mill to George W. Tate (John L. Tate's dad)

1882 – J. W. Robson is deceased and his wife Mary sells the **Robson Homestead** to James Blacknall

1905 – James Blacknall sells the **Robson Homestead** to Frank Couch

1913 – J.L Tate has to liquidate the **12 acre mill site** holding due to estate settlement – Robert Dickson buys it.

1925 – Robert Dickson (single) sells the **12 acre mill site** tract to Erwin Cotton Mill Corp.

1925 – Frank Couch sells the **Robson Homestead** to Erwin Cotton Mill Corp

1926 – Erwin Cotton Mill Corp. sells **12 acre mill site** & **Robson Homestead** mill and 12 other tracts of land for $100 to Duke University.

Mill Operation Time Line

1793 – 1811 – George Johnston (18 years of operation)

1811 – 1873 – William Robson/James W. Robson (62 years of operation)

1873 – 1913 – Sharp and Tate (40 years of operation)

Locations

Before diving into the details, here are some maps, and aerial images, that assist in describing the location of these two mill seats. New Hope Creek meanders through Orange County (south east of Hillsborough) which ultimately crosses into Durham County. There are a number of mill seats on this river.

The Johnston Mill, as it is known today, was preserved, and opened to the public in 2001, thanks to the effort of the "*Triangle Land Conservancy*". This park (Johnston Mill Nature Preserve) has a nature trail that passes the mill remnants, and other areas of this old plantation. The USGS map (below) shows the location of the Johnston Mill, and the Robson Mill. The Robson mill site was preserved via the Duke Forest program, which acquired this property from Erwin Cotton Mill Corp, (Durham Co. Corporation) in 1926. In fact, Erwin Cotton Mill Corp sold 13 tracts (86/181) of land totaling 839.14 acres for $100 to Duke University.

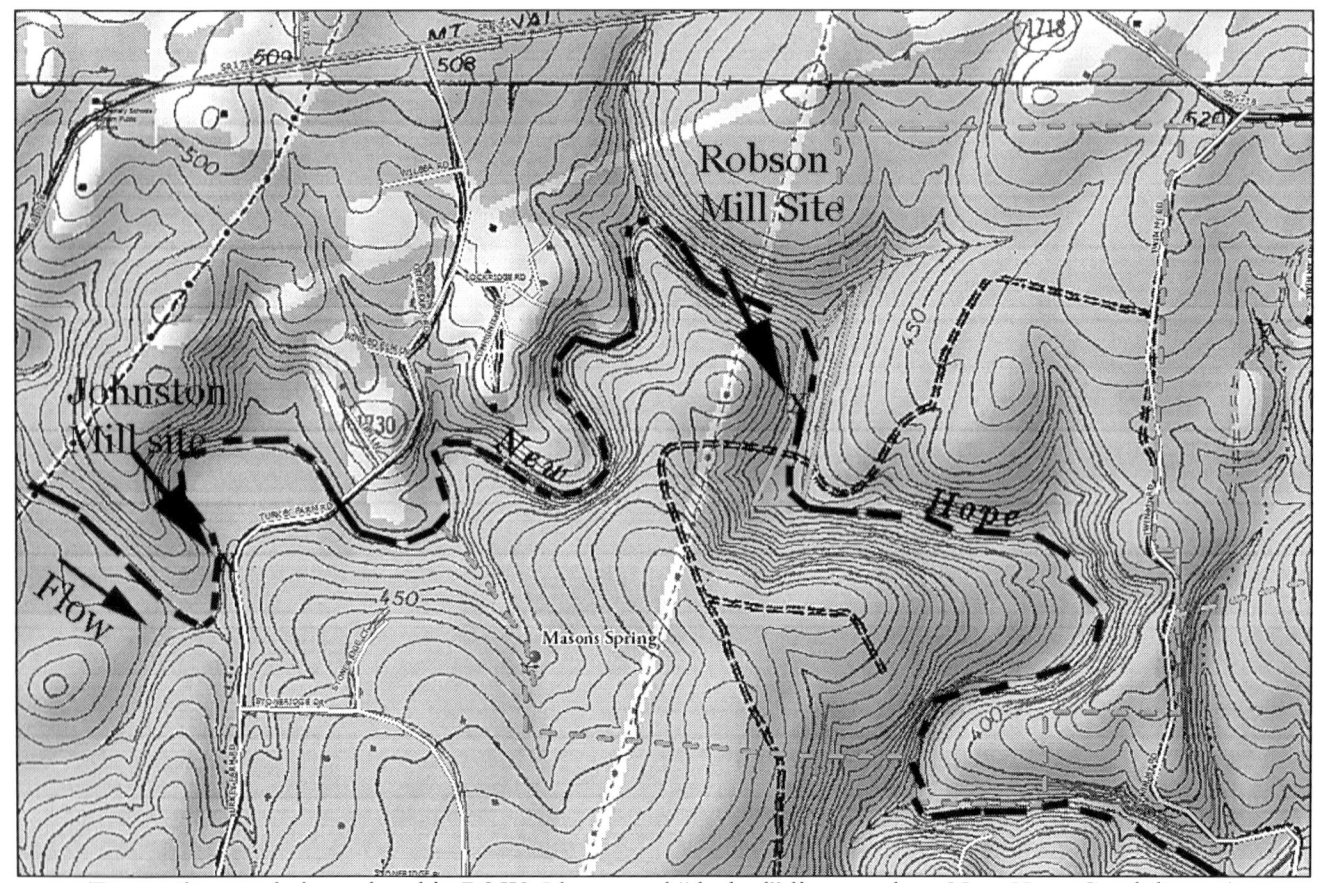

(Due to the map being printed in B&W, I have used "dashed" lines to show New Hope Creek better.)

Here is the 1938 image of the Robson land, and mill seat. Interesting to note the power-line right-of-way existing in 1938.

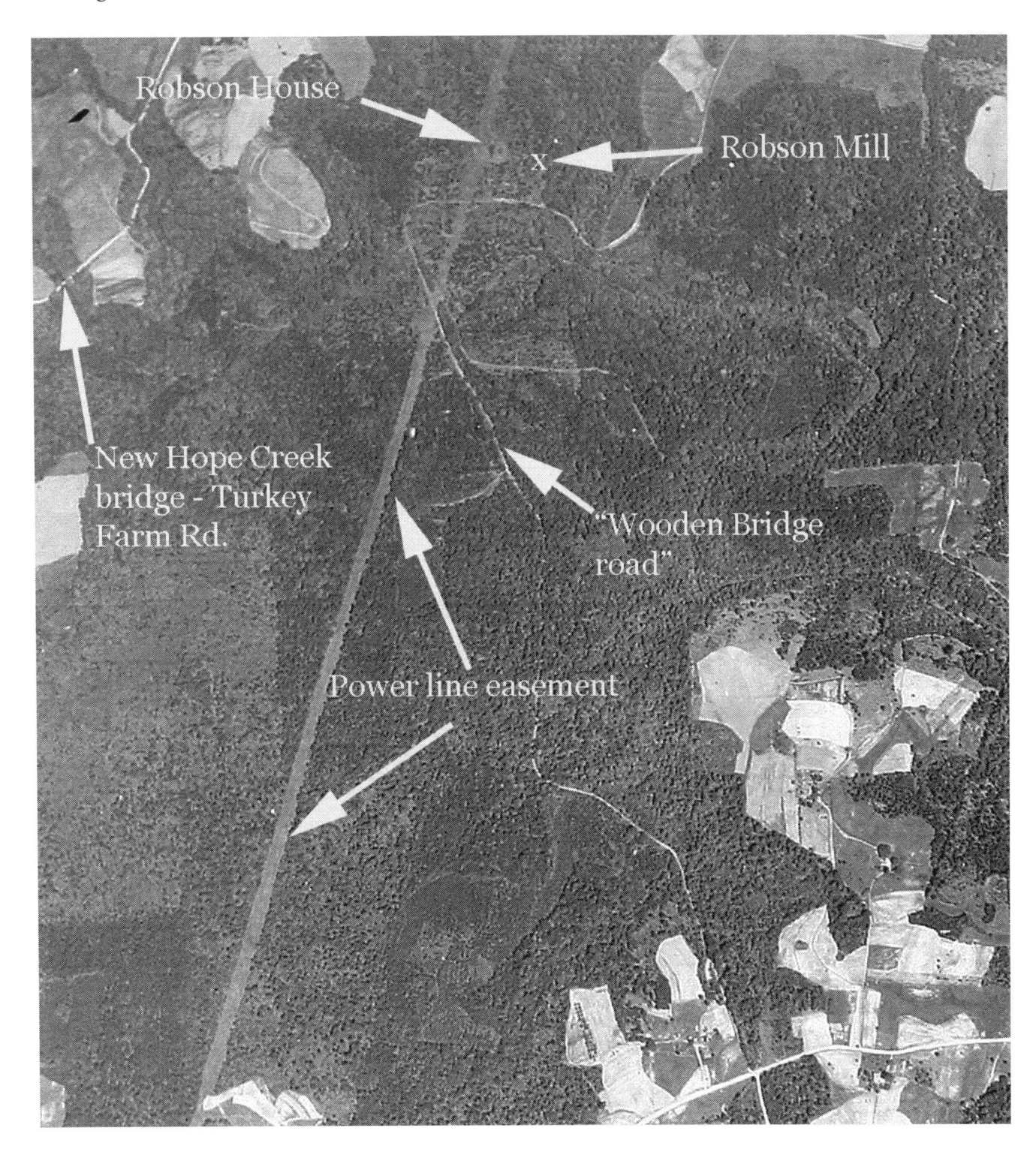

Moving to the modern time, the GIS image shown below illustrates the Johnston Mill seat off of Turkey Farm Road.

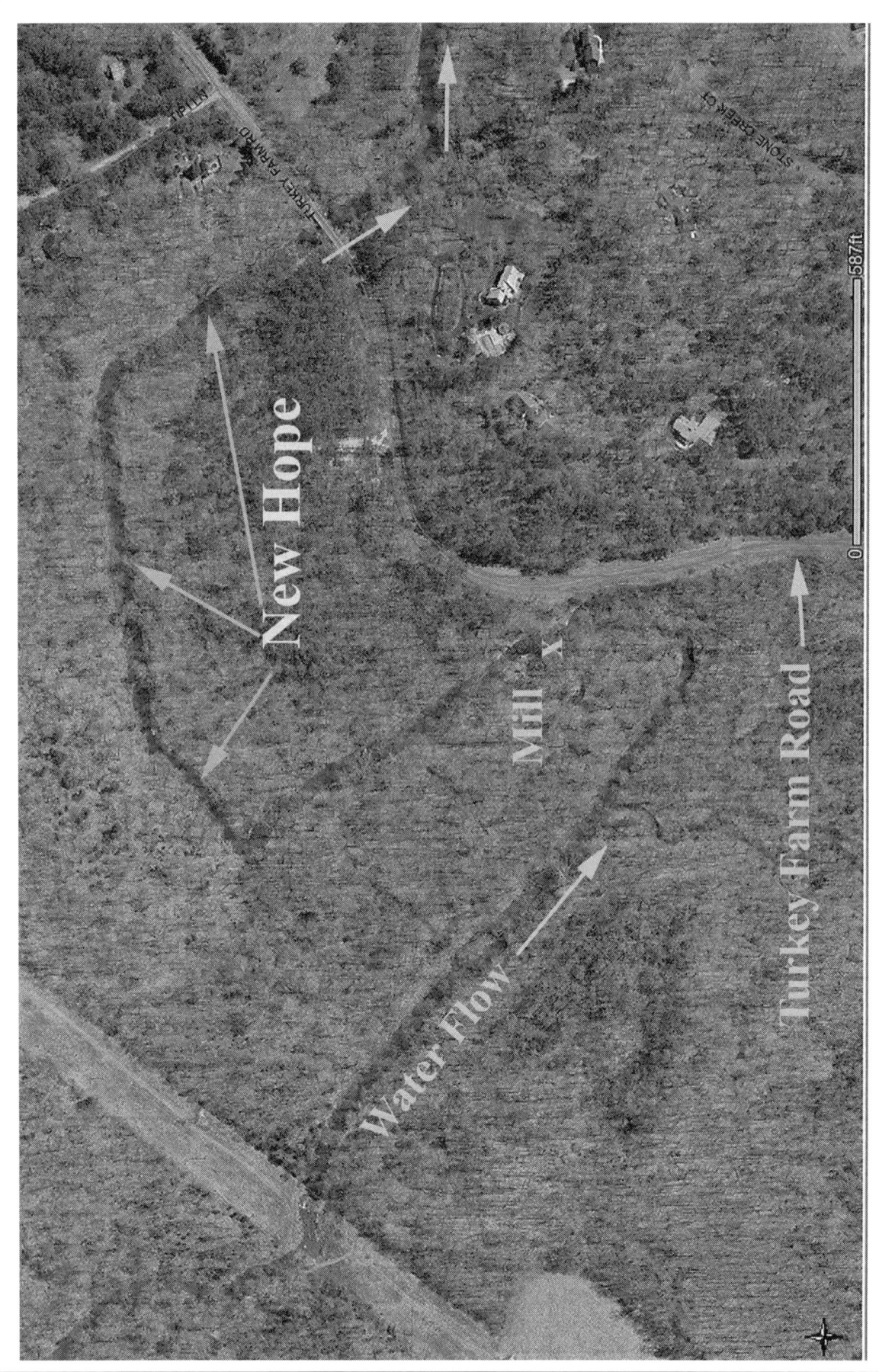

Here is the 1938 Aerial photo of the same area. Note that New Hope Creek goes around the area that looks like a field. The "x" marks the mill area. Note what looks like a road near the mill site.

Here is a close up of the Robson Mill tract. I have included notes on the "M" mill site, and "H" for the possible home site of the Robson's. A dedicated section on the home site is give later on.

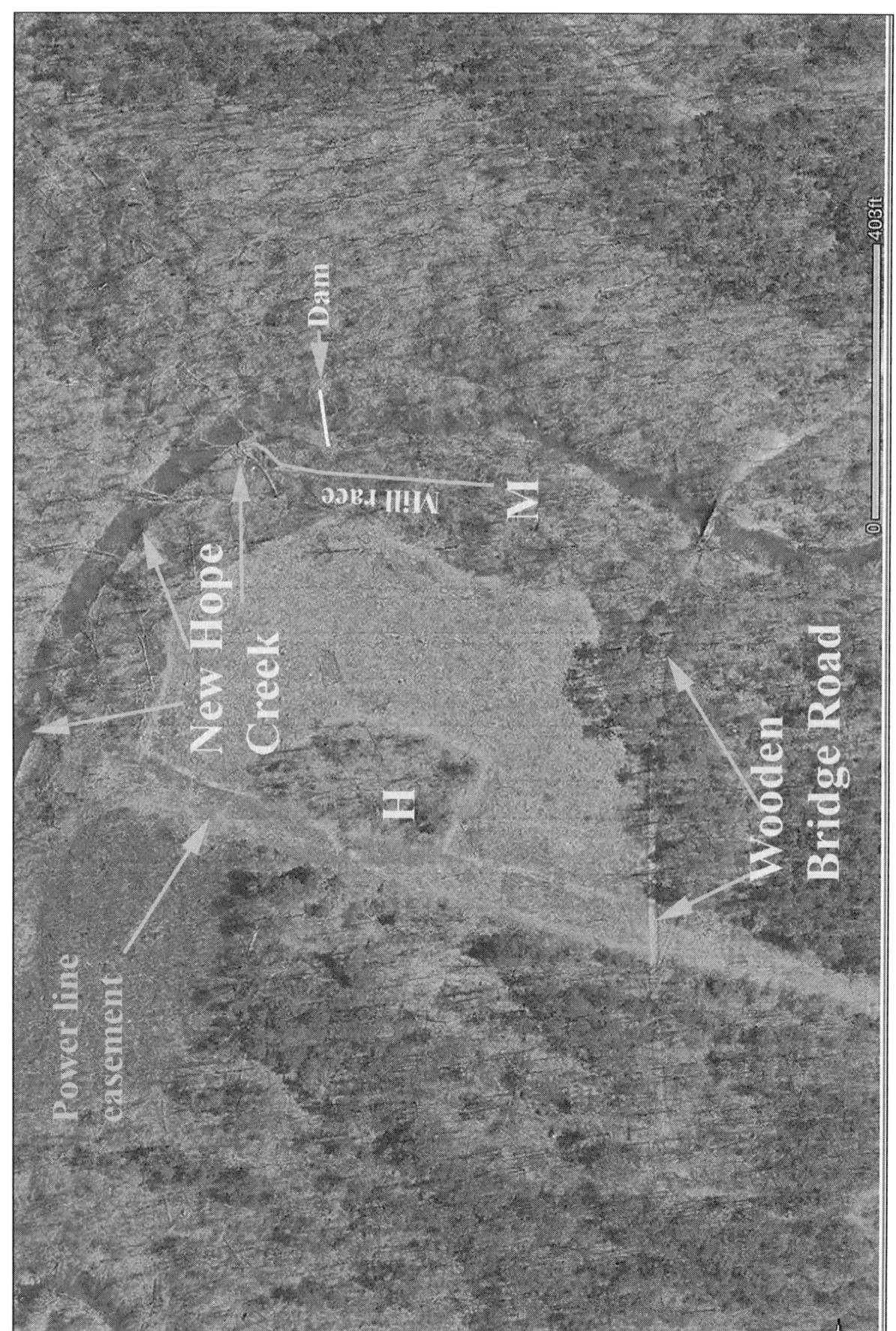

18

Here is the Orange County Soil Survey of 1918. The roads are somewhat different when comparing to the 1938 aerials. However, the locations, and possible house site, is interesting to note (or ponder).

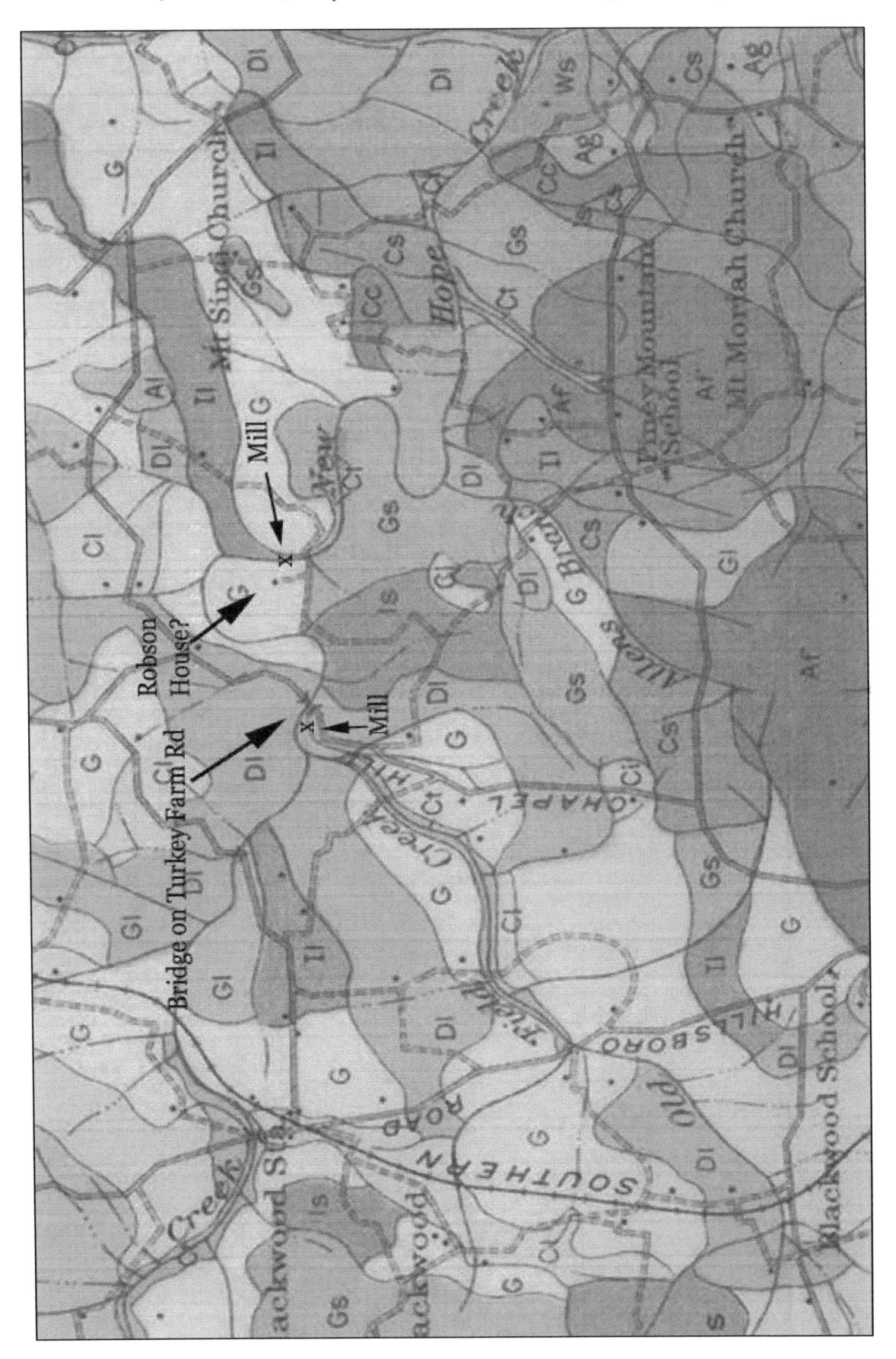

Here is the plat from a deed book. It shows Babs Branch, and the location of Masons Spring! It also shows the 12 acres mill tract.

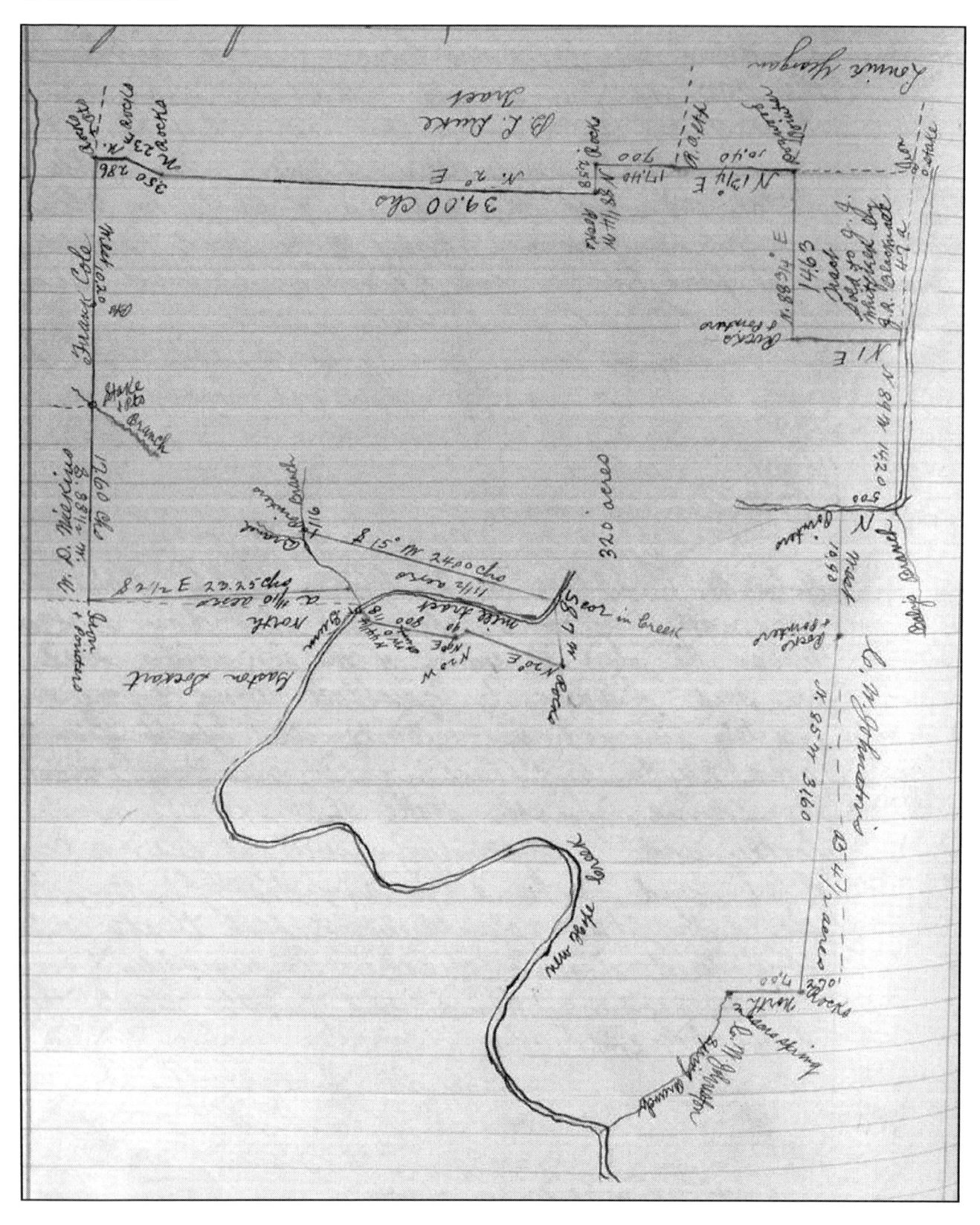

The Mill Story Begins - 1793

May 28, 1793, George Johnston Sr. petitions Orange County Court to erect a mill on the waters of New Hope. *"To the Worshipful Court of Orange County…whereas your petitioner hath an intention of building a mill on the waters of New Hope and the lands being my own therefore prays your worships to grant me an order to erect a mill on said premises and your petitioner as in duty…"*

What is unfortunate, we don't have any operational information about this mill. In fact, the only information beyond the petition is the sale of this mill, and some surrounding land to William Robson in 1811. In the deed it states, *"…both a merchant mill and grist mill…"*. This deed included 143 acres of land, and was sold to Edward, and William Robson, for $3,500. (See Deed 14/367) According to the book *Water Rights Determination – An Engineering Standpoint* (Jay Whitman – 1918) he states, **"The distinction between grist and merchant mills has many times been recognized in contracts and deeds…build a merchant flouring mill for grinding and packing flour as is usual in what is called a merchant mill…(Recorded Jul 23, 1828…)…"**
Here we see that Johnston defined it as both, in the simple ability to grind meal, and the more involved process of providing flour (bolting cloth etc.). Let's take a look at this "merchant and grist mill" that George built, by looking over the ruins that remain to this day.

Mill Site

This site is located on the Duke Forest property, and the gravel road accessing this section is called "The Wooden Bridge Road". A short 1 mile hike will take you to the wooden bridge that crosses New Hope Creek. Leaving this road you will follow a trail (called Primitive Nature Trail) along the river. On your left, you will start to see stone embankments. Pictured below is one such embankment. In one of the surveys of the mill tract, it mentions the "old stone wall", which is shown here.

Mill Building

After traveling the path (just 235 feet) on your left you will see more stone walls. This time, it's the mill foundation. It was amazing to me, how accurate the measurements turned out. That said, in some places it will be clearly seen where the foundation has settled, and shifted. This is what caused some of the measurements to vary from wall to wall (or side to side, front to back). It is difficult to tell (without a real site dig/excavation) to ascertain if the front of the foundation was opened (as we see it today) or just general human interaction with the ruins.

Here is a view from near the where the water wheel would have been (foreground), showing the back wall (right), and one of the side walls. On the left is part of the wall facing New Hope Creek.

The east wall is not complete, as mentioned earlier, maybe this was a door way. Although, today, you enter the mill foundation via the stream path, I do not believe this was the location of access during the time-period this mill was in operation. Yet, I could not find a well defined roadbed from any location. Clearly, the stream would have flooded its banks and you could not be driving wagon in that area.

Facing the back of the foundation, the wall was obviously "cut into" the ground, so this would eliminate any location for egress but that may have been accomplished via stairs (inside). Never the less, the ground behind the foundation has another stone wall, which I assume was placed there to ensure stability of the upward sloping land. Maybe it was erected to divert water (from rain) from running down into the mill building. Below this area, the corner of the foundation is intact, and the joint is an amazing piece of mason artistry.

The next interesting aspect of this area, was the intersection of the mill "race way" to the mill, and the wheel well. Shown here is the location of the raceway as it flows to a 90 degree bend, and then along side the mill. In addition, the raceway, as it falls from the raceway to the wheel well is a rather steep drop…and will be shown in more detail further on. Note the wall, and corner is damaged on this side of the mill building foundation.

Corner detail shown here.

Wheel Well

As the water plummets from the mill race, it will strike the wheel. It is certainly probable, that a wooden plume (or chute), would have channeled the water in order to strike the water wheel at the top, or at the middle. An overshot wheel was well known as the most efficient means to operate a water grist mill. Next (efficient) would be a breast wheel, which would channel the water to the middle of the wheel. Last, but least efficient, was the undershot wheel, in which water simply passed underneath the wheel. *I believe this was an over-shot wheel configuration.*

Also note the settling at this part of the foundation as well as the stone embankments surrounding this part of the mill structure. Certainly, they would not allow a large flow of water directly against clay or soil, or erosion would have been too great. Therefore, stone embankments were installed. Still visible are some of the stone embankments which were strategically placed, as opposed to some natural stone being present during excavation.

Here is a view standing in the raceway from the top looking in the direction of the water flow. Annotated was one particular tree (Sweet Gum) which is rather old, and certainly was present during the mid to late 1800's.

The point of this picture (left) was to illustrate the location of this very old tree in line of the outflow of the wheel well. My first look would assume it was in-line with the wheel well, but this is not true. It was clearly to the right, and out of the way of the outflow (if this was the direction – or straight course to New Hope Creek).

Pictured below, is the stone wall showing that sides were developed in order to prevent erosion from the wheel well. Although the wheel well varied in width, the distance between the mill foundation (wall), and this stone wall-embankment would be fairly accurate, as to the original width (approximately 6 feet wide).

Unfortunately, it is difficult to follow the outflow canal from the wheel well to the river. From the very back of the stone embankment of the wheel well to the end of the well defined canal is 31 feet long. The more I studied the ground (at this 31 foot location) it is possible the canal *may have* turned, as opposed to continuing straight to the river. If it continued straight, it would have easily intersected the river, which is as at my back when taking this picture, although an additional 53 feet away. All of the land in this general vicinity looks to be subject to river flooding which is possibly why the canal is "buried", and not visible.

Once again, proper excavation or archeological dig would answer this question.

As to the river flooding the mill site, it is interesting to see two tiers of stone work near the mill foundation. Moving from the mill towards the river, there is one tier at 18 feet, and the second tier at 37 feet, with the river being 76 feet from the mill foundation. It appears they knew the river could flood, and provided some general land excavation as well as stone work to protect from that situation.

Mill Race

The mill race transports the water from the mill pond (behind the dam) to the water wheel. From the remnants found, the mill race is over 350 feet long. As it meets the mill wheel, there is a significant drop in elevation. This will increase the force of the water as it strikes the wheel. It is deduced that this was an overshot mill, due to the high elevation of the raceway. This is the most efficient, and it also required elevation so the water can strike the wheel at its apex. The total fall from the bottom of the mill race to the bottom of the wheel well was 8 feet (8'- 6" to be exact). It is possible this height could infer a 10 foot wheel.

The wheel well would house the water that falls from the wheel, but the water would then flow away from the wheel well back into New Hope Creek. As the water wheel spins, obviously there will be currents, and churning of water, thus the stone reinforcement in the banks of the wall's in this area of the construction.

Pictured on the right, is a view from the top of the mill race looking towards the wheel well, due east towards the river (New Hope).

Here is a little more detail of where the water from the mill race would flow onto the wheel. Since there is erosion from the elements over time, the foundation wall is missing, and makes it a little difficult to view this area. Then again, being open you can view the details of the race, and the stone embankments that were placed at this part of the well.

Below is the view of the mill race looking towards the dam, or (approximately) north. The western wall (on the left) was always much higher, and the eastern wall (to your right) was lower in height. It seems that, excavation material from the mill race was piled up onto the right hand side, as it was cut out of the naturally sloping hill towards your left.

Here is my site survey drawing showing the location of the river, race, and mill foundation. I also measured the top of the mill race (eastern side) embankment to verify width. Without a surveyor, as near as can be determined, the mill race is straight (line of sight), then the river makes a slow turn towards the race entrance.

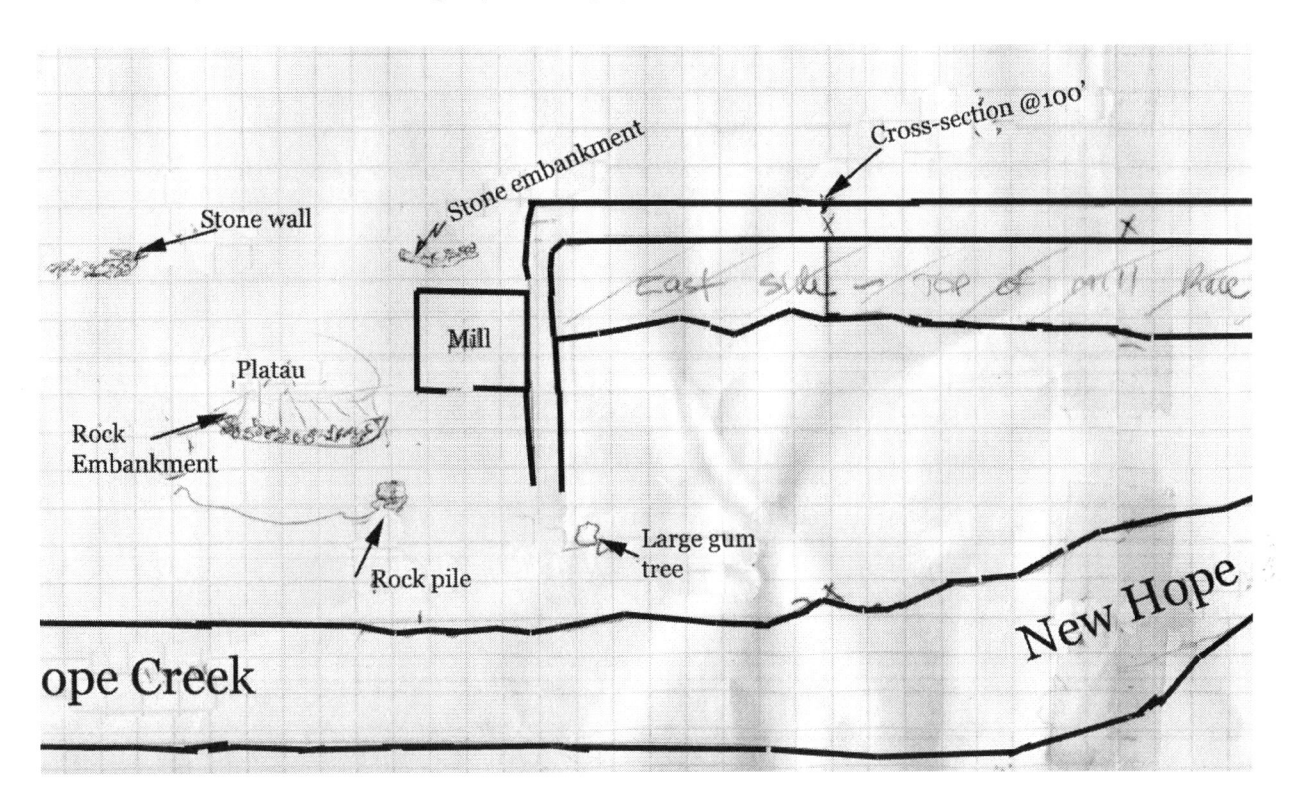

Here are the GPS markings of the mill race. The way-points were made typically under 17-20 +/- feet accuracy (per the GPS).

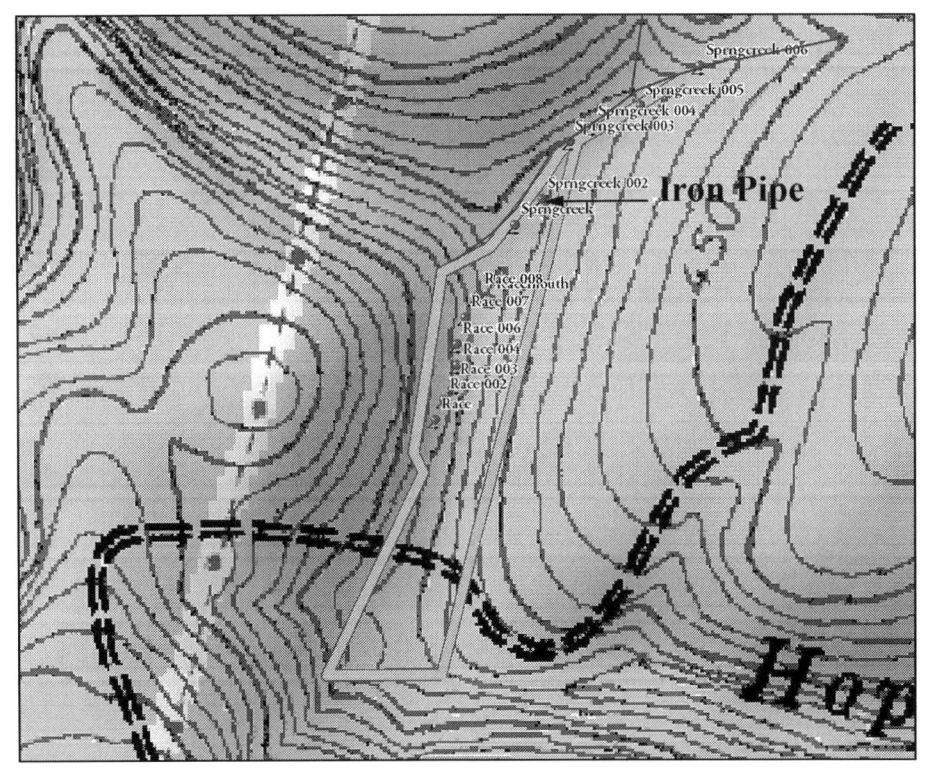

Even the sides of the race had stone embankments to protect from erosion. This was found in one particular area, and no other locations were spotted. Yet, the race itself (in a number of locations) had a number of very large boulders or rock outcroppings that must have been uncovered during excavation. As to whether this was blasted is difficult to tell. I did *not* see any drilling or tooling marks on the exposed surfaces. Also note the steepness of the bank on the left side as to height, and steepness. Again, clearly the natural lay (fall or slope) of the land.

Measurements were made at two locations, detailing the shape and steepness of the race at 100 feet, and 300 feet down the race.

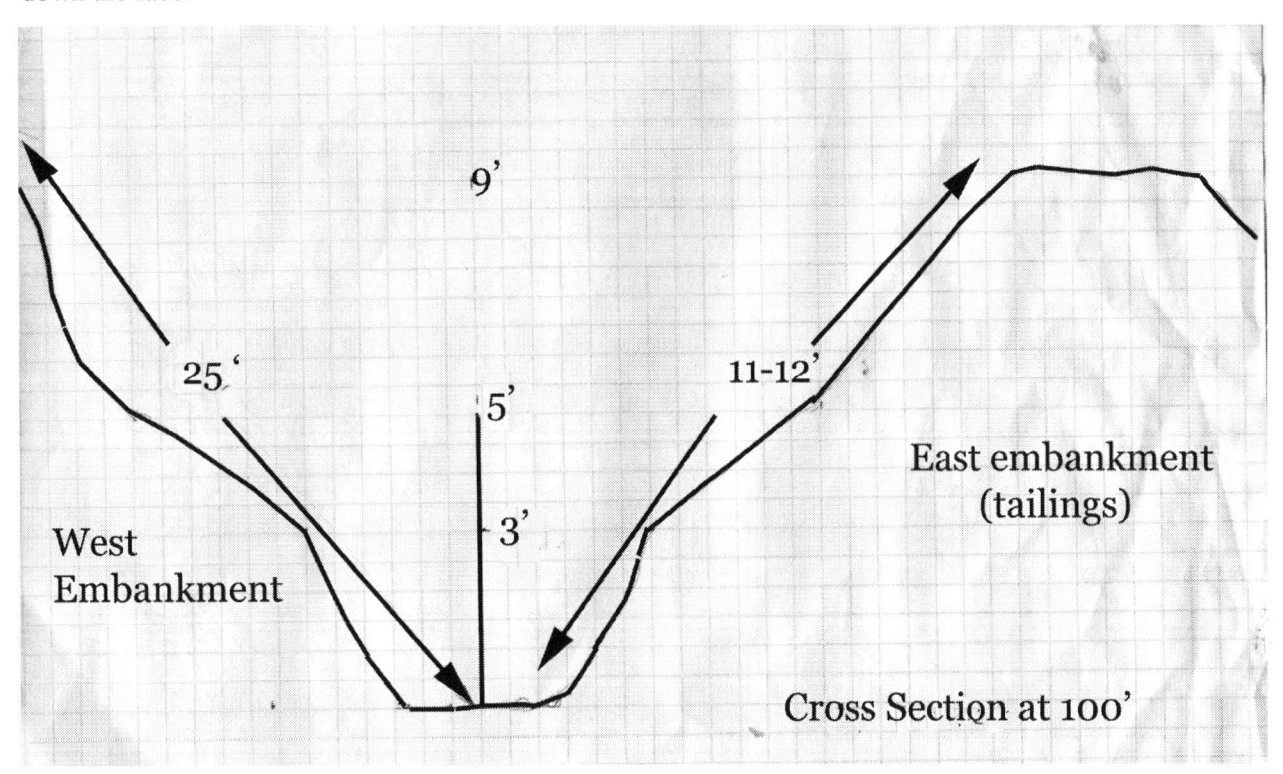

Cross Section at 100'

West Embankment — 25'
9'
11-12'
5'
3'
East embankment (tailings)

Towards the end of the race, the walls were getting shallower and the breadth of the race flatter, less "V" shaped. This was probably due to the drop of the race in elevation. As the race near the beginning (at the mill pond) would have a slope downward, as it flowed towards the mill (wheel). I think the design was also to go from a broad or wide race, and then make it narrower as it got closer to the mill.

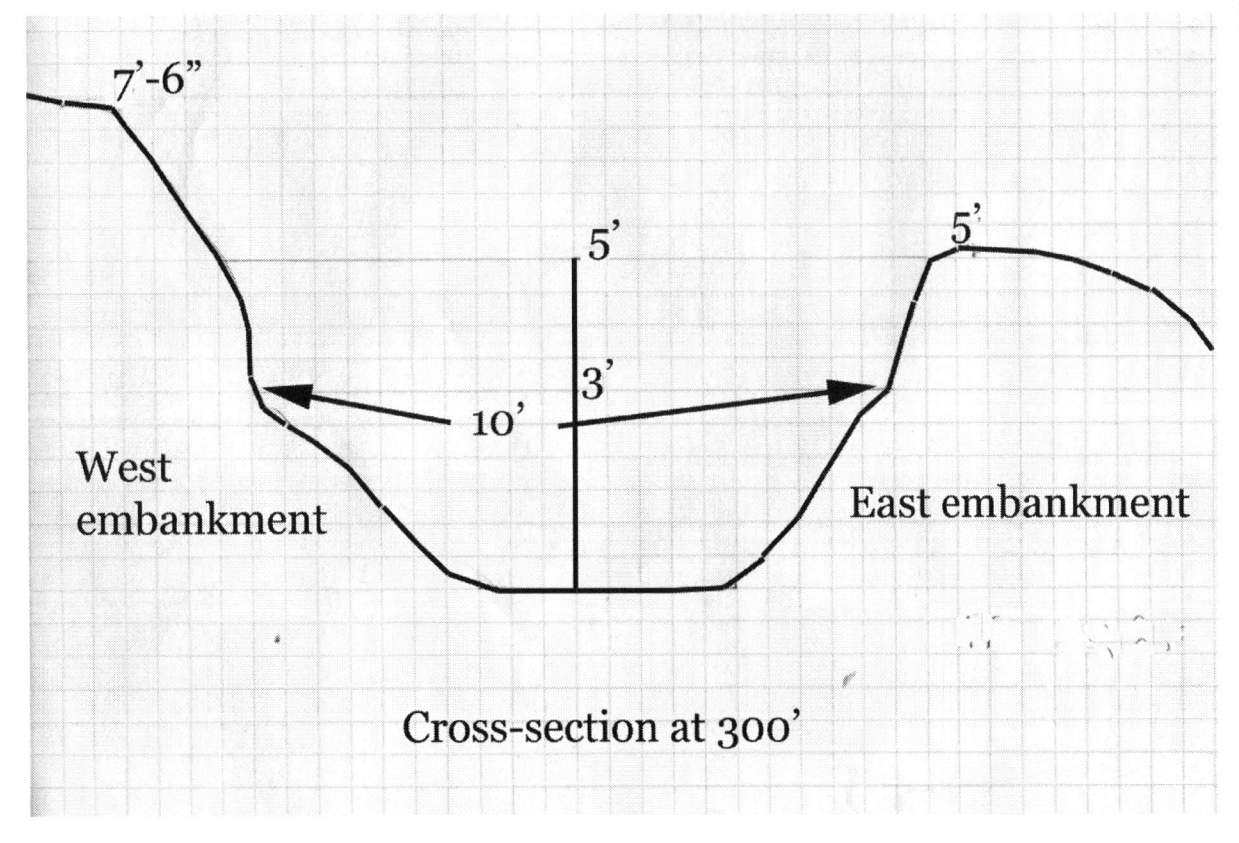

Cross-section at 300'

7'-6"
5'
5'
10'
3'
West embankment
East embankment

Here is an image at the 300 foot mark, looking back towards the mill (south) with my back to the entrance of the race from the mill pond.

Here is a view at the 100 foot mark. There were rock (boulders) exposed in the mill race from the sides, which looked to be rather large, although naturally projecting (as apposed to falling in place from erosion). This is a negative attribute to a mill race, since it would impact the flow (if this was not a modern erosion remnant).

The top of the mill race bank, the part that was on the eastern side, or probably "tailings" was very flat. It typically held a 20 to 30 foot width. I digitally altered this photo to remove trees, limbs etc., to expose the flatness of the ground.

Here is another altered photo looking towards the river (due east) illustrating the elevation difference between the race height, and the river (New Hope Creek is barely visible in the background).

At the end of the race, or the beginning (entrance) the race makes (approximately) a 45 degree bend towards the river, or what would be the mill pond. Although my arrows are pointing towards the race entrance, the actual water flow would be in the reverse direction.

Here is a view of my site survey as the race finally makes the bend into the mill pond. Here you can see the relationship between the mouth of the race, and the mill pond, versus the dam location. The dam is located about 80 feet below the entrance of the race. The opening of the race into the pond is heavily damaged, and a lot of fallen timber in the mouth. It is very difficult to determine its original form.

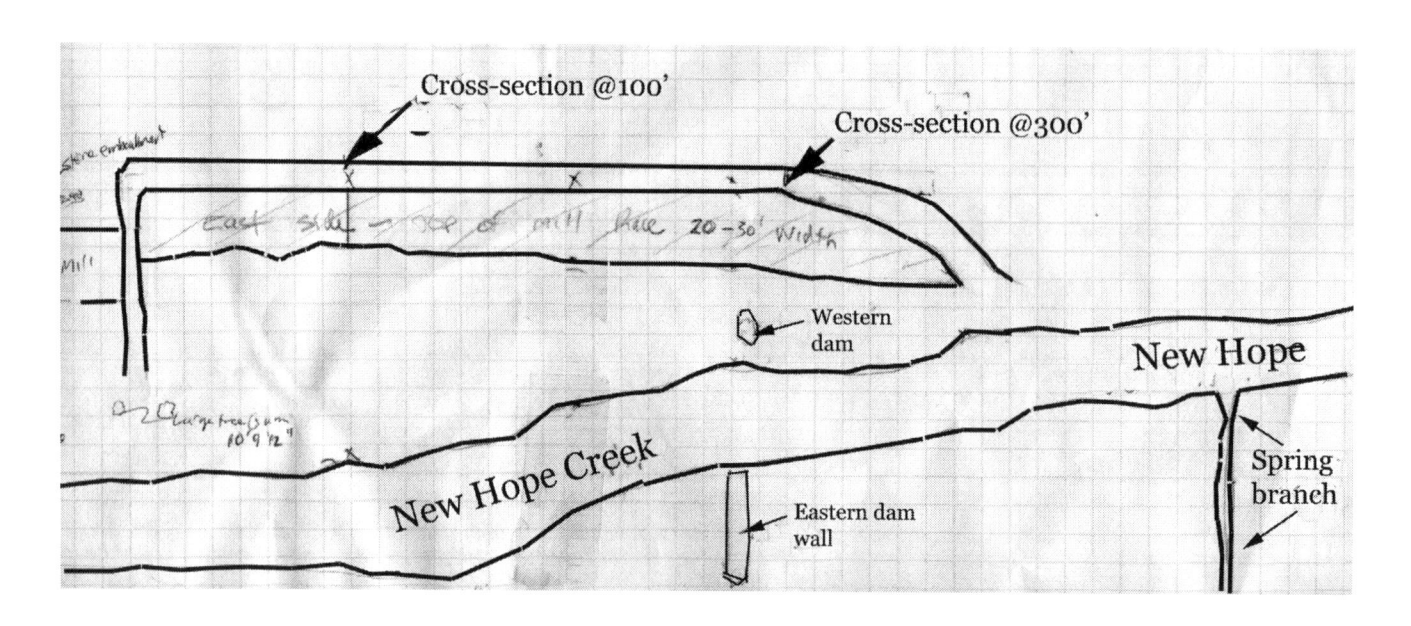

Millwright Commentary

The Millwright Handbook (*The Young Millwright and Millers Guide - 1860*) states the area of the canal should remain the same. Depth was not the focus, but area. "*Much expense may be oftentimes saved, by making the canal deep where it cannot easily be made wide enough, and wide where it cannot easily be made sufficiently deep.*" Of course he points out that depth (being too shallow) has some restriction during low water, so don't design a very shallow, although very wide canal.

Another discussion about mill races in *Leffel's Construction of Mill Dams – 1881*, it stated the material of the race, that being sand or clay, was an important concern. In addition, this book documents, the steepness of the walls of the race could be greater for clay (than sand, for example).

The mill race channels a volume of water, and the cross section that was measured is used to calculate the volume of water that can be transported to the mill wheel. This volume is necessary to know, in order to match the water demand from the mill. In a certain sense, the calculation of "horsepower" requirements, start from the size of the millstone. The average millstone is 4 feet (diameter), followed by a 5, and a 6 foot stone. In addition, some mills could house more than one stone. It is deduced, from the size of the foundation, this is a one millstone operation. Adding to the assumptions, it is presumed a 4 foot stone was utilized. Once the stone size is calculated, then the wheel size, and type will be calculated, in coordination with the amount of water that can be offered to the wheel.

The millwright handbook recommends 1 to 2 feet per second velocity (flow) in a canal (race), and he makes another point about velocity, "*…but the slower the better, as there will be the less fall loss…*". He also states, "*…As to the size and fall necessary to convey any quantity of water required to a mill, I do not find any rule laid down for either.*" He finally documents that his observations were, "*….I conclude that about 3 inches to 100 yards will be sufficient, if the canal be long, but more will be requisite if it be short…*" Finally he ends with this comment, "*…for the shallower the water, the greater must be the velocity, and the more fall is required.*"

Based on the 100 foot cross section of the raceway, a 3 foot depth would allow 12.75 sq feet, and with a 1.5 foot per second flow (velocity) a calculated 19 feet per second (flow) is obtained. Using the typical 2 acre mill pond, and the dam being approximately 6 feet high, the volume of water in the pond is 522,720 cubic feet. Based on typical mill demands (somewhere between a 4 to 5 foot millstone, and an overshot wheel) 16 cubic feet of water per second, the mill can operate 9 hours. Of course the flow of the river should be replenishing the pond as the water is being used. However, this illustrates the reason for a mill pond, and more importantly, the height of the dam. In addition, the ability to raise the height of the dam would extend mill operation. True to the point, adding one additional foot in height to this configuration, would add 1.5 more hours to the operation. The other aspect would be to increase the millstone size, or increase the operation to multiple stones, and this would demand a larger mill pond. In addition the mill pond would fill up with silt, thus lessening the volume it held. Thus the common increase in the dam height over time (for most mill sites) which tended to cause ramifications to land upstream (e.g. flooding).

Dam

This mill seat utilized a stone dam. There are many dam types (even in the 18th century) that could have been used. In the book, *The Millers Millwrights and Engineers Guide* by Pallett (1866) he states, *"A rock dam I believe to be the best in use, if there is sufficient rock near for building materials, and with a rock bottom to the stream."* He continues, *"By building a rock-dam, if properly managed, it will be perfectly tight. I would recommend you to use a large rock as you conveniently can move; building this wall from four to six feet thick, according to the length of the dam, with jams or buttresses every place where they are needed to strengthen it. I would make true joints to these rocks, especially on the ends, so that they may join closely together."* Not to quote the whole chapter, but he provides a lot of common sense insight to mill operations. He also makes two other points about the dam, *"Mill-dams entail a heavy expense in keeping them in repair, when not constructed properly, or when poor materials are used. When building a dam, you should select the most suitable place. If you can, conveniently, place it across the stream, near a rock bluff, so that the ends of the dam may run into the bluff. This will prevent the water from running by at the ends of the dam."* In this chapter on dams, he ends with this comment about the mill, *"I would not recommend any mill to be built close to the stream of water, for this reason: they are in danger of being carried away by heavy floods. Besides, by digging a race, you can build them where they are easy to be got at, giving better roads, with plenty of room."* Road access to and from the mill (hauling of goods), is an interesting aspect (without 4-wheel drive), if they were to navigate along a stream bed.

The picture on the right illustrates the "cross-section" of the stone dam. The river-side of the dam is earthen as it slopes down towards the rivers level. Of course without seeing the dam, and the mill in operation, it is difficult to know the exact design.

The purpose of a dam is to raise the water (in the river) height behind it, causing a pond to be formed. The term is called "ponding" of the river. The mill pond becomes a reservoir of water, which the mill race channels off towards the wheel. The mill pond turns a rapid flowing river into a (somewhat) stagnant pool. This allows the silt, and debris to settle. If the water wheel was directly in the river, and a dead tree was to float down the stream in a heavy rain storm, it could damage or destroy the wheel.

When the river hits the pond, it produces some resistance to the flow. Never the less, the excess water will flow over the dam, and continue down the river. The pond remains at a constant level. However, this can be altered by raising the dam height. This in turn increases the pond size. Depending on surrounding land, this could flood or damage neighboring land, and the primary cause of all law suits that I have transcribed (generally speaking).

Therefore, the raceway enters the pond at some location mid-way or a third of the way back from the dam. This allows floating debris to bypass the mill race, and either flow over the dam, or get "hung-up" at the dam (and eventually removed). At this site, the entrance of the mill race was 80 feet up-stream from the dam. In this picture below (standing in the center of New Hope), the remnant stones of the dam are shown on the left, and right hand side. It appears the dam was erected on an angle, and not perpendicular to the rivers edge.

For some reason, the dam stone work on the western side of the river was more or less destroyed. Yet, as shown in this picture, you can see some of the stone work as it intersected the raceway embankment. However, that was not true for the eastern shore of New Hope.

Here is a picture (below) that shows the stonework for the dam on the eastern side. Clearly the stone work is well preserved, and required fording the stream to see it in person.

As illustrated in this photograph, the dam (remnants) is rather high, although the ground was not very level, thus it varied in height. Due to the silt build-up, erosion over the many years, it will be difficult to say what the actual dam height was. Never the less, the 46 foot long stone work was impressive to see.

This photograph shows the intersection of the dam into the bank of the surround land. This is a rather hilly location. It is very unique, in that, as you go further upstream, towards the pond, the land flattens out, and almost like a field. Clearly, this mill seat was properly located.

Mill location to the Duke Forest trail – which is known as the "wooden bridge road".

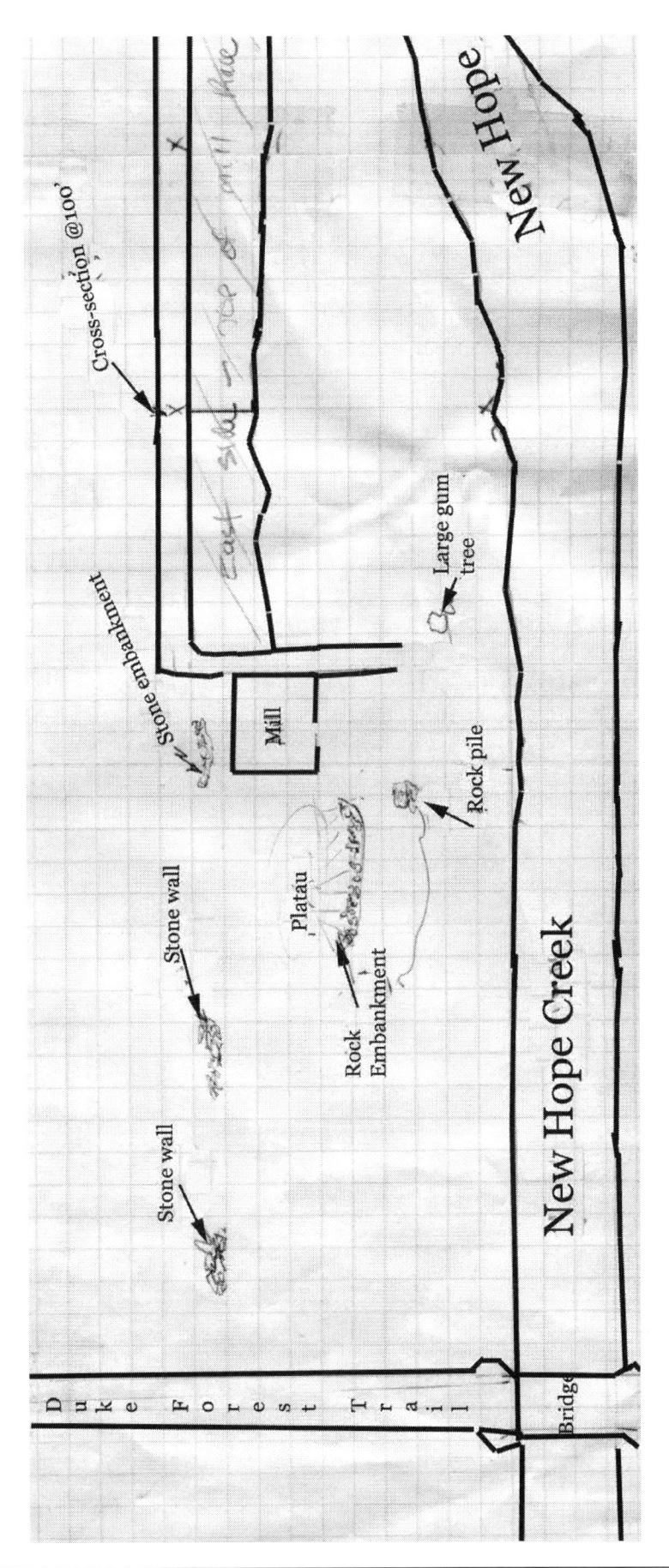

House Site

Not much information was found about the Robson home location, except for ruins, and remains that identify the home site. However, the family cemetery was very helpful in identifying this as Robson's Plantation. Even in the 1930's the home site was disturbed by the power line right-of-way as it was cut, and clearly visible in the 1938 aerial photograph. Yet, it looks as if some of the home or outbuilding remained as annotated here. It is difficult to tell what exactly this area was, other than it seems to be cleared or grass/field, and two objects appear. Also to the right is a bright white object, which is also unidentifiable.

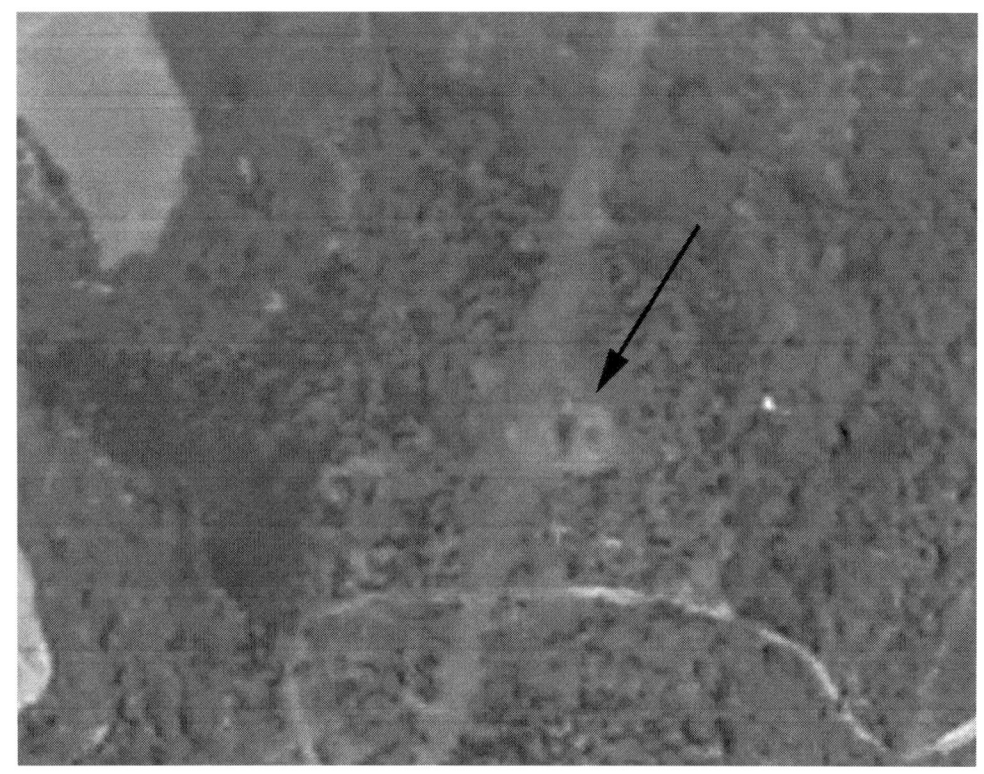

The modern visible image (GIS image) shows this same general area was forested, and the same (island looking) area was left alone. Why? A short walk from the gravel road to this area revealed a possible house site. Even across the power-lines was another stone wall area that seemed to be part of the "plantation". Only a detailed archeological dig will answer the question, and possibly establish dates.

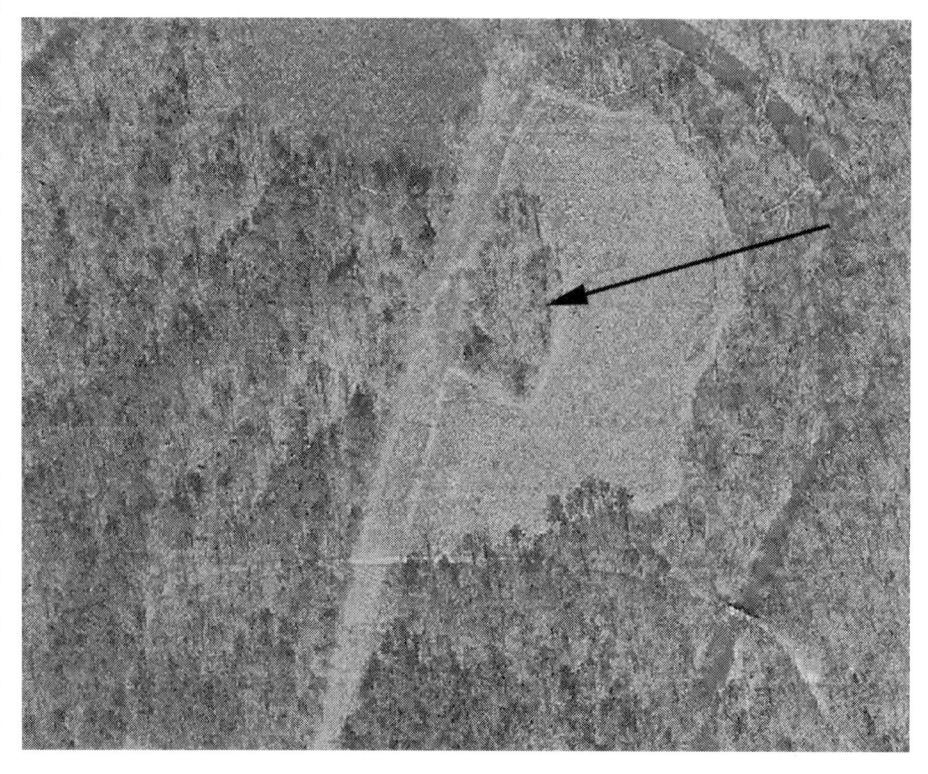

Today, the forested area is now grownup with young pine trees, and is virtually impossible to hike through, due to vines, briars, and the like. The GPS

46

coordinates show that this "home site" is very close, and directly west of the mill. If you could walk it, it would be a rather easy (and short) trip to the mill from the house.

Digressing a little, the road (Wooden Bridge Road) that is provided for hikers to follow, near the entrance, the old roadbed is visible on your left. It will remain that side, until a clearing (on your left) disturbs the bed. Due to this clearing, I was unable to follow its route, nor can you located it again. I assume, the old road merges with "Wooden Bridge Road". When you come to another road on your right, kept up by Duke Forest, the old road bed appears (again, now on your right), and even stone walls are not visible. As you follow it, it is cut-in-half by the power easement as shown in the map below. Crossing the power easement, you can easily find the roadbed, as well as the signature stone walls, and embankments as the old road way continues towards the "90 degree" bend. It is at this point in which the old road bed *splits* - as shown in the GPS waypoints below. One roadbed heads towards Robson's homestead, and the other heads for the mill site. However, on the way, near the river, another house foundation becomes apparent.

The map below is labeled with many landmarks. Also note that I have altered the USGS map by removing part of the "modern" gravel road because the map became too busy, and I wanted to illustrate the old road heading towards the mill. Thanks to my visit with the Duke Forest staff, I re-visited the site to ensure this is accurately marked. Both "house ruins" have a chimney pile (remnants) that is easily visible.

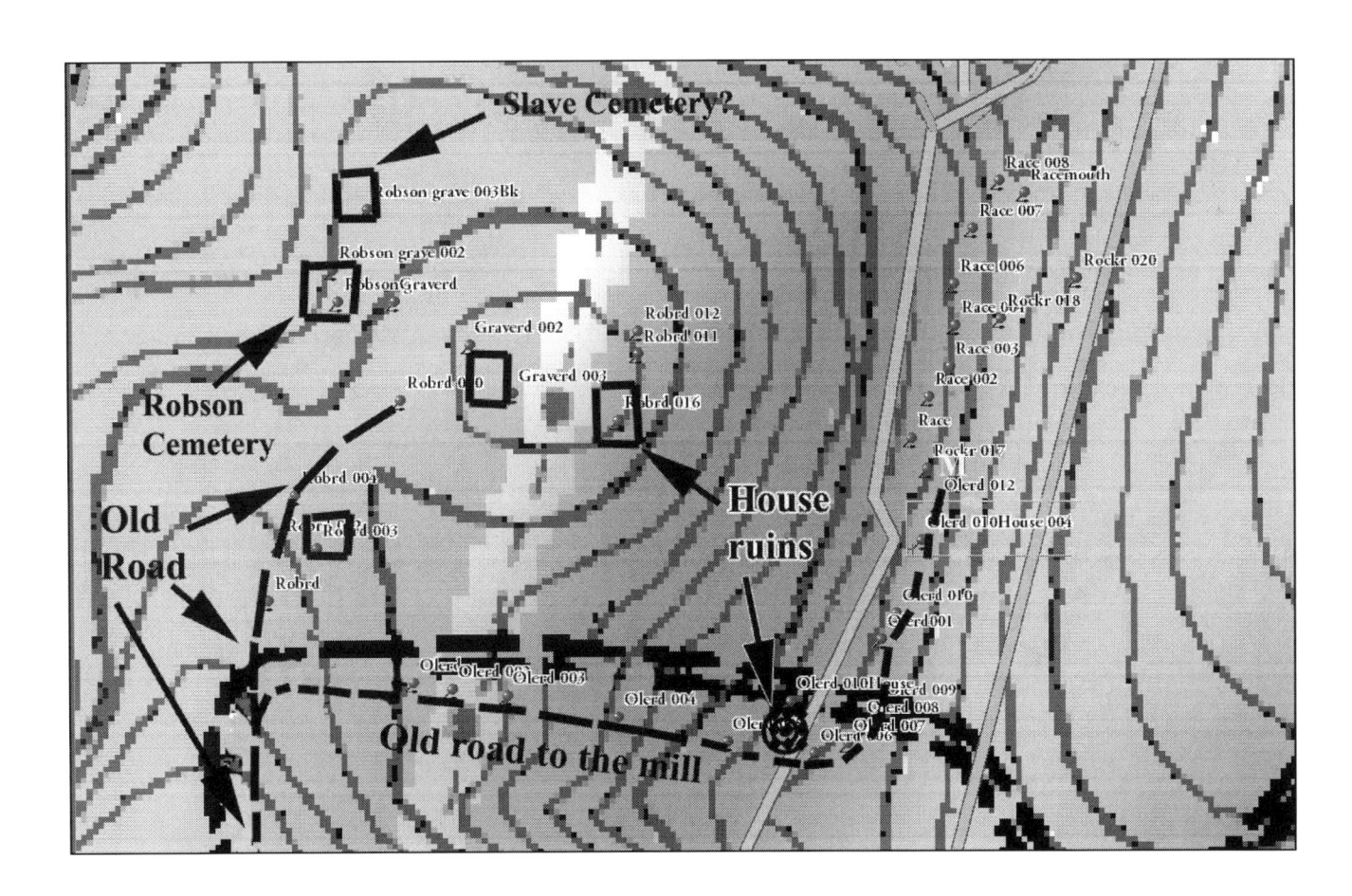

For a short distance, the roadbed (as it crosses the "Wooden Bridge Road") is easy to follow, mainly from Robson's continual use of stone walls (fence). Then you run upon a stone foundation that has a lot of downed trees from either the hurricane or the ice storm of years past. It is difficult to walk, hike or measure. Trees were down everywhere you looked. The road becomes very difficult to find in this mess. There are a series of survey stakes (1/2" pipe) that were followed, but it seemed to head off into the wrong direction, as the waypoints will show. Retracing my direction, the road bed was located, thus moving in an easterly direction, the power-line easement, was easily seen. Another stone wall/foundation on the edge of this easement was apparent. Directly across from this stoned area is the house (or whatever it is) foundation. Of course you have to cross the power-line easement.

Here is a piece of the wall that winds around the property. This will be found at the mill, the house area, and along the roadway.

Although not as high as the prior image, the wall can be seen along the old roadbed. This image was taken from the old roadbed, facing the gravel hiking road, and just prior to the power-line easement. If you don't look into the woods, you will never know this roadway follows the gravel road.

Not easily seen, is this foundation just off the gravel road, and prior to the power-line easement. Toppled with trees, a chainsaw would be the first tool required to expose the area clearly.

Note the numerous downed trees.

This area seems to be another building foundation, as opposed to being a property wall or fence. However, due to the downed trees this site is difficult to discern as to its purpose. It's possible this was a barn, just before the house. If this area was thoroughly cleaned, proper archeological work could document what this location was used for.

Once across the power-line easement you enter into a grassy area. Immediately this "pit" catches you eye. The depth in the center of this pit is 4 feet measured in the middle (10 feet in from the side). At one end is a pile of stones that look like a chimney. There are bricks visible in this area. Part of the stone foundation has been left alone, and is intact, shown below.

Is this a chimney? Maybe this was a large smoke house. Since this "pile of stone" is rather broad, I measured it to be about 8 feet thick, but that is taking into consideration that debris (stone) is spreading out as it is falling down. Never the less, call it a 19 foot wide, and 8 foot deep pile of stone (with some brick, and metal lodged around).

It is at this location (only) that brick appears. Everywhere else, only stones are apparent.

As you can see, metal, and other debris are seen in this area. More, and more brick.

Towards the back of this area, I found another wall or "fence".

A nice view of both mill sites, and the general area from 1938.

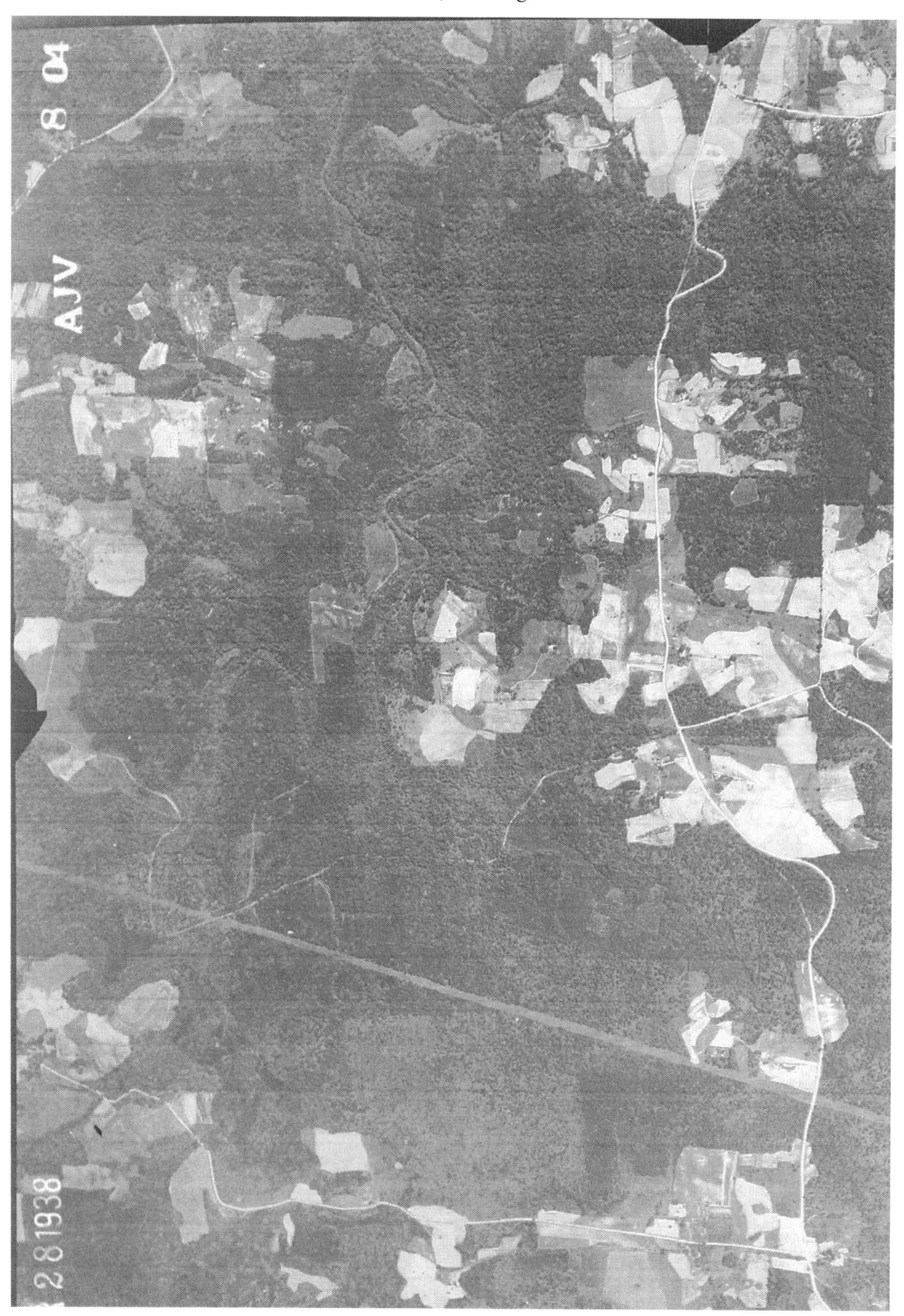

Home or an Ordinary?

As mentioned earlier, there is another chimney ruin on the old roadbed that meanders down to the mill. This old road bed is easily followed from the power lines nearing the bend in Wooden Bridge Road. The road bed then splits. One heads straight across Wooden Bridge Road (not bending to the right), which leads to the homestead. The other bends to the right, almost parallel with the bend with Wooden Bridge Road and basically follows it down (down in elevation) as it heads towards the bridge across New Hope Creek. The picture on the left shows the roadbed as it heads towards New Hope Creek. With all the growth, it is not easy with a camera to view the "U" shape to the road. In addition erosion over the years has taken its toll on the road, making it (in places) look like a stream bed.

Finally, you will see on your left two piles of stones. In front of you will be the river. Here is a plat of the location of the chimney pile, and another stone pile near by. The one stone pile represents a chimney, and would allude to a home site. The question is, whose, and when? Some speculate that this may have been an Ordinary on the roadway before fording the stream or going to the mill. If it was an ordinary, a bond had to be applied for. Court minutes would reflect the bond being (either or both) applied for or approved. Neither the bond, nor any entry in the Court Minutes (Orange Co.) reflect any Robson or Johnston Ordinary (Tavern). Of course you could speculate it was illegally run, but I have seen a number of fines for selling illegal "spirituous liquors" without a license, so it was certainly enforced. The only answers could come from an excavation (if any information can be found) that could date the foundation. Could this be a millers house? Could this have been one of Robson's sons?

Here are pictures of both stone piles. The one below is of the chimney, and is about 6 feet wide.

Here is the other pile of stones in the area. The surrounding land (in the immediate 100 foot perimeter) is rather flat, and somewhat level.

Finally the road makes a gentle bend, and makes the downward move to the rivers edge. The "bright white" to the top of this image is the reflection of the sun from the river (New Hope Creek).

Despite the unknowns, what is known, the road way makes a bend around this house site, and heads slowly down-hill to the rivers edge. If Wooden Bridge Road was not there, the old roadbed could be seen following the edge of the land as it heads straight for the mill. This roadbed "hugs" the wall, and Robson (could have been Johnston) put stone embankments to prevent the walls from falling into the bed. The distance from the river is about 75 to 100 feet, and the elevation is such, that it should be free from flooding.

Here are a few pictures that show the stone embankments above the roadbed.

George Johnston Sells Mill to William and Edward Robson - 1811

October 16, 1811, George Johnston sells his mill, and 143 acres of land to Edward, and William Robson. It is this deed that identifies (for the first time) in the metes and bounds – Masons Spring. This spring, and spring branch (which flows into New Hope Creek), will become the western boundary for this tract of land for decades to come. Where did the name Masons Spring originate? Unknown. (See dedicated section on this topic) From this time forward, the mill site will now be known as - **Robson Mill**.

Robson Family

Bear with my slight detour. The Robson family is very difficult to track. I could not find any genealogy or family history about them on Ancestry.com (that is – family tree information). Court records do not mention them, generally speaking. Yet, William is born in England, after the Revolutionary War. When he comes to America is unknown (although an Emigration index states that he signed naturalization papers in 1811 in NC, as did Edward Robson). His first land purchase was this mill (Oct 1811) before the War of 1812. Never the less, I did find some basic information, primarily from census records.

1783-1859

William Robson, who is sometimes referred to as Rev. William Robson, was born in Royal Oak, England on May 25, 1783. His wife Ann was born in NC, on September 21, 1795. It looks as if the McCain family in Caswell County will become the female choice of the Robson men. John McCain, who died in the 1850's surfaces the probable marriage. Nancy Robson was listed as one of his daughters, and then I found a marriage bond for William Robson and Nancy McCain – August 25, 1817 in Caswell County. Yet, all the Census records, and even her tombstone documents her first name as Ann. In addition, in this will, it also mentions that one of the sons (of John McCain) was Hugh McCain. In the will of J.W. Robson, his wife Mary C., (1850 Census lists Mary C. McCain as 18, daughter of Hugh A. McCain – Caswell Co.) states that her dad was Hugh McCain of Caswell Co. Further, William G. Robson marriage record documents another McCain female, America L. McCain (Caswell Co.) September 14, 1865. Certainly there was a close relationship with the McCain family in Caswell County. If they were related, close friends or the like, why did Robson not live near them in Caswell Co.? I found a marriage record (William Flintoff to Rebecca Hogan Aug 8, 1842) which stated the marriage was consummated by Rev. William Robson. Why wasn't he a minister in a local church? Why did a minister sue in court (Geo. Johnston)? Coming from England to America in the early 1800's, was he affiliated with the Church of England?

In the 1810 census they had 1 slave, and by 1820 they had 4 slaves (2 male and 2 female). By 1840, the census shows the family content includes; 4 boys, and 3 girls, excluding mom and dad. Unfortunately, their eldest son (John) dies June 28th, 1842 at 23 years of age, thanks to a headstone! I looked through the 1842

Hillsborough Recorder (newspaper), and did not find any death announcement. This was unusual, since they would publish all deaths in the area, as well as marriages.

For some reason, they do not appear in the 1850 census. Searching the census (around their neighbors), and nothing was found. The index for the census does not list them. In a newspaper it stated that Alexander Hogan is marrying Matilda Robson, daughter of Rev William Robson on November 9, 1854. Here was proof they resided in the County in 1854, however, the 1850 census does not identify them. I have searched ALL states in 1850, with every version of spelling, and even with "Soundex", and nothing. Somehow, he was missed. Even searching his wife's name, which was always listed as Ann, and I found nothing. I tried searching under the children's names or even the salves names, nothing. There are two missing females from the census records (1840) that I cannot account for. The missing 1850 entry has hampered my ability to identify their names. They were not listed in any Orange Co. marriage record either.

1860 – 1870 (Civil War)

In the 1860 Census, it shows that two of their children remain in their house, Milton (26yrs) and William G. (21 yrs). Louise Burroughs was "head of the household" (next door), and Robson's other son was listed in that household – J.W. Robson (35yrs). William G. Robson enlisted in Company D, NC 1st Regiment on April 6, 1861 and mustered out November 12, 1861. His brother, Milton B. Robson enlisted in Company G, NC 27th Infantry Regiment on June 22, 1861. He was mustered out (private) December 13, 1862 at Fredericksburg, VA. He was wounded. He died later from these wounds (it is assumed he is buried in VA). William G. Robson marries America L. McCain on September 14, 1865 (She was the youngest daughter of Hugh McCain – 1850 census). Now the youngest son begins his family. This leaves dad with two boys (living), the eldest James W., and the youngest child, William G.

1870-1880

In the 1870 Census, William Robson (now 87 years old) remains on the home plantation, with his son, James Wesley Robson, and his wife, Mary C. They have one son living with them, John who is attending school at age 17. The next "house" is Lynn Robson, mulatto (70 yrs – male), and his wife Rebecka (60 yrs), is black. Their three children are all listed as mulatto (Cora, female 25, George M, 35, Calvin M, 40). The next "house" is Squire Robson (45 yrs, male) Black, and his wife Lydia (34yrs), listed as black. Their first child is Eddie, black, and Charles Green, and John W. are all males, but listed as mulatto (ages 4, 2 and 3mths). 1872 brings the death of William Robson.

1880-19xx

My experience with the US Census has revealed the spelling of the Robson name as Robison (and even Robeson). It was difficult to follow the family. As I searched with the name spelling anomalies I would locate them in Orange County census records. By the 1880 census, people were all over the place, and the "black/mulatto" Robson's were appearing in other people's homes. The 1880 census does not show James Wesley Robson alive, although his wife (Mary C. Robson) is listed as a widow. His will (Book H, Pg. 170) was written December 2, 1876. It was a very simple will, all goes to his wife, if she remains single, otherwise she gets $100, and the estate goes to his relatives (who his relatives are – was not stated in the will). There is another document referenced in the *Orders and Decree* Book (pg 408-10) entitled – "Articles of Agreement" dated April 21st, 1877. Here is another date that narrows the death date of J.W. between December 2, 1876, and April 21, 1877. This agreement starts to define relationships. It begins with who the agreement includes. Between Mary C. Robson, William G. Robson (J.W.'s brother) Louisa E. Burroughs (assumed sister of J.W.), Matilda W. Hogan (known sister of J.W.), and Franklin X. Burton, and his wife Alice Burton (unknown relationship, Alice was Alice Shelton). Finally the agreement states, *"..and the other parties to this agreement who are the heirs at law and next of kin of the said J.W. Robson that there should be a division of the property of the said J.W. Robson so that the several parties may hold their estates in fee simple..."* It also mentions that Mary C. Robson inherited land in Caswell County from her dad – Hugh A. McCain. Unfortunately, none of the other people are identified in terms of relationship to J.W. Robson. Yet, I did find Matilda's marriage record, but the 2 other sisters remain unknown. It is probable that Louisa E. Burroughs is one. The three page agreement is very involved, but it looks as if the other family members must have contested the will, since the will is very clear – ALL goes to my wife. Yet, they divide the land up.

Mary C. Robson sells the home plantation to James R. Blacknall, October 3, 1883 - this ends the Robson plantation story. This would also answer the black/mulatto question, as their land/housing I assume was on the plantation somewhere, and when Mary C. Robson sold it, they (blacks) had to move on. I cannot locate Mary C. Robson.

William G. Robson and his wife America S. [note the middle initial was squeezed in, and the index lists it as "P" and looks like a "S" or maybe a "L"] were located in the 1880 census, with their daughter, Mary C (1 year old). They were listed in the *"Chapel Hill District"* and lived between W. Pendergrass and Alivs Andrews, next door to Martha Blackwood (71 yrs old). His occupation was listed as farmer. Thanks to the Cemetery Index (online), W. G. Robson tombstone was located in the *Cedar Grove United Methodist Church Cemetery*. The tombstone provides Williams' vital statistics (b. Sep 5, 1839 – d. April 13, 1907). His wife has not been located, but adjoining "W.G." was a Lula S. Robertson (b. 1879 – d. 1961). Was this his daughter who was listed in the 1880 census as 1 year old (although a clear "C" for her middle name)? Yet, she is listed to another Robertson, who could have been her husband (Flem Robertson - b. 1876). The 1900 census does not list any of these family members (no Lula Robertson, no Robson/Robsin/Robeson etc.).

Edward Robson (mystery man)

Edward Robson (who jointly purchased the mill site from Johnston) was William's brother. The 1810 census has Edward in the 16-25 year bracket. Edward Robson buys land in Orange County before William. In fact, his first (registered) purchase was December 9, 1807 on Phills Creek (13/177 – 262 acres from William Hogan for $3700!). He purchased land in 1810, and 1811. Edward sells land for several years, with his last transaction, June 6, 1817. At this point in time (and forward) Edward Robson no longer appears in Orange County records. June 14, 1814, Edward Robson sells his half-interest in the mill to William for $800, (See Deed 15/10). Was this sale a sign of Edward leaving the area, or was this due to ill health? Reading the Hillsboro Recorder (Newspaper) I ran into Edward Robson being listed in the February, and March 1823 Term (Court) Legal notices. It stated that *"...Edward Robson is not an inhabitant of this state..."*, There were 2 suits (in equity) against him, one by Jerret Yeargan, and the other, Pleasant Henderson. One thing is for certain, I NEVER found Edward Robson (with ANY spelling variance) in any state. My guess, he returned to England.

Robson Family Tree

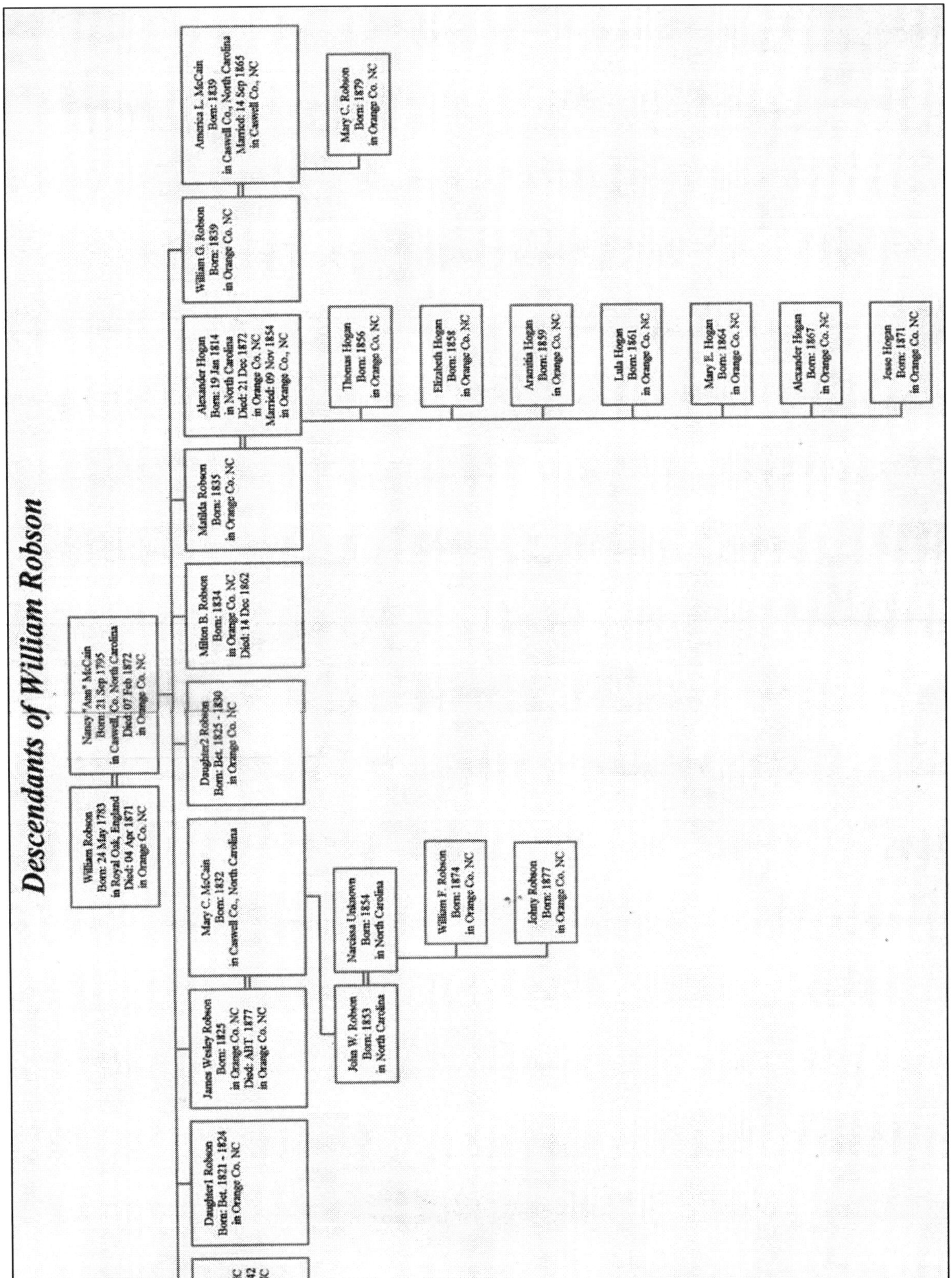

Descendants of William Robson
William Robson
Born: 24 May 1783
in Royal Oak, England
Died: 04 Apr 1871
in Orange Co. NC
Nancy "Ann" McCain
Born: 21 Sep 1795
in Caswell Co. North Carolina
Died: 07 Feb 1872
in Orange Co. NC
John Robson
Born: 1819
in Orange Co. NC
Died: 24 Jun 1842
in Orange Co. NC
Daughter1 Robson
Born: Bet. 1821 - 1824
in Orange Co. NC
James Wesley Robson
Born: 1825
in Orange Co. NC
Died: ABT 1877
in Orange Co. NC
Mary C. McCain
Born: 1832
in Caswell Co., North Carolina
John W. Robson
Born: 1833
in North Carolina
Narcissa Unknown
Born: 1854
in North Carolina
William F. Robson
Born: 1874
in Orange Co. NC
Johny Robson
Born: 1877
in Orange Co. NC
Daughter2 Robson
Born: Bet. 1825 - 1830
in Orange Co. NC
Milton B. Robson
Born: 1834
in Orange Co. NC
Died: 14 Dec 1862
Matilda Robson
Born: 1835
in Orange Co. NC
Alexander Hogan
Born: 19 Jan 1814
in North Carolina
Died: 21 Dec 1872
in Orange Co. NC
Married: 09 Nov 1854
in Orange Co., NC
Thomas Hogan
Born: 1856
in Orange Co. NC
Elizabeth Hogan
Born: 1858
in Orange Co. NC
Aramilia Hogan
Born: 1859
in Orange Co. NC
Lula Hogan
Born: 1861
in Orange Co. NC
Mary E. Hogan
Born: 1864
in Orange Co. NC
Alexander Hogan
Born: 1867
in Orange Co. NC
Jesse Hogan
Born: 1871
in Orange Co. NC
William G. Robson
Born: 1839
in Orange Co. NC
America L. McCain
Born: 1839
in Caswell Co., North Carolina
Married: 14 Sep 1865
in Caswell Co., NC
Mary C. Robson
Born: 1879
in Orange Co. NC

Robson Family Cemetery

Near the house (albeit below), is the family burial ground. About 100 feet further away is the slave cemetery. Both of these locations are on Duke Forest Property.

Robson Cemetery GPS (+-15 feet) – N35° 59.676 W79° 2.231

Below is the marker of the eldest son followed by a marker with no indication of a depression in the ground.

Below, is an image of the stone marker, and then just past it towards the top of the image, is a deep-depression, as if the body were removed. Moving leaves around the "removed" plot, at the head, I found another square stone, although very short, in the ground. Is it possible that this stone marker was moved?

Although out of order, here is the last grave, the one on the far left, as you face the tombstones. This head stone, and foot stone, are clearly visible. This grave (like most of them) has a clear body-depression in the ground. It is my opinion this is the grave of James Wesley Robson (J.W.). He dies in 1877, and his wife sells, the plantation.

The plat/drawing below represents the Robson Graveyard. It is very difficult, to be exact, without some serious land clearing (which really needs some attention) in order to plat this exactly. Never the less, based on the tombstone death dates, the burials are from right (oldest or first) to the left.

Based on my brief research, their son (Milton) who was wounded in Fredericksburg, and died from his wounds in the Civil War, was buried there, and not brought back home.

This leaves two unaccounted graves. However, there are 1 or 2 daughters that are still unaccounted for as well. More research is required. The last grave (far right) clearly looks as if it has been removed.

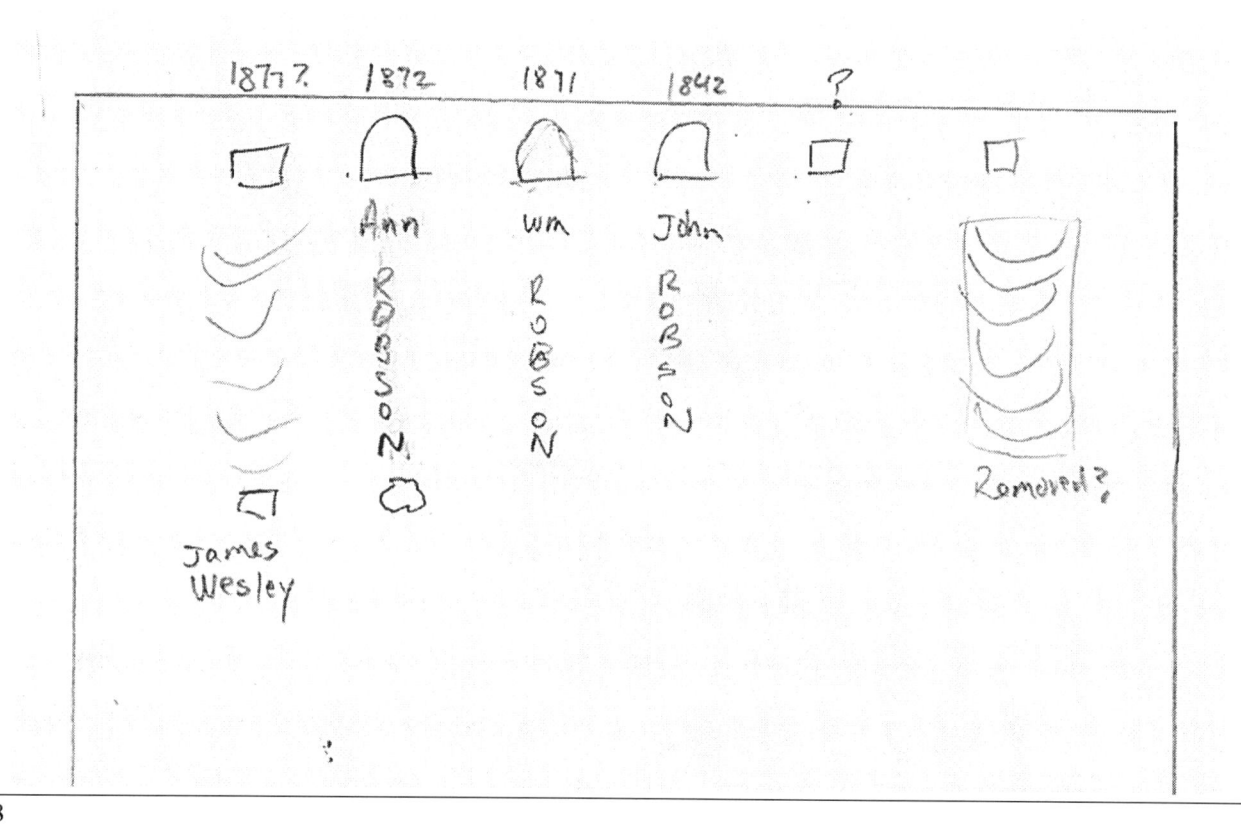

Slaves

The Robson family had slaves. They were listed in the 1810 census as 1 slave, 1820 they had 4 slaves (2 male and 2 female), 1830 has 3 (damaged census image), and in 1840, they has 9 (6 male and 3 female). It is possible that (based on the census) Lin (Lynn) was their first slave who would have been born in 1800. Rebecca is next, 1810 followed by Squire, 1825 and Lydia, 1836. The 1840 census provides a detailed breakdown of his slaves (by age), but cannot reconcile the 1840 to the 1870 census. There are less slaves in 1870. Of course at this point in time, they are free people. So maybe the rest left the area.

In the 1870 Census we get a better idea of the two black families. The first listed, next to the Robson Family, is Lynn (or Lin) Robson, and his wife Rebecka. Lynn (male) is listed as mulatto, and Rebecka is black. Lynn is listed as working on the farm (cannot write, but can read), Rebecka is keeping house, and she cannot read or write. In this same dwelling, is Core (Cory) who is mulatto, 25 yrs old, and is listed as a domestic servant. She cannot read or write. Next if George, who is 35 years old, mulatto, working on the farm, and Calvin, who is 40 years old mulatto working on the farm. Neither of these men can read or write.

The next dwelling house is Squire Robson (45yrs old) black, and his wife Lydia (34 yrs old) black, and neither of them can read or write. He is listed as "working on farm", and she has "keeping house". Next is Eddie a 7 year old female (black), followed by Charles who is 4 years old, and a mulatto, then Green 2 years old, and a mulatto, and John W., who is 3 months old, and is a mulatto. Lastly there is Lyzie who is listed as a 25 year old female, black, and here occupation is listed as "at home", and she cannot read or write.

Friedman's Marriage Records (Negro Cohabitation Certificates) documents, Lin Robson (Lynn in the census) cohabitating with Rebecca – Aug 25, 1861. Then Squire Robson with Lydia on Aug 25, 1857. To me this continues to emphasize these two "couples" could be those which are buried on the plantation.

As I surveyed the surrounding land (near the Robson plots), I found more body-sized depressions. Upon closer examination, I found head and foot stones for at least 2 people, maybe 3 (could be larger). As I scrapped away the leaves with my hands, I found what looks to be a rock border around the graves. I firmly believe, with appropriate equipment, this cemetery could be cleaned up, and carefully restored, which may provide some more details.

Black Cemetery (GPS coordinates +-20feet) – N35° 59.690, W79° 2.220

Since it is difficult to provide details with images, I have drawn lines on the stone border to help illustrate what the eye can see.

On the left, the two arrows are pointing to the headstones. The dashed line shows the area where the stones appear that could have been established as a border to the cemetery.

The picture directly below take from another angle showing where the stones are that seem to outline the graves.

On the left the arrows show one head, and foot stone. The depression of the body (area) is not as visible in this picture, as they (both) are when you visit the site.

Pulling the leaves away by hand, revealed the foot stones, more so than the headstone. The depressions are present for two graves, but there looks to be either three of four head/footstones in the general area. This part of the graveyard is clearly segregated from the Robson Family plot, but only about 100 feet.

The Robson Plantation has been disturbed over the years, primarily from the power-line easement. Yet, on either side of the easement, immediately you discover stone walls or foundations. On the eastern side, towards the mill, there seems to be a chimney remnant along with other foundation stones. In addition there are signs of roadways, although seemingly modern. Based on the 1938 aerials, this land was altered, as the power line easement was already established. Then in more modern aerial images, the eastern side of the plantation (towards the mill) was forested. This just adds to the disturbance of the ground, probably removed the road remnants. However, the foresting did not disturb the stone remnants. They have not disturbed the western edge, which ultimately meets the cemetery.

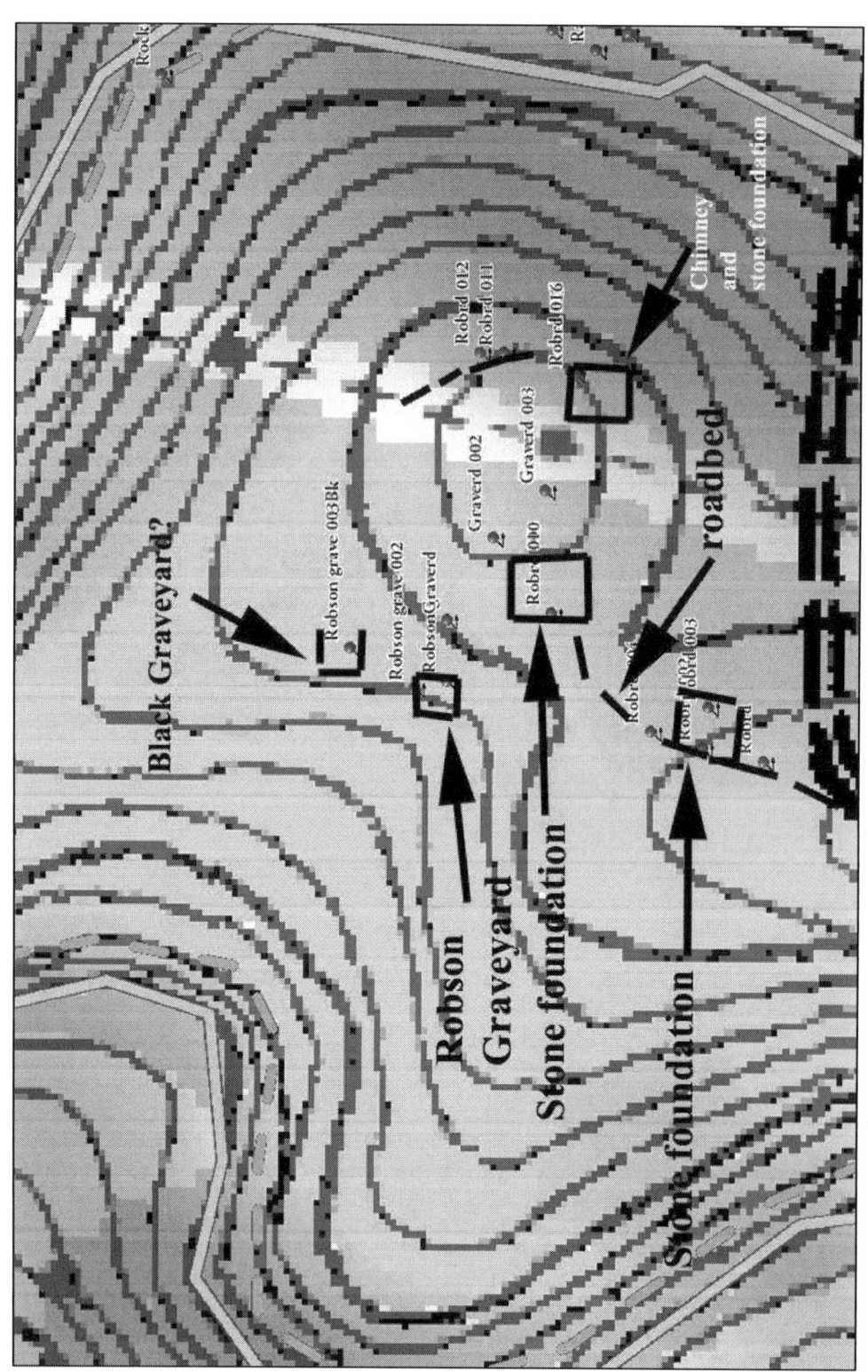

As you walk "Wooden Bridge Road" on the east side there is the original roadbed are (every once in a while) stone walls. The original roadbed ultimately crosses "Wooden Bridge Road". If you look closely on your left, you can see it wander off. Following this a short distance, you run upon (previously discussed) what looks like a stone foundation, covered in fallen trees. From this point on, the roadbed comes, and goes in visibility. Then another stone foundation appears.

George Johnston Erects a Saw Mill on New Hope - 1820

January 1820, George Johnston Sr. and his son George Jr., begin erecting a saw mill on New Hope, southeast (down stream – about 1 mile – stream distance) of the Robson Mill location. In fact, there is land between Johnston, and Robson, that of Boroughs (Burroughs), and Blackwood. This insulation is interesting to note, in that, there is a fair distance between them, as far as the river course is concerned. I was unable to locate any mill petition, nor in the minutes of the Orange County Court Records, for this saw mill. This could be due to a number of reasons. A private mill did not have to be petitioned. However, reading the minutes for 1818 to 182, not a single mill petition, or any complaint in the Court minutes (dealing with mills). It seems to me that this might allude to a change in process for Orange County (towards mills) at that time.

May 6, 1820 William Robson purchases 1.5+ acres of land, sort of an island in the middle of no where, from William Blackwood. This drawing from the Robson-Johnston law suit, including my added information, shows the area in discussions. Note the odd-shaped dotted area. This is the recent land purchase by Robson. It also clearly documents the other land holdings, and their relationship to this purchase. To the north is the Boroughs land which isolated Johnston from Robson.

May 1823 (Court Term), William Robson files a law suit against George Johnston Sr., and George Jr. He represents their saw mill has impacted William's land which was purchased for a mill seat. A mill seat is a term for a piece of land situated on a river/stream that is suitable to house, and operate a mill. However, Johnston disagrees, and states that this mill seat is not a valid mill seat at all. In fact, Johnston provided witnesses that were timbering the land, and stated that Robson requested them to timber *all* the land, since it was the only reason he bought it. Johnston stated, the saw mill was in operation for years, prior to Robsons complaint.

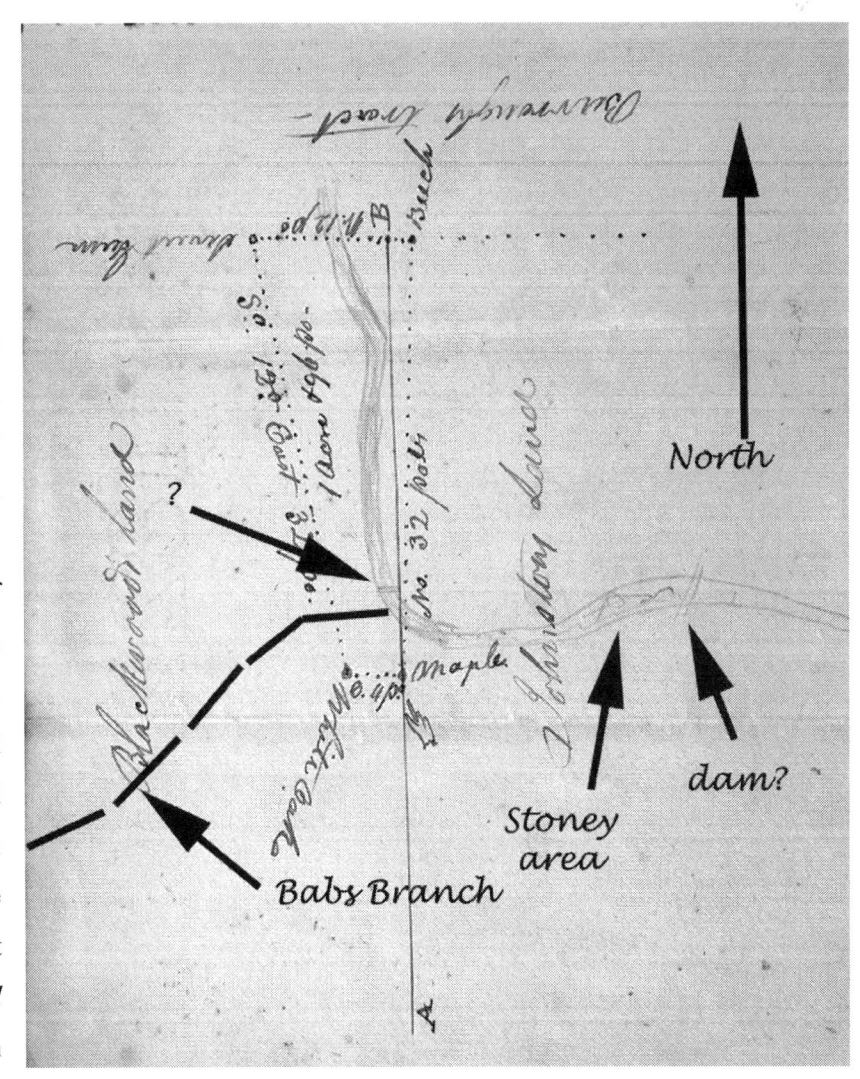

73

As the prior map illustrates, the N-S part of the river divides the lands of George Johnston from Blackwood, and Burroughs. The map below was another drawing found amongst the law suit papers. This shows the bigger picture. I have added Babs Branch, and labels to keep it consistent with the other drawing.

However, some anomalies appear. His drawing of New Hope River is rather crude, and seems to allude to a "bend" in the river in which the Saw Mill resides on, and then scribbles it out. Was this super condensed? Or was he trying to show the saw mill was just further down the stream? The stream runs (more or less) due east-west (flowing eastwardly) after the bend near Babs Branch.

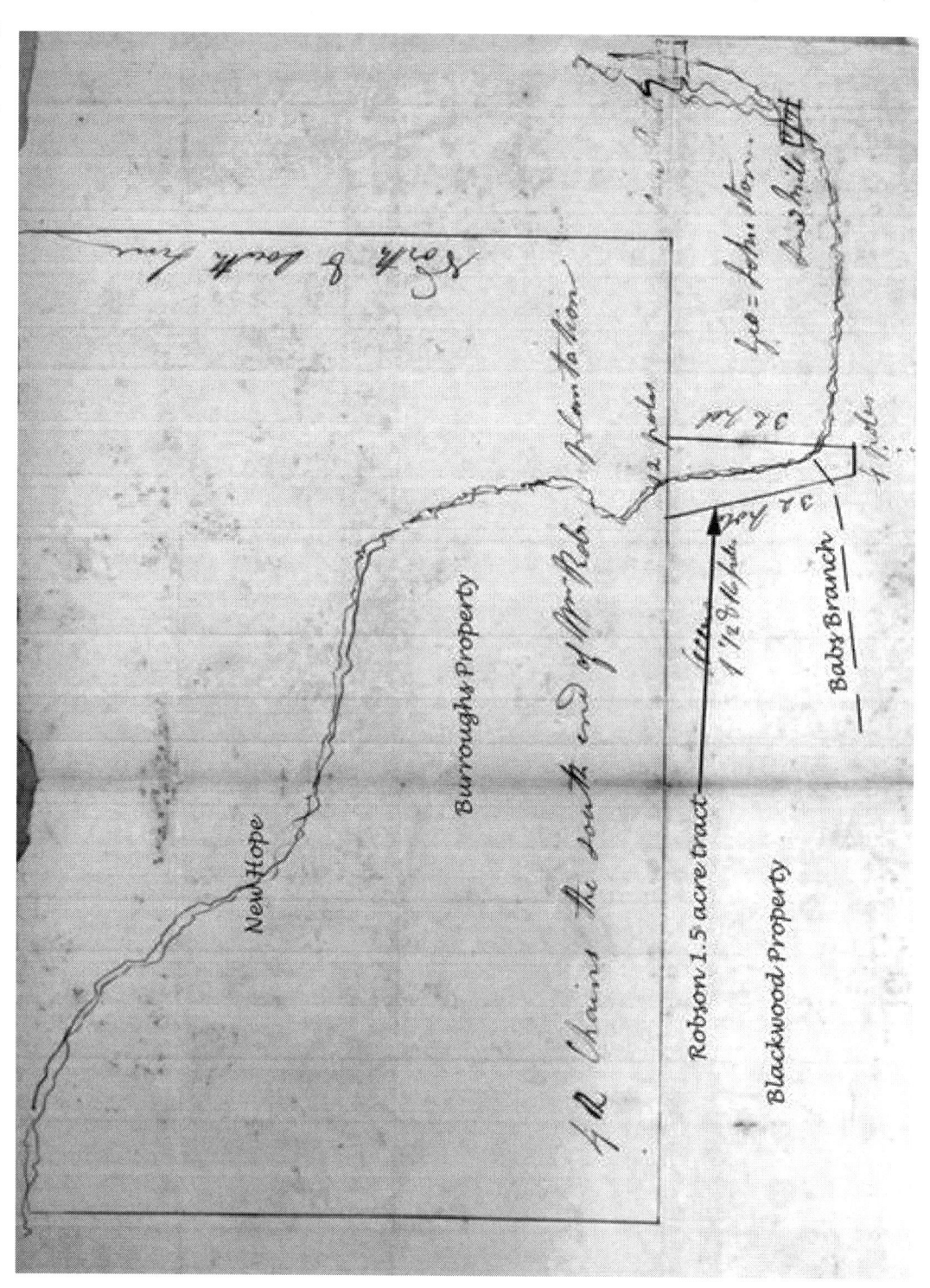

Here is a modern Topo map showing the same general area. Note the bend in the river towards the far right hand side (east). Was this where the Saw Mill was located, was this the bend he was attempting to show? (Note: Due to New Hope Creek being drawn in blue, this B&W book image was highlighted using large-black dashed lines to represent the creek).

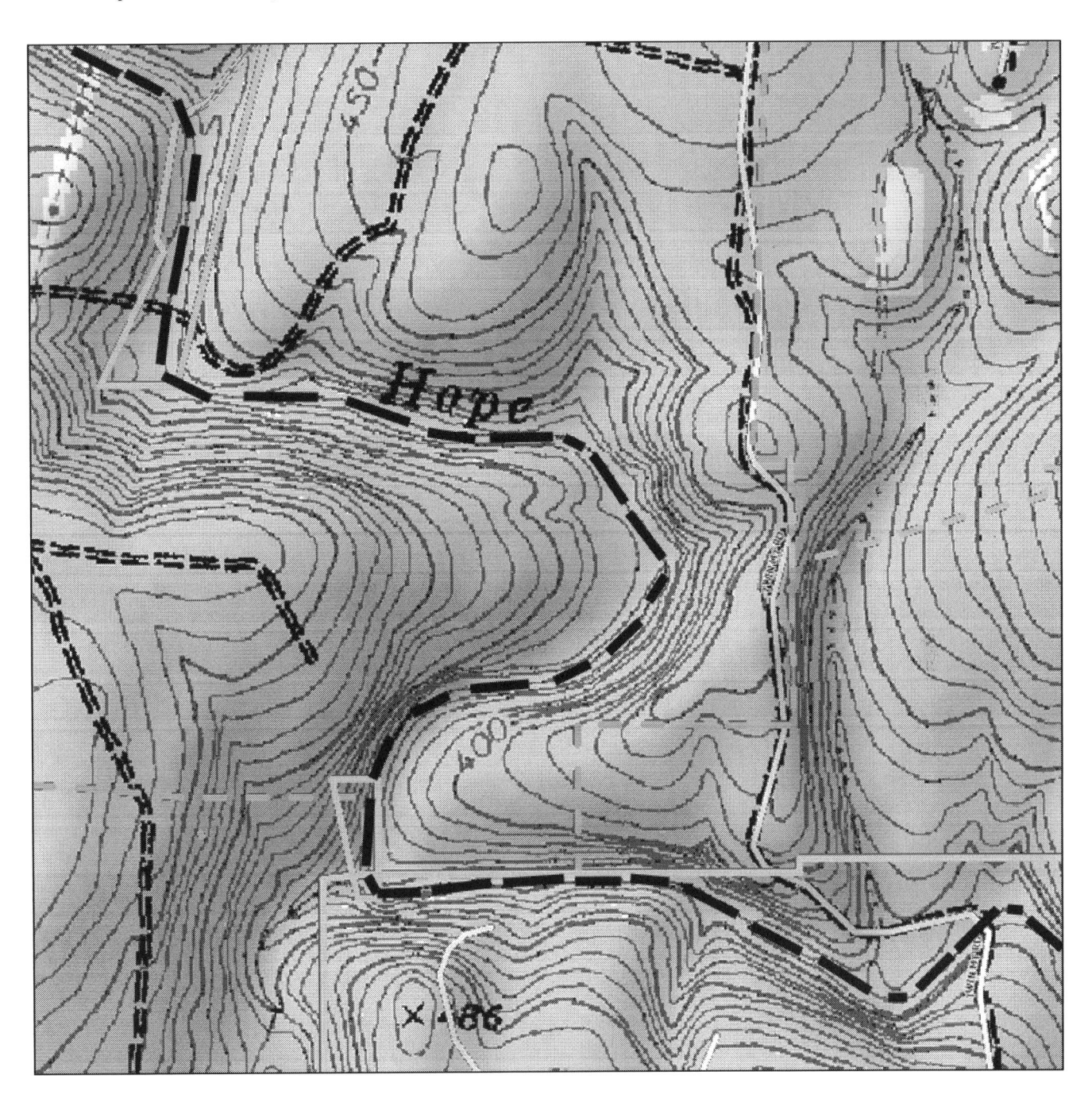

Search for the Saw Mill

In searching for the saw mill that George Johnston Sr., and Junior had erected, I followed the New Hope Creek from Babs Branch almost to Erwin Road. Certainly there were not any remnants like Robson's Mill or even like the mill near Turkey Farm Road. However, there were some possible remnants or stone foundations located along New Hope Creek.

During my search, I kept two perspectives in mind. Foremost in thought was "access". Secondly, a valid mill seat or possible mill race. Yet, it seemed that access was the most difficult to envision. New Hope meanders through some very diverse geography. At one point you can visualize a possible road, and then in 100 feet further there is a massive stone cliff rising out of the stream. Banks so steep nothing but a mountain goat would traverse the sides.

The map (above) shows my GPS marks as I scoured the sides looking for the mill. For this general area, the south side of New Hope is just too steep. On the north side, there seemed to be remnants of a road bed in front of the stone wall in which the Robson's had erected for several hundred feet. As with most walls (fence) they begin, and end abruptly. So did this wall. The land (as the topo-map illustrates) is a "slopping" land, and could easily be traveled by horse or wagon. However, not a single road bed, just flat gentle pine forest land. The road by the stone wall ends due to (as annotated on the map) a steep stone wall that goes into the river. (Pictured here on the right.)

I found an area at the bend of the river, near the mouth of Babs Branch, which looked like a short mill race. But it is very difficult to tell if this is man made or from the force of a flooding river, as it resists this 90 degree elbow. Yet, a wall on one side seemed to have a flat top that seems to be man-made. But Johnston's drawing shows a dam like mark further down stream (not at the bend or elbow of New Hope Creek).

Further down stream, the situation reverses. The north side becomes steep cliffs, and the south side has a low area that moves to a general steep side (not a cliff, however). On this southern side I ran into a stone embankment in a pine forest area that looked man-made. As I scoured the sides of the land, before they start a steeper rise, I did not find anything else. As you continue on this eastward course, you get closer to the old road (now called Concrete Bridge Road). Was this an original road that was reused for more modern access? Was this the road that was used to, and from their saw mill? In addition, was this bend in the river (the upward curve) which George Johnston was drawing in 1823? I continued to follow the stream, and again, now the north side became much more level, and possibly able to support a road, but nothing definitive was found. Neither was their anything that would resemble a mill seat or raceway.

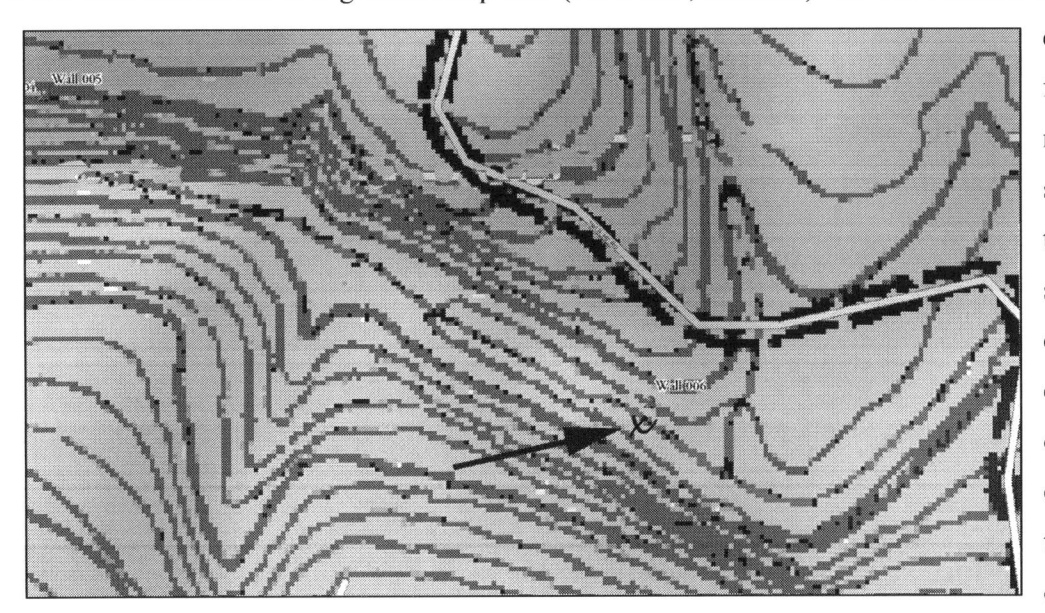

(Stone embankment marked via GPS on the above Topo map)

Here is another view of the stone embankment, and surrounding land looking south. As you can see the ground is somewhat level, and the rise upward rather gradual.

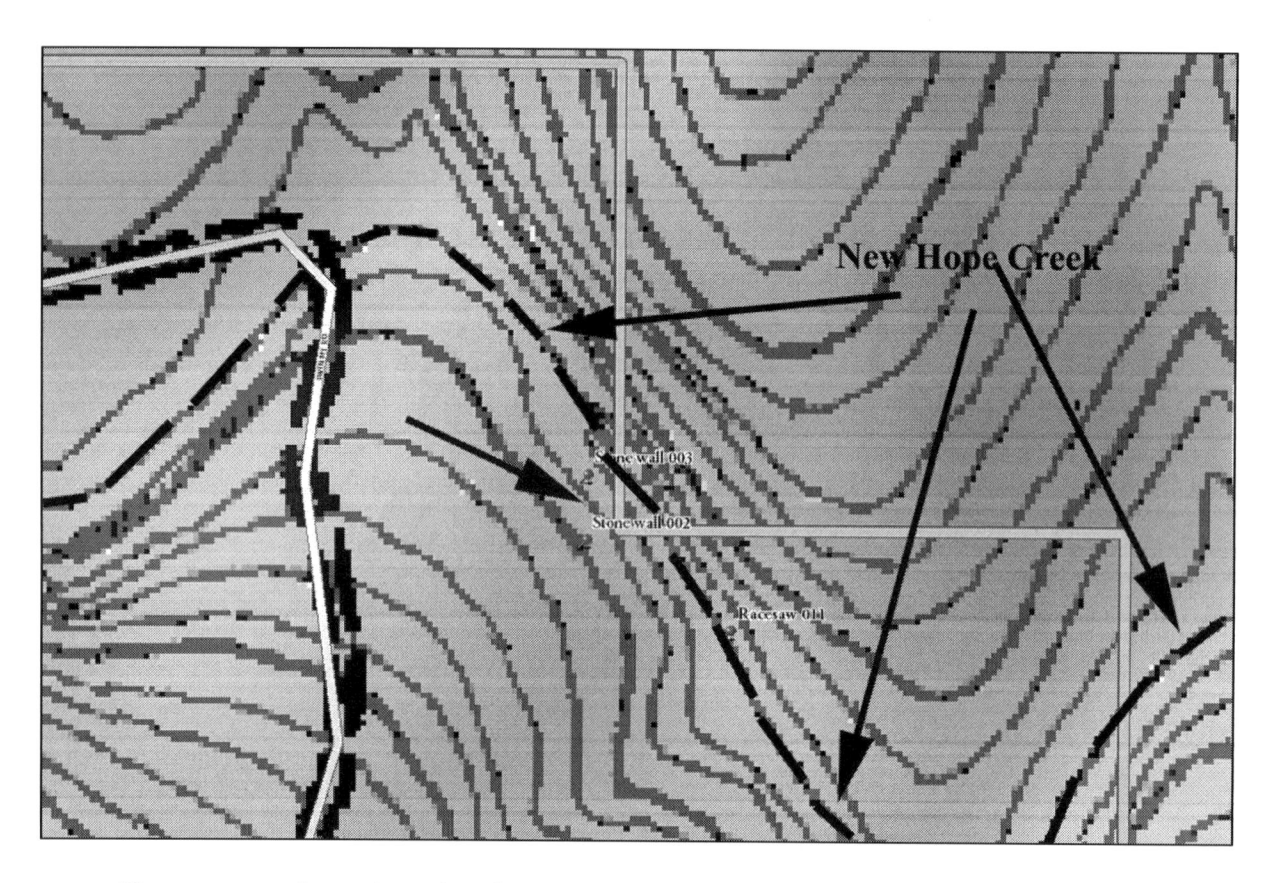

The topo map shown here, has the Courtney property line drawn, to show the "stair step" attribute. In his original plat, it was annotated there was a saw mill (and the text stated – and a paper mill), and this was near the "stair" and New Hope Creek. There was a large area of a stone foundation, as well as a roadbed. The river looked to have a raceway similar to that of Turkey Farm Road, which formed an island. It is possible that this was the old Courtney mill site, or even the Johnston Mill site. Regardless of who or which, this location merits detailed research to come to a better conclusion as to what was there. Certainly something was located at this site. **(* SEE PLAT SECTION for more detail – including more pictures and a diagram *)**

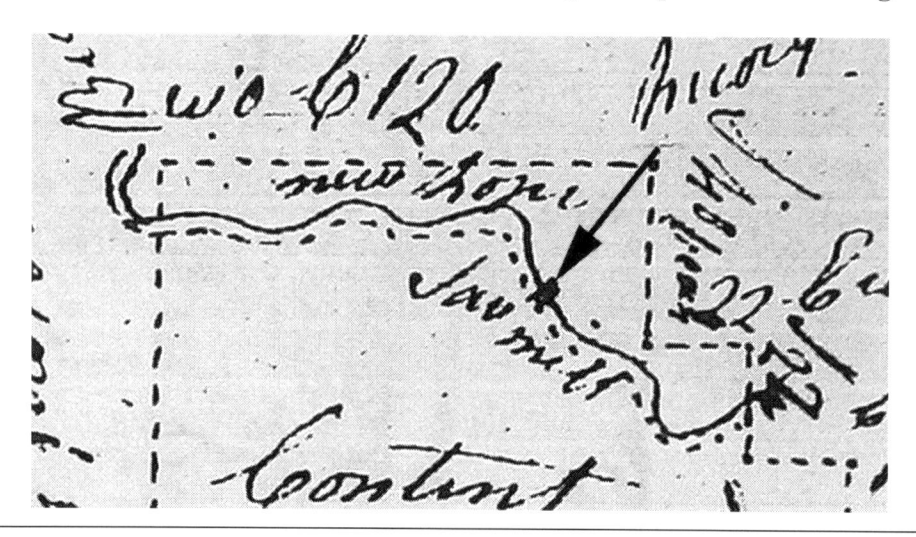

In addition to stone foundations or embankments were a number of roadbeds that were heading south from this area. This whole area, in general, looked level, and numerous roads, and stone pile.

Based on what I saw in this area, these were *not* stone fences, that are so prevalent to Robson's land, and this is certainly not on his land. Could this be the old Courtney Mill foundation?

William Robson vs. George Johnston Law Suit - 1823

This law suit provides a lot of insight into this saw mills history (although unable to precisely locate it). It also illustrates the contentious situation between Johnston and Robson. This law suit uncovers who were millwrights in the county area, and documents the neighbors, and workers, providing some insight to the general activity in Orange County during the 1820's.

The law suit was initiated by Robson against George Johnston Sr. and Jr. Robson represents that he too wants to have a mill erected, and that George Johnston's mill dam has backed the water up in New Hope Creek, flooding Robson's land such that he cannot erect his mill. Johnston hires Millwrights (designers of mills, including researching mill locations, river flow/fall, etc.) who testify that Robson's proposed location for a mill is invalid. Johnston finds out from workers (woodsmen) Robson was attempting to stop his mill operation. Why? Nothing documents Robson's side of the story, as to personal views, and opinions. However, Johnston's letters document a lot about his opinions towards Robson. In one heated letter to Judge Ruffin (retired judge, and in very ill health at this time) George Sr. states he fought in the Revolutionary War, and Robson has not sworn allegiance to America. William (born in England) migrated to America after the American Revolution, and before the War of 1812. George didn't take kindly to a Brit suing him.

An interesting comment in the law suit was William Robson's claim of what he was attempting to build, or type of mill he wanted to construct with the following statement, "*...by building a public mill and a tilt hammer with a view of profit...*" A tilt hammer is a steel forging tool. From an encyclopedia (*Penny Cyclopaeida – 1846*) it states, "*TILT-HAMMER, a large hammer worked by machinery, impelled either by a water wheel or a steam-engine. Such hammers are extensively used in the manufacture of irons and steel, and the name tilt-mill is sometimes applied to the mechanism of which they from the principal feature.*" And then it continued with this description, "*When tilt-hammers are impelled by water-wheels, it is advisable to fix the cams or arms upon a separate shaft, which may revolved at any required velocity without increasing the velocity of the water-wheel itself, by the intervention of suitable cogged-wheels.*"

> "...William Robson...a parcel of land lying on both sides of New Hope Creek in the County aforesaid with an excellent mill seat thereon, which he commenced improving and intended to improve by building a public mill and a tilt hammer with a view of profit to himself and accommodation... (cont)..."

"...to the neighborhood but has been forced to desist from such his undertaking for the cause hereinafter set forth. Since the purchase of the said tract of land by your petitioner and since notice was give to the neighborhood generally and in particular to the defendant by your petitioner of his determination to build as aforesaid on the said mill seat, the said defendant has built a mill on the same stream to wit New Hope, some distance below and have backed their pond water upon the said lands of your petitioner so as materially to lessen the value and use of the same and in particular to render wholly useless the said mill seat. Your petitioner charges that by reason of said pond water he is disappointed in his intended improvements as well as injured seriously in the value of his said lands. Your petitioner therefore prays your worships to order a writ to be issued to the sheriff commanding him to summon a jury agreeable to law to meet on the premises and assess what damages your petitioner has sustained and what sum he shall receive as an annual compensation...."

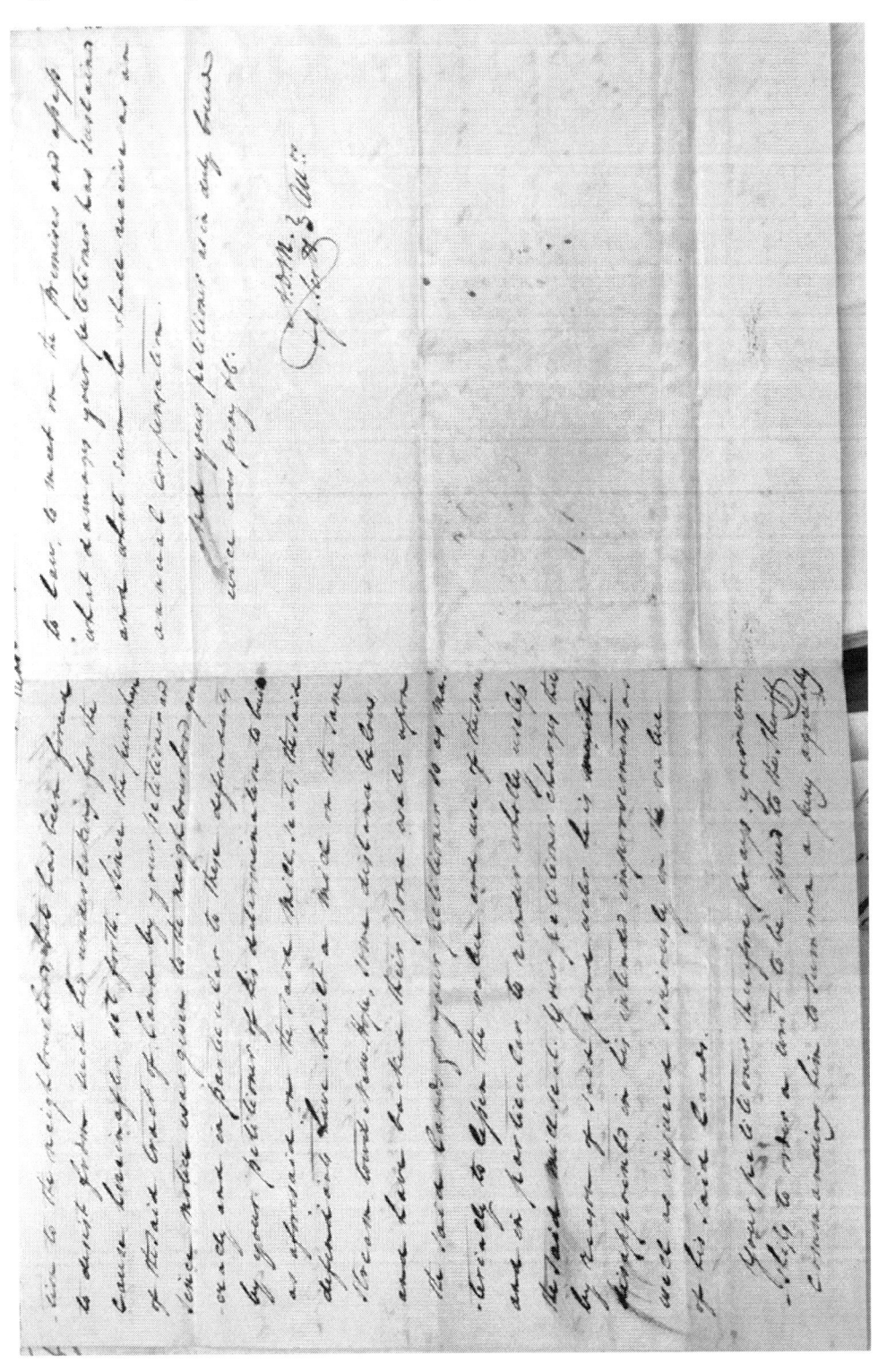

Jury Report – June 14, 1823 – "…find that William Robson aforesaid has not sustained any damage…"

William Robson
Geo Johnston Sr
Geo Johnston Jr

We the undersigned Jurors being duly sworn and empannelled well and truly to enquire whether William Robson aforesaid hath sustained any damage by reason of the pond water belonging to the mill complained of by him in his petition against George Johnston Sr & George Johnston Jr aforesaid and having attentively viewed and examined the premises heard the evidence on both sides do find that William Robson aforesaid has not sustained any damage — Given under our hands and seals this 14th day of June 1823

Alexander Gatlin (Seal)

Lewis Bantis (Seal)

Thos. his + mark Hutchins (Seal)

Josiah Athens (Seal)

S. Corick (Seal)

Fred Reeves (Seal)

John Buril (Seal)

Sam B Lisph (Seal)

John Henderson (Seal)

Alfred Boothe (Seal)

James Shepard (Seal)

Jos. Morcom (Seal)

Deposition of Mrs. Margaret Blackwood, wife of William Blackwood. *"…Question by defendant – Did not you William Robson when he came to purchase the land of your husband that perhaps that you (viz) Robson wished to build a mill? Ans. That I did tell Robson so that if he Robson built a mill there it would be as bad as if George Johnston was to build there. Question – What was Robson's reply to you? Answer - That Robson said that he should not build a mill there neither wanted any other person to build there. Further, this deponent saith not…"*

Here is the notice to Robson that a deposition from Mrs. Blackwood will be taken.

July 19th 1824

Mr Wm Robson,

Sir, you will please to take notice that on the 21st day of August next. We shall take the deposition of Margaret Blackwood (the Wife of William Blackwood Senr) of Orange County. between the hours of Ten & twelve o'clock A. M. of that day. at the house of the said William Blackwood. to be read as evidence in our behalf in the suit now pending in the superior Court of Law in the said county of Orange. Wherein you are plaintiff and we are Defendants. When and where. you may attend & cross examine if you think proper.

Yours &c
George Johnston
Geo M Johnston

The above notice was served on _____ Johnston, maketh oath. that on the 3d day of August 1824. I delivered to William Robson a true copy of the above notice.

Sworn to before us 21st Aug 1824

W Blackwood J.P.
W. N. Pratt J.P.
John McCauley J.P.

C.W. Johnston

"In the year 1820 about the 15 or 17 January I began to build a saw mill on New Hope and employed a man (James Copley) to dig the pit and also employed Mathew McCaulay (smith) to make the irons both of these men began the work for me about the same time. Mr. Robson purchased on the 27th May afterwards, of Mr. Blackwood a small parcel of land (say 2 acres) above my seat and then ordered me (or my workman James Copley) to stop digging the pit. I then applied to Mr. Norwood who was then at the Court for counsel who told me to go on and build any sort of mill I thought proper. But not feeling willing to get into a law suit I got a millwright and traveled down the creek until we found a seat which would admit of a dam of 5 feet without backwatering Mr. Robson's land but in starting the foundation of my dam to bring it up with a proper slope I raised the dam 4 feet which causes the water to be dammed a small distance above my land (as will appear from the amended report of two millwrights which I had to travel the creek and to know how much I dammed back the water on Mr. Robson's land) but not out of the bed of the creek. I can prove by Margaret Blackwood that when Mr. Robson was making the purchase of her husband W. B. she observed to him, that George might as well build a mill there as him (he observed, that he never intended building neither did he want any other person to build there) Mr. Blackwood was opposed to any person building a mill or dam if built where I first designed or at Mr. Robson's land would stop up a cow ford of hers. I can prove by Archibald Brockwell who was in Robson employ that when the act of cutting the timber off said land for he had given a great price for the land and it (the timber) was all he expected, he would get unless he could stop Geo Johnston from building a mill (cont)…"

"...on Robson land at the place where he says he wants to build is not a proper place to build at as it is below the fall of water and that there is no place for a mill yard as his land is not more than five rod wide at the place he wishes to build at and also that a road to his place can not be had without trespassing on other persons land. But it is their opinion that about five rod above this place is a much better seat where my back water would not injure him and where a good millyard can be had and where a mill have more space of ground as his land widens as it extend up the creek – this I confirm by Stephen Gappins and Thomas Carter millwrights, these millwright who leveled and examined this place together with Col Joseph Woods who surveyed and platted it I wish you to examine particularly as they have been on it and can give all necessary information respecting this mill seat of Robson's. N.B. At the place which I mentioned before where my eddy water was one foot high being 7 rod [115.5 feet] above my line is the place where Robson designs to build and 3 rod above that place my eddy water as I mentioned before runs out. Will it be necessary to mention the cause why Mrs. Blackwood observed to Robson that if he build a mill it would be as bad as if Johnston was to build - if so - the cause is this. That her husband has above both seats a cow ford which either dam would stop up and she wished not a mill to be built as it would deprive her of the advantages of the ford."

"I have had according to an order from the Supreme Court the land owned by Mr. Robson surveyed by Col Woods a plat of which he has and at some time had the 2 millwrights mentioned before to level the creek to ascertain how much I damaged Mr. Robson by back water and the following is a copy of their report, to wit: –'The elevation of the creek from Johnston's saw mill up to where the line crosses which divide the lands of Johnson and Robson's mill tract is 2 feet - from the line up to the head of Mr. Robson's race is one foot elevation in meanders of the creek a distance of seven poles[115.5 feet] – When Johnston's dam is properly and completely full. There will be a back of dead water at Robson's dam of one foot. – N.B. from Robson's intended dam up to the head of dead water is 5 rods[82.5 feet] nearly opposite to a large poplar on the creek. We suppose and believe that there is a better mill seat on Robson's, tract about four or five rods above the other seat of Robson's which would not interfere with the back water from Johnston's Mill'. Opinion of Stephen Gappins and Thomas Carter."

Frances L. Hawks Letter – "*Sir as you have been informed of my request to employ you in a suit in the Superior Court to defend me against Rev. William Robson. I have taken this matter to give you a statement of the whole business. Sir in the year 1820 in the month of March I commenced preparing to build me saw mill and employed James Copley to dig my mill pit also Mathew McCauley to make my mill iron which circumstances these men can provide and with which Robson was acquainted and also the time above mentioned on the 27th May in the same year which the records will show, said Robson purchased from William Blackwood Sr. a small part of the creek above my mill seat when I then was at work and ordered me not to raise the water on his mill seat. At the time Robson made a purchase he did not own one foot of land east west south or north of that part of the creek neither had any land adjoining it, - I believe he purchased this spot of land merely to stop me from building. – I can prove Peggy Blackwood wife of William Blackwood Sr. whose deposition is now in the hands of Mr. Ruffin (being so old and infirm that he cannot attend court) that when said Robson was making the purchase from her husband William Blackwood she observed to him that George Johnston might as well build a mill there as him for if he build a mill there it would stop a ford on the creek which was useful to them. Robson reply was he never intended to build there. I can prove by Archibald Brockwell and John Bowers that when in the act of cutting the timber of the land that Robson purchased of Blackwood there was one poplar tree inconvenient to come at and the hands refused cutting the said tree replied they must cut all for he had given a large price for the land and the timber was all he expected to get except stopping old George Johnston from building a mill – when Robson forbid me from building at that place, I found a seat down the creek and did not want to lose the timber and iron I had prepared neither wishing to…(cont.)*

"... enter into a law suit with him I commenced building my said mill and my back water flows back on his seat one foot. But Sir he has pitched his seat at the lower end of his fall which is quit uncommon. Had he not done so he has a better seat six or seven rods above where my back water would not interfere with him. But his intention being to stop me from building he pitched his seat at the lower end of the fall at the same time my back water does not go out of the channel of the creek or banks of the creek – On this head I want you to examine Stephen Gappins and that Carter (Millwrights) who have reviewed this seat of Robson very closely – whether it was ever a custom with them to pitch a mill at the lower end of the fall, call on the same millwrights if they do not think that a better seat could be got six or seven rods up the stream. Also call on them if the do not think that my saw mill dam above Robson's Mill is a benefit to Robson Mill as the stream is small – when both the dams are empty in the summer season and a good rain falls so as to fill both dams as his discharges my dam may re-supply his which enables him to grind longer. Ask John Blackwood Esq. when his father made a deed of this said land to Robson ask if my saw mill is not a benefit to the neighborhood and to Robson himself for he has had as much lumber sawed at the mill as any one neighbor – When Robson purchased this said land from Blackwood they ran into my land and made a beach tree a corner when my old corner was a dogwood a few paces west of this beach a dispute arose and I agreed that the beach should be the corner provided it canceled all disputes – All the land that I was willing to give up at that time is not worth five cents but gives Robson a little more room. I observed to you that all this time my dam was not made at the lower place and perhaps it might be policy in me not contend for that land..."

"...for it is all a bluff. Did I contend for it and he gain it he would through me in the cost of the whole suit Col Joseph Woods and Col Hugh Mullholland can show the plot of this land.

Witnesses

James Copley and Mathew McCauley to show when I began to work at my upper mill seat. John Blackwood Esq. to prove when Robson made the purchase from his father William Blackwood also if the saw mill is not a benefit to the neighborhood.

Peggy Blackwood wife of William Blackwood by deposition in the hands of Mr. Ruffin to prove that Robson when he made the purchase from Blackwood that he never intended to build a mill there neither did he want any other person to build.

Archibald Brockwell and John Bowers to prove that when in the act of cutting the timber that Robson purchased of Blackwood there was one tree a poplar not convenient to come at they refused to cut it. Robson observed he had given great price for the land and all he expected to get was the timber except he could stop old George Johnston from building a mill – call upon William Adams to establish what he heard Bowers assent to."

"…that your petitioner William Robson is seized and possessed of a valuable tract or parcel of land lying on both sides of New Hope Creek in the County aforesaid with an excellent mill seat thereon which he commenced improving and intended to improve by building a public mill and a tilt hammer with a view of profit to himself and accommodation to the neighborhood but as been forced to desist from such his undertaking for the cause herein after set forth; since the purchase of the said tract of land by your petitioner and since notice was given to the neighborhood generally and in particular to these defendants by your petitioner of his determination to build as aforesaid on the said mill seat, the said defendants have built a mill on the same stream to wit, New Hope some distance below and have backed their pond water upon the said lands of your petitioner…Whereas lately in our Court of Pleas…held for the County of…(cont)…"

"…Orange William Robson hath complained to us that he is injured and aggrieved by the erection of a mill on New Hope Creek used and owned by George Johnston Jr. and George Johnston Sr. and he having petitioned us to provide for him a fit remedy in that behalf and we being willing to do what is just in the premises of therefore command you that you summon twenty four freeholders unconnected with the parties …and the sheriff of our said County on that day returned to us our said writ…viewed and examined the premises heard the evidence on both sides, do find that William Robson aforesaid has not sustained any damage. – Given under our hands and seals this 14th day of June 1823 – Alexander Gattis - John Bevill"

"The said report being returned as above stated, the same was confirmed by the Court and judgment rendered thereon accordingly, as also for costs of suit but the said William Robson the petitioner being dissatisfied with the verdict of the jury and judgment of the Court aforesaid, prayed an appeal to Orange County Superior Court of Law, and enters into Bond and Security accordingly."

David Southern adds, "More freeholder names: Lewis Partin, Thomas Hutchins, Josiah Atkins, Samuel Couch, Frederick Reeves, John "Jack" B. Leigh, John Henderson, Alfred Boothe, James Shepard, and Joseph Marcom [or Markham]".

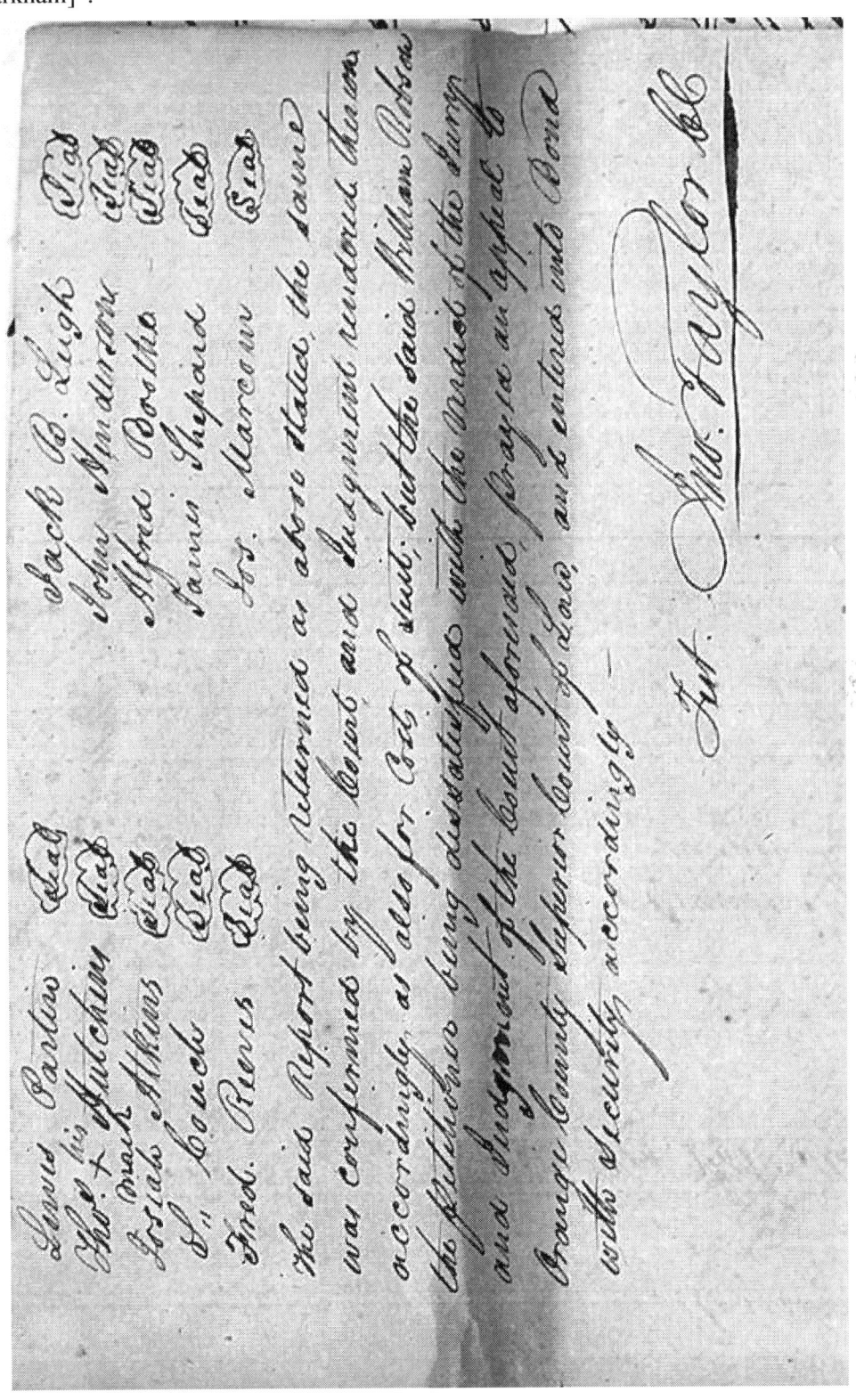

William Robson
vs.   } appeal
         3 Petition
Geo. Johnston Sen.r & Jun.r

To Orange Superior Court
September Term 1823.

filed 2d Septem.r 1823 —
            A.B.B.

Petition		10.
2 Copies		13.4
1 Subpoena		1.6
Writ to Shff		10.
verdict space		3.
determination		7.6
appeal Bond		6.
Transcript		8.
		2.19.4
Shff Watts & Witnesses		15.
Do 24 Jurors		2.8.
atto. Ruffin		2.
	£	8.4.4
Wm Blackwood wit		7.
Margaret Blackwood		7.
John Bevill Juror		11.
Sam.l Couch "		11.8
Tho.s Hutchins "		12.4
Tho.s Hogan "		11.
Wm Pearson "		15.8
Christ.r Barbee "		11.8
Tho.s D. Adams "		12.
Wm Barbee of F. "		14.4
Jno. Henderson "		12.4
Fred. Reeves "		15.
John B. Lugh "		13.
Alex.r Battee "		11.
Josiah Atkins "		17.8
Jos. Marcom "		16.4
Alfred Boothe "		15.8
Lewis Partin "		13.8
Barnes Shepard "		15.8
	£	20.8.4

Johnston – Ruffin Letter - 1823

George Johnston writes to Thomas Ruffin – "*Mr. William Robson has began to harass me again by his suits and et cetera of which I will inform you he has notified myself and son George that he will petition this May Term for a jury to assess annual damages and lay me under an annual tax to him – It appears to me that if Robson is under the necessary to notify myself and son, in this way, that we have a right to object to his petition. We do object on this ground, that after I had began my mills upwards of three months [before] he the said Robson made a purchase of a small tract of the creek above me from Mr. Blackwood Sr. and ordered me not to raise the back water on his part of it, notwithstanding at that time Robson did not own one foot of land adjoining it or near it when he had made the aforesaid purchase from Blackwood and it appears to me that his purchase was a malicious one and our only to stop me from building or to force me to pay an annual tax to a British alien, he is not a subject for he has not taken the oath of allegiance yet, I count myself a true American and have fought in the Revolutionary War. If Sir you think proper as my agent in all matters of litigation whatever, I wish for you to act for me in this affair. I will justify you to your satisfaction your friend…*"

The outside of the former letter.

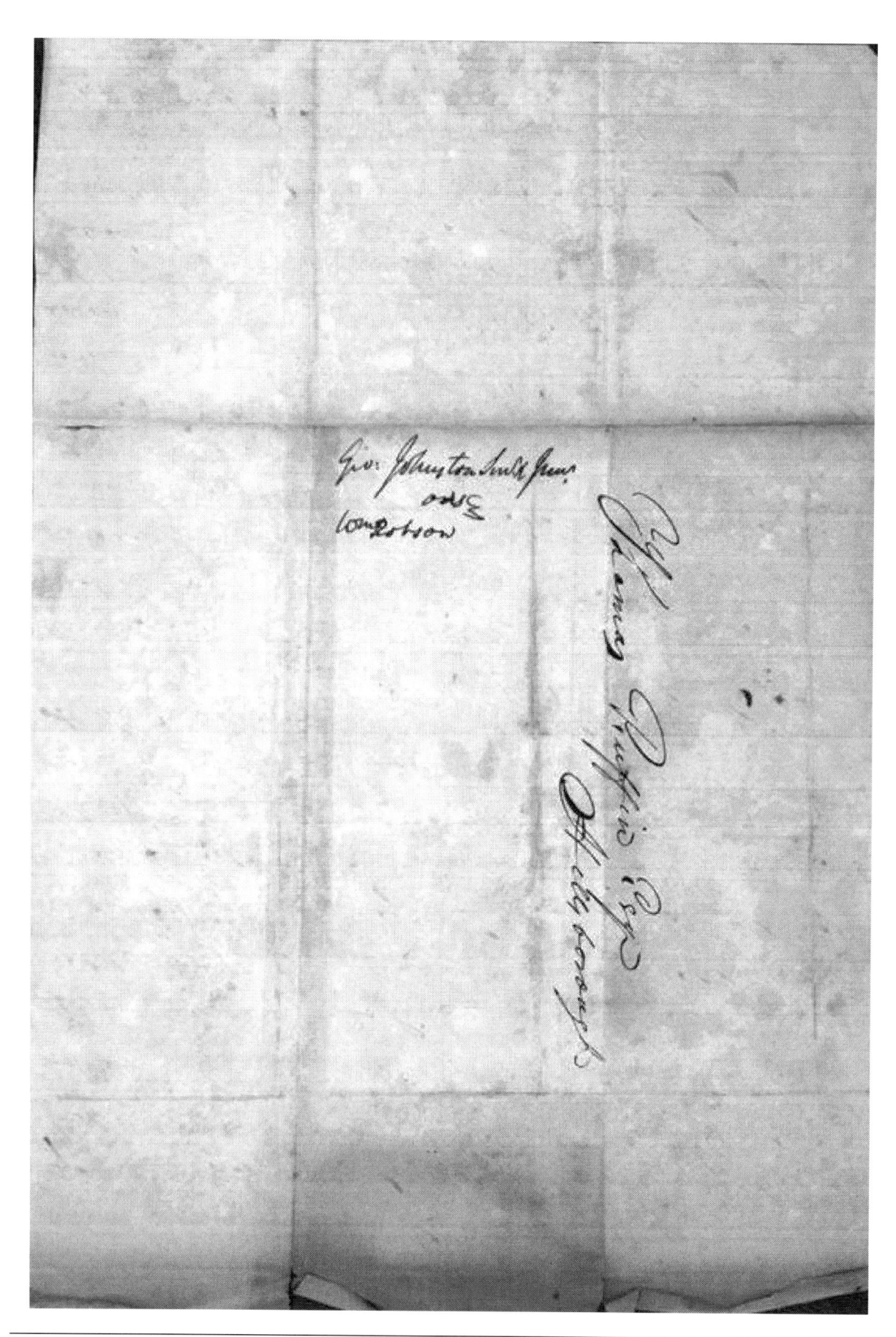

Here is a letter found in the Southern Collection of UNC library. This letter is located in the Dr. James Webb collection, in the Miss Mary Burke files. I have no idea why, but as I was working on Burke research, I found this letter that caught my eye, written by George Johnston discussing the law suit with Robson.

New Hope Sep 10th 1824

Dear Sir

Having a suit in our ensuing Superior Court wherein William Robson is plaintiff and myself and son are defendants which is about a mill that I have on New Hope Creek I would be glad you would assist my attorney Mr. Ruffin in defending us – and as I probably not have an opportunity of seeing you before court. I will state to you the case as plainly as this opportunity will admit so that you may be the better prepared to defend us, which is as follows. That wishing to build a saw mill on New Hope and having very good millseat on said creek, I in the year 1820 about the 18th or 20th January commenced preparing my millerons and digging the pit for a mill as can be proved by Mathew McCauley the smith who made the irons and by James Copley who dug the pit – William Robson who has a grist mill about a mile or thereabouts below me wishing to prevent me from building my mill above him purchased of William Blackwood Sr. in the month of May about the 27th of that month 1820 a small parcel of land consisting of Bluffs containing about an acre above my millseat and in a few days after he made the purchase, came and forbid me damming back the water on his millseat. This I can prove by John Blackwood Esq. and also prove by him that at the time he (Wm Robson) made the purchase of Mr. Blackwood he owned on neither side of the land he purchased my land – Now I wish it to be made appear that Robson design in making this purchase was not to build on it himself, but solely to prevent my building the saw mill which I think can be proven from the following circumstance – That when Robson was in the act of trading with Wm. Blackwood for this land Mrs. Margaret Blackwood his wife observed to Robson that if he built a mill there (??? On the land he purchased of her husband) it would be as bad as if Geo Johnston was to build – Robson replied that he never intended building there neither wanted any other person to build there. This can be proven by Mrs. Margaret Blackwood who was unwilling that either of us should build as either would stop up a cowford which she had a small distance above both seats – and that when Robson some time afterwards was in the act of cutting down the timber off this land a certain poplar tree being on the land which was inconvenient to get at the hands objected to cutting it – Robson replied that it must be cut as the timber and preventing Geo Johnston from building was all he expected to get after paying fifty dollars for the land. This can be proven by Archibald Brockwell who was at that time in Robsons employee and was one of the hands assisting in cutting the timber off the land.

When Robson forbidding me building a mill or damming back my water on him – I not wishing to enter into a law suit with him about it and unwilling to lose the materials I had prepared and wanting a saw mill – began to build some distance down the creek and the back water of my saw mill when the dam is completely full dams back on the dividing line between Robson and myself about 2 feet eddy water seven rod further up the creek only one foot and 3 rods still further up my eddy water runs out and it is the opinion of the millwrights which I had to examine this millseat of Robson that Robson land at the place where he says he wants to build is not a proper place to build at, as it is below the fall of water and that there is no place for a mill yard as this lands is not more than five rods wide at the place where he designs to building which is 7 rods above my line, and that a road can not be had without trespassing on other persons lands – But it is their opinion that about five rods above this place is a much better place for building a mill where my back water will not injure him where a good mill yard can be had and where he can have more space of ground as his lands widens as it extends up the creek. This I can prove by Stephen Gassins and Thomas Caster millwrights – These millwrights who leveled and examined this place and Col Jno Woods who surveyed and platted it. I wish you to examine ??? as they have it in their power to give all necessary information concerning this place as they have been on it. This suit is an appeal of Robson from the decision of a jury which he had appointed to assess the damages he sustained from my back water which jury reported no damages sustained and as I never have damaged him. I am unwilling to suffer in any shape whatever from this suit and hope you will find it in your power to be serviceable to me in this suite. My son George can give you all necessary information concerning this case if I should not have it in my power to see you myself.

"September 8, 1824 By the consent of William Robson and George Johnston…the parties mutually consented for the deposition of the Archibald Brockwell to be taken in consequence of his leaving this State for Tennessee and cannot possibly return in sufficient time to give personal testimony in behalf of the said defendants at our next Superior Court…"

Question – Were you not in the service of William Robson when you were cutting the timber of the land that he purchase from Mr. Blackwood Sr.? *Answer* – I was.

Question – Do you recollect the conversation that Mr. Robson had with yourself and the other hands when cutting on this ground? *Answer* – I do recollect the conversation and it was this. That in the job [task] of cutting the timber and taking it away from this ground there was an objection made by the hands in cutting a poplar tree down, it being unhandy to get to. Mr. Robson said to us his hands that it must be cut down for the timber on the ground was all that he expected to be profited by this ground except the timber and preventing Old George from building there after paying fifty dollars for the land.

Question by Plaintiff. I understand that you say that Mr. Bowers and Mr. Harril was there? *Answer* - That they were present at the time this conversation took place.

Question – Had not Mr. Johnston build his saw mill before this conversation took place or some ??? him before this conversation? – That it was where it now stands.

Continuation of the deposition.

Question By plaintiff I understand that you say that Mr. Bowers & Mr. Harril were there.

Answer By Deponant That they were there present at the time this conversation took place

Question By plaintiff. had not Mr. Johnston built his saw Mill before this conversation took place or some considerable time before this conversation —

Answer by deponant That it was where it now stands

And further this deponent saith not Duly sworn to and subscribed before us Acting Justices of the peace for the aforesaid County the day and date first above written

W. A. Pratt J.P.   his
                                Archibald X Bradshaw
H Johnston J.P.   mark

Question by the plaintiff What was your idea of my intention when this conversation took place

Answer By Deponant that it was my idea that it was your object &c by plaintiff

The forgoing Deposition was taken in the presence and by the consent of the parties both being present signed in the Presence of us W. A. Pratt J.P.   Wm Robson
          H Johnston J.P.   Geo Johnston

Wm Robinson
vs
Geo Johnston   William Blackwood summoned to
attend as a witness in the above case in behalf of
the Defendant ~~Charges~~ 1 days attendance   £n. 6— — 1 —
                                                              ——————
this ticket   — 7 —

Test
J D Watts Sh ff

Wm Robinson
vs
Geo Johnston   Margritt Blackwood summoned to
attend as a witness in the above case in behalf of
the defendant ~~Charges~~ 1 days attendance £n. 6— — 1 —
                                                              ——————
this ticket   — 7 —

Test
J D Watts Sh ff

Robson Appeals - 1823

Here is the official paperwork to file for an Appeal by Mr. Robson.

State of North Carolina.

D. Heartt, Printer, Hillsborough.

KNOW ALL MEN BY THESE PRESENTS, That we William Robson, William Kirkland & John M. Cawley are held and firmly bound unto George Johnson Senr. & George Johnson Jr. in the sum of One Hundred Pounds to which payment well and truly to be made we bind ourselves, our heirs, executors, and administrators, jointly and severally, firmly by these presents. Sealed with our seals and dated this 28th day of August A. D. 1823

THE CONDITION of the above obligation is such, that whereas lately in a suit prosecuted in Orange County Court of Pleas and Quarter Sessions, wherein the said William Robson is plaintiff and the said George Johnson Senr. & George Johnson Jr. defendants, a verdict was rendered in behalf of the said Johnsons ~~for the sum of~~

and judgment of said court was rendered thereon accordingly, as also for costs of said suit: but the said William Robson being dissatisfied therewith, prayed for and obtained an appeal to the Superior Court of Law to be held for the county of Orange Now if the said William Robson shall well and truly prosecute his said appeal with effect, and in case he be cast therein shall well and truly pay all such sum or sums of money as shall be awarded against him, and costs of suit, then the above obligation to void; else to remain in full force and virtue.

Wm Robson
J. M. Cawley
Wm Kirkland

Final Judgment of the Appeal - 1825

The final piece of the puzzle comes from the Superior Court records (NC Archives). As shown earlier, Robson appealed and here is the final judgment. – George Johnston was NOT Guilty.

George Johnston Sells land – 1821 to 1826

Now that all the legal issues have been settled, it is time to move forward. Actually, we first have to review some key land sales prior to the legal mess, and just after. All in all, this section addresses the last years of George Johnston Sr. life.

George Johnston Sr., stops purchasing land in 1815, except for the Cabe Mill purchase, which is a very interesting situation, in 1826. It will be easier to just quote the information found in the deed record (23/27), *"…undivided 3rd part of a certain tract of land including a merchant and grist mill on Eno River formerly the property of John Cabe deceased … and since his decease has been laid off and allotted to Lydia daughter of said John Cabe deceased now the wife of Charles W. Johnston and by the said Charles and Lydia conveyed to George M. Johnston by deed bearing date June 1, 1825 and by the said George M. Johnston conveyed to George Johnston Sr. by deed January 21 last. Viz the 1/3 part the other 2/3 part to Mary wife of Mann Patterson and Margaret wife of John W. Caldwell daughters of the said John Cabe deceased by commissioners appointed for that purpose by order of court. Adjacent the land of Abraham Nelson lying on both sides of Eno River, beginning stake S43C PO, E6C BO, S46C PO, E38C PO, N40C WO, W5C WO, N40C to Spanish Oak, W39C to beginning. Contains 304 acres in the whole three parts be the same more or less…"*

George starts to sell off his land holdings to his children, starting October 3, 1821 when he gives 255 acres to his daughter Mary. Then on October 20, 1821 when he gives 333 acres of land (22/439) to Elizabeth Johnston (minor), and 574 acres of land to his son George M. Johnston (20/129). Three years later he transacts two more pieces of land on August 25, 1824. First he sells 373 acres of land to his son-in-law William Dusken, and his wife Mary Johnston Dusken (21/301). Then he gives part of his Tennessee (speculation) land to son-in-law Gray Huckabee 400 acres (25/187) in Haywood County on the Hatchee River. June 1, 1825 he gives 900 acres of land to his son George M. Johnston (23/22) also part of the (2500 acres) Tennessee land he bought from John Rice in 1789. He then gives 300 acres to each of his youngest, Elizabeth, and Sarah (23/50 and 23/51).

George Sr. last two sales are to his son-in-laws. In another interesting twist, George Sr. originally wanted to give the land adjoining (east) William Robson, to his Gray Huckabee. However, it turns out that he sells it to William Robson, and has William pay his son-in-law (Gray) for the land. It is my assumption that George Sr. asked Gray if he wanted the land or the money, since it would be certain the last thing he would want to do, is sell land to the man who just sued him! Never the less, 261 acres of land was sold (21/546) to William Robson, and Gray Huckabee (wife Martha Johnston) received $500 from William, per the deed. In fact, it states in the deed, *"…I designed giving to my said son in law…"*

Unfortunately, George Johnston Senior dies November 5, 1830, at age 68.

George Johnston Land Information

	Year	Date	Book/pg	Acres	Name	Notes
George Sr. buying	1784	18-Dec	3/73	357	John Young	New Hope land
George Sr. buying	1784	14-Dec	3/74	100	John Young	New Hope land
George Sr. buying	1786	8-Nov	4/330	640	Mathew McCauley	Davidson County land
George Sr. buying	1787	6-Jan	3/174	640	Alexander Duggar	Orig Andrew Peterson land 3/1/1786
George Sr. buying	1789	9-May	4/329	2500	John Rice	Western Dist (TN) Haywood Cty Hatchee River TN
George Sr. buying	1790	13-Sep	9/165	300	Samuel Strudwick	Land on McAdams Creek
George Sr. buying	1792	13-Jul	4/710	520	David Merideth	New Hope land
George Sr. buying	1793	16-Oct	5/84	1	UNC	Lot #11 University (Chapel Hill)
George Sr. buying	1795	18-Sep	5/488	240	Samuel Allen	
George Sr. buying	1795	4-Dec	5/502	200	Thomas Connally Sr.	
George Sr. buying	1796	5-Jan	5/505	132	James Blackwood	adjacent to Connally
George Sr. buying	1796	21-Nov	6/156	627	William Courtney	3 tracts of land on New Hope
George Sr. buying	1796	27-Feb	6/226	22	James Patterson	Partner Samuel Hopkins - includes a saw mill on Bolins Creek
George Sr. buying	1797	24-Feb	6/204	22	William Rhoads	New Hope land
George Sr. buying	1797	19-Jul	7/322	40	Land Grant #1274	New Hope land (Aug 29, 1786)
George Sr. buying	1797	19-Jul	7/323	51	Land Grant #1275	New Hope land (Dec 27, 1792 per plat)
George Sr. buying	1797	7-Aug	6/327	12.5	James Patterson	Partner Samuel Hopkins - Bolands creek near University
George Sr. buying	1802	12-Jan	10/65	218	John Barbee	New Hope land
George Sr. buying	1806	15-Apr	13/105	10	Mathew McCauley	Bolands Creek land, Saw Mill and timber rights
George Sr. buying	1811	16-Feb	13/451		James Rainey	
George Sr. buying	1815	26-Dec	19/35	331	James Johnston	Haw River and Meadow Creek
George Sr. buying	1826	1-Jan	23/60		George W. Johnston	Cabe Mill Purchase

	Year	Date	Book/pg	Acres	Name	Notes
George Sr. Selling	1794	25-Jul	5/123	1	John McCawley	Lot #11 University (Chapel Hill)
George Sr. Selling	1797	13-Jan	6/333	132	Mathew McCauley	Hightower, to Blackwood to Johnston.
George Sr. Selling	1798	3-Dec	7/429	141.5	Thomas Couch	this is half of the Mack Patterson tract
George Sr. Selling	1801	5-Mar	9/285	12.5	Samuel Hopkins	sells his half-interest (see 6/327)
George Sr. Selling	1811	16-Oct	14/367	143	William Robson	Sells the mill on New Hope
George Sr. Selling	1819	25-May	17/279	614.8	Charles W. Johnston	gives this land to son, bounded by Freeland, Blackwood, New Hope
George Sr. Selling	1821	3-Oct	20/124	255	Mary Johnston	to his daughter Mary
George Sr. Selling	1821	30-Oct	22/439	333	Elizabeth Johnston	minor - daughter of Geo, land adj to Mann Patterson
George Sr. Selling	1821	30-Oct	20/129	574.3	George Johnston Jr.	home land to son (see 22/355) Geo Jr. sells to son C. W.
George Sr. Selling	1824	25-Aug	21/301	373	William Dusken	Son-in-law (daughter Mary) land by Buroughs and Geo sr
George Sr. Selling	1824	25-Aug	25/187	400	Gray Huckabee	Son-in-law (piece of the Western Dist Land)
George Sr. Selling	1824	25-Aug	23/50	300	Sarah B. Johnston	Haywood Co. TN - Hatchee River land
George Sr. Selling	1824	25-Aug	23/51	300	Elizabeth Johnston	Haywood Co. TN - Hatchee River land
George Sr. Selling	1825	1-Jun	23/220	900	George Johnston Jr.	Haywood Co. TN - Hatchee River land
George Sr. Selling	1825	8-Oct	21/546	261	William Robson	Gray Huckabee paid by Robson, Geo Sr. sells
George Sr. Selling	1826	21-Sep	23/27	304	Mary Dusken	Eno River land (daughter) John Cabe Mill 1/3 interest

William Robson and - New Hope Land – 1825-1833

As stated earlier, George Sr. sells some adjoining land to William in 1825 (although Gray Huckabee was paid). Then in 1833, George Johnston's (now deceased) daughter Elizabeth (now married to Charles King) sells 330 acres of land (26/123) to William Robson.

William Robson gives the Estate to his Sons – 1862-1867

Since William Robson is much younger than George Senior, he lives well into the Civil War era. His two sons (who were living) get all the land, that being, William G. Robson, and James W. Robson (typically just – J.W.). The first transaction occurs April 6, 1862 when he gave 430 acres (40/329) of land to J.W. Robson, which includes the Mill. The next land transaction occurs April 20, 1863 when he gives 300 acres (40/33) to the same son. Finally he gives 281 acres of land (37/410) to his son William G. Robson January 1, 1867.

William Robson Land Information

Here is a table of the land transactions of William Robson. From this table you can find the deed transcript in the back of this book.

	Year	Date	Book/pg	Acres	Name	Notes
William Robson Buying	1811	16-Oct	14/367	143	George Thompson	Buys the mills from Geo Sr. $3500 (Edward and William Robson)
William Robson Buying	1814	14-Jun	15/10		Edward Robson	Edward - William's Brother, sells his half interest in the mill - $800
William Robson Buying	1820	20-May	20/246	2	William Blackwood Sr.	land adj Johnston, law suit over flooding
William Robson Buying	1821	28-Nov	19/203	428	Joel Cloud	Combs Creek Land
William Robson Buying	1825	8-Oct	21/546	261	Geo/Gray Huckabee	Gray Huckabee paid by Robson, Geo Sr. sells
William Robson Buying	1833	23-Dec	26/123	330	Thomas King	New Hope - King married Eliz Johnston (see 22/439)
	Year	Date	Book/pg	Acres	Name	Notes
William Robson Selling	1843	6-May	31/145	99	Charles King	Morgans Creek land
William Robson Selling	1867	1-Jan	37/410	281	Willaim G. Robson Jr.	Sells New Hope land to son (adj Blacknall and Freeland)
William Robson Selling	1862	6-Apr	40/329	430	J.W. Robson	Sells the mill and New Hope land to son
William Robson Selling	1863	20-Apr	40/330	300	J.W. Robson	Sells moreNew Hope land to son

After William dies at a very old age (abt. 87), his two remaining sons (J.W. and W.G.) have all the land holdings. For some reason J.W. (James) has the largest amount of land, and includes the family estate. J.W. dies at a young age (abt, 52), and his wife Mary C. Robson then has control of the large land holdings. She ultimately sells it all.

Selling	Year	Date	Book/pg	Acres	Name (buying)	Notes
J.W. & M.C. Robson	1875	19-Oct	44/123	1	NHD Wilson	Part of Lot #6 Hillsboro
J.W. & M.C. Robson	1876	15-Feb	48/51	58	Henry Cole	Bolins Creek Near Chapel Hill
J.W. & M.C. Robson	1873	6-Sep	42/17	12	Sharp and Tate	Mill and 12 acres
J.W. & M.C. Robson	1876	30-Oct	44/545	44.5	H.P. Smith	Land on Oxford Rd
M.C. Robson	1876	15-Mar	48/485	55	Nash Booth	land on Mill Road to Patterson's mill
M.C. Robson	1883	3-Oct	48/22	403	James R. Blacknall	Robson Homestead Place
M.C. Robson	1884	19-Dec	48/197	1	James E. Jones	Part of Lot #25 Hillsboro
W.G. Robson	1882	4-Mar	49/491	3	Lloyd and King	3a and a mill - Railroad/New Hope and a stream
William Robson	1829	29-Dec	25/360	80	Mary Flintoff	Part of Zachias Burroughs land
Wm Robson	1843	11-May	31/145	99.5	Charles King	Morgans Creek property
Wm Robson	1867	1-Jan	37/410	281	W.G. Robson	Great Branch propery
Wm Robson	1862	6-Apr	40/329	430	J.W. Robson	Geo Johnston-Huckabee land
Wm Robson	1863	20-Apr	40/330	300	J.W. Robson	Geo Johnston-King- Robson land
Wm Robson	1877	11-May	45/173	1	Alice Burton	part of Lot ?? In Hillsboro
Wm Robson	1877	11-May	45/258		Mary C. Robson	

Mill Site Transition to Duke Forest

As time moves on, people pass away, and land gets sold off. Nothing different for the Robson Family. William amassed a large estate, and financially survived it all. His son, J.W., inherits the mill, and most of the land, especially the estate (home).

Robson to Sharp and Tate (1873)

J.W. Robson sells the mill tract (mill, and 12 acres of land) in 1873, while he is alive. Was this due to health issues? Was it operational? The deed documents this very well:

42/17 – 9/6/1873 – On waters of New Hope Creek adjoining the lands of J.W. Robson, Johnston and others, known as Robson Lower Mill Tract. Beginning at white oak along race on the south side of the mill pond S9°W 8C to peach tree then S20°E 90 links to corner of a rock fence near the mill then S20°W 9C to rock pile thence E5C 62L to a rock in the middle of the creek, N15°E 24C to Spanish oak on a small branch, down said branch as it meanders to the mill pond and across said pond to beginning 12 acres…includes mill home fixtures and all the appurtenances thereunto belonging together ….with all the necessary privileges of said mill seat and ….privilege to raise the mill dam two feet higher then present standing without further charge for damages…"

Note the deed provided a title for the tract – *Robson Lower Mill Tract*. Secondly, the deed clearly allowed the new owners the right to alter the dam height, and absolved them from any "damage" law suits from Robson. This was certainly important to have, written into a contract, let alone the deed. However, the dam height (2 feet) clause implies the buyers had recognized the need (immediately or in the future) to increase it's height. This might have originated from past experience, or maybe Robson mentioned to them, that silt buildup or operational issues occurred, and agreed to add this clause for them. Despite these theories, the buyers received a great clause in their deed.

Sharp & Tate to Robert M. Dickson (1913)

Robert Sharp, and John L. Tate purchase the mill for $800, September 6, 1873. In the 1880 census of Orange County, John L. Tate is listed (with his wife Henrietta) as 26 years old, and his occupation was "Machinist". Imagine 7 years earlier he was 19 years old! Does a 19 year old buy a mill operation? Was his occupation (machinist) why he was a partner? In the 1900 census (still owning the mill) John is still listed as a machinist, renting a home in Hillsborough. Deed records prove that John L. Tate's very first purchase of land was this mill. However, his dad George W. Tate gives him some land on Haw Creek in 1880, and he sells this in 1884. This sale lists (his wife) Henrietta, which proves this is the correct person. Yet, legally, his dad was his partner, or at least ½ owner. George W. was 50 years in the 1880 census, and 8 children still at home! In fact, George W. resides with his daughter, and son-in-law (via the 1910 census) at age 80. His daughter's (Margaret C. Lynch) name helps understand the settlement issue, later on (legal issues).

Robert H. Sharp, on the other hand, states in the Census that he is a farmer, and he too was very young, just 28 years old, making him 21 when they bought the mill. Was this an investment? Was life that simple, that two very young men (a machinist and a farmer) buy, own, maintain, and operate a mill?

Not very long after their joint-purchase, Robert H. Sharp sells his half to George W. Tate (John L. Tates's dad) for $580.00 on December 31, 1874, just 4 months after buying it. He sold his "half" for more than half of the original purchase. Was this due to valuation (property appreciation) or was this due to business being such that warrants the increased valuation? We will probably never know. In the census records, George W. Tate is also listed (occupation) as a machinist. Certainly, from a mill maintenance viewpoint, being a machinist would be a valuable skill.

Never the less, the mill is owned for 40 years, from 1873 until 1913 when the settlement of the estate (George W. Tate's death) forced them to liquidate this property. Searching old books, I did find a reference to George Tate. It was an act to establish grade school boundaries for Orange County. It stated, (1903) *"...thence south to railroad, two miles east of the depot thence with line of T.M. Cheek and George W. Tate to creek above G.W. Tate's Mill-pond; thence down said creek to Henry A. Wilson..."* Many questions come to mind about "Tate Mill". Was it successful? Did they expand or improve the mill? I have searched the internet (and other resources) looking for a mill under their name, either individually or as a combination, and did not find anything. How do you operate a mill for 40 years, and no one documents a thing?

George W. Tate dies (September 28, 1911), the estate gets settled, and the mill is sold. March 17, 1913 the land, and mill, are sold to the highest bidder at the Hillsboro Courthouse. The deed states, *"**Judgment of the Superior Court, John McAdams was appointed commissioner. J.L. Tate and others, devisees of George W. Tate deceased against Mannie (sic?) Lynch and others...**"*. It was sold for $150 to Robert W. Dickson. Another date associated with the legal proceedings was April 30, 1913. Knowing that George Tate's daughter was a Lynch, helps understand who was suing, and why.

	Year	Date	Book/pg	Acres	Name	Notes
Mary Robson (J.W. deceased)	1883	3-Oct	48/22	403	James R. Blacknall	Robson Homestead place, masons spring, $1500
James Blacknall	1888	17-Mar	52/343	403	W.E. Martin	Robson Homestead place, masons spring, $3000 *** DEAD DEED***
James Blacknall	1905	6-May	59/584	400	Frank Couch	Robson Homestead place, masons spring, $3000
Frank Couch	1925	2-Feb	83/622	365	Erwin Cotton Mill Corp.	Robson Homestead place, minus 125a to Maj Trice
Erwin Cotton Mill Corp.	1926	3-Jun	86/181	365	Duke Land Co	Robson Homestead place tract
J.W. Robson	1873	6-Sep	42/17	12	Sharp and Tate	12 Acre Mill Tract
Tate forced sale Court House	1913	30-Apr	84/59	11.5	Robert Dickson	12 Acre Mill Tract
Robert Dickson	1925	17-Feb	85/71	11.5	Erwin Cotton Mill Corp	12 Acre Mill Tract
Erwin Cotton Mill Corp.	1926	3-Jun	86/181	11.5	Duke Land Co	12 Acre Mill Tract

Dickson to Erwin Cotton Mill Corp (1925)

Why did Robert Dickson buy this? Was this an investment? Once again, searching the Census records, I located the ONLY Robert W. Dickson, as a young man (35 years old in 1913) whose occupation was listed as - Railroad Engineer. He was living at home. In fact, he remains living at home for many years. When Robert M. Dickson sells the mill, the deed record includes this comment - *"unmarried"*. Here we have another unknown – why would a single guy (living at home) buy a grist mill? What is known, he retains ownership for 12 years, and then sells the mill (1925), and land for $10.00 to Erwin Cotton Mill Corp. One year later Erwin Cotton Mill Corp. sells all their companies land holdings in 1926 to the Duke University. This ends the land transaction, for the "Robson Mill" tract. Why did Dickson sell it? Buy it for $150, and sell it for $10 (buy high – sell low) – was this a depression issue? Searching the internet, and all the historical resources (books) I could, I found – nothing.

Erwin Cotton Mill Corp.

As near as I can determine, this company was formed around 1893. In a report documenting all the cotton mills in North Carolina, stated that Erwin Cotton Mill Corp., was currently under construction. Then it appears for many years thereafter. In a State Labor report (1915) Erwin Cotton Mills of Durham was manufacturing denim, pillow cases, and material of all kinds. The President was Brodie N. Duke. This was a large textile corporation in western Durham. Although formed by Duke, they named it after their new recruitment – William Erwin. Erwin came from Alamance County, formerly employed by the Eugene Michael Holt mill company.

Another book states this about the company (1898), *"...On the newly macadamized road which runs from Durham westward past the Erwin Cotton Mill, at a spot two hundred yards or more below the point at which the county road passes under the railroad, is a place which has a certain weird interest for those people who like to know the legends of the past. It is known as the Redmond Place, and because of a fine spring of clear water it is frequently visited by some Durham people who have never heard of the dark traditions concerning it which have come down in the minds of old people in the community."* The story continued to tell about the Peeler family killing people, and disposing of their bodies in the well. The place was given the name "Peeler Cross-roads." Never the less, here is another book that documents the time when Erwin was in operation.

It was interesting to note that in 1925 they bought all the land, which they would sell (below) in 1926, just one year later. In fact, the pages were sequential (book 85 - pages 70-74), and covered all the land holdings between the dates of February 9 to the 23rd. Oddly, *all* transactions (purchasing) were for $10, despite the acreages. Most deeds were for multiple lands acquisitions. Why did they buy all this land, and one year later sell all the land? Erwin Mill's was in operation until 1986. This disproves the idea they sold all 13 lots of land in this area due to "closing their doors". Based on the deed (86/181) the vice-president of Erwin Mills was John Sprunt Hill and K. P. Lewis was assistant secretary for the Corporation (in 1926).

Because this was a Duke (B.N. Duke) owned company, is this why all the land was sold to Duke University?

Here is the sale of all pieces of land for Erwin Cotton Mill Corp in 1926 – one deed.

86/181 – June 3, 1926 – 13 tracts of land (839acres) **Erwin Cotton Mill Inc to Duke University ($100)**
1) New Hope Creek – high bluff near Blacknall's corner, 60A (74/84)
2) 31acres (74/83)
3) Sinai Baptist (colored) Church near 2.4a (78/400)
4) Upper Mill - 365 acres from three pieces (59/584, 72/245, 83/622) Frank Cole, from J. R. Blacknall
5) Late C.W. Johnston and Frank Couch corner – Allen's Branch to Yearagin's line, mouth of Allen branch and New Hope creek – 180.61a (73/341)
6) Willow Spring, near Levi Carden and Couch property 35.5a (74/409 & 85/73)
7) New Hope and the mouth of Willow Spring Branch – 31a (79/473)
8) 0.83a (85/8 & 85/73)
9) New Hope – 15a (85/70)
10) 4a (85/70)
11) New Hope, spring branch in Carden's corner, old Whitfield line – 88.8a (82/108 & 85/75)
12) North side of New Hope – 13.5a (85/75, 56/229)
13) Lower Robson Mill Tract – 11.5a (84/59 and 85/71 which points to 42/17) – "begin WO stump along mill race and in the edge of the old mill pond S9°W 8c stake (peach tree in the old deed) S20°E 90 links on the east side of an old rock fence with fence S20°W 9c to rocks, E5.62C rock in middle of New Hope then N15°E 24C to Spanish oak on spring branch down branch as it meanders to said creek then across said creek S44.75°W to begin 11.50acres, known as the Lower Robson Mill Tract.

This deed (the main one – 86/181) had one exception – Crawford Stake and Handle Company has timber rights to land #11 and #12. (82/108)

Misc. Notes:

In one deed (73/341) I saw the name of Charles Hughes Johnston and wife Nell B. residing in Illinois (Dec 1, 1916) selling land to John T. Johnston, called Lot 1 and Lot 7 and the home place of the late C.W. Johnston. Based on information from Will Book J, page 582. Plat (none referenced) was provided by James Webb August 29, 1916.

Deed 85/71 (Feb 17, 1925) states that Robert Dickson is single.

The 1925 land deals (Erwin Cotton Mill Corp buying):

85/70 – Levi Carden $10.00 1)15a (56/361) and 2) 4a (73/280)

85/71 – Lower Robson Mill Tract - $10.00

85/72 – Frank Couch $10.00 – 1)60a 7/84, 2)31acres (74/83) 3)Colored Church 2.4acres (78/480)

85/73 – Trice - $10.00 1)35.5 acres (74/409), 2) Willow Spring (70/473), 3) 13.5acres (56/229)

85/74 – John T. Johnston $10.00 – 180.61 acres (Charles H. Johnston to John T. 73/341) * See above

85/75 – J. K. Timman $10.00 – 1) 88.8 acres (82/108) 2) 13.5acres (56/229)

Key Locations

In order to locate old property boundaries, it takes time, patience, and good luck. The surveyor can make or break the "good luck" by how much detail he adds or leaves out, during the survey. Fortunately, two key locations were mentioned many times. Babs Branch, and Masons Spring where real important land marks. That was due to consistent use or reuse of these landmarks even into the 20th century. This next section shows these locations in further detail.

Mason Spring

In my deed research, the property metes and bounds (as provided by the surveyor), when working with the Robson property, always referenced Masons Spring. In fact, the very first time this spring name is used was 1811. I have been unable to reconcile the name "Mason" to this spring. (One theory is that George Johnston was a Mason – i.e. Masonic Lodge). Typically, you would expect the spring to be named for a former land owner (and this would be his spring). Yet, all this land dates back to land grants of Young and Allen. Then George Johnston owned it, and then sold it to William Robson. In addition, the spring does not seem to be associated to a nearby house, but a location feeding a stream (in the stream bed) below a land drainage area. My point is, this is low land, and not a good home site. During the wet season, you would have a difficult time traversing this low, wet ground.

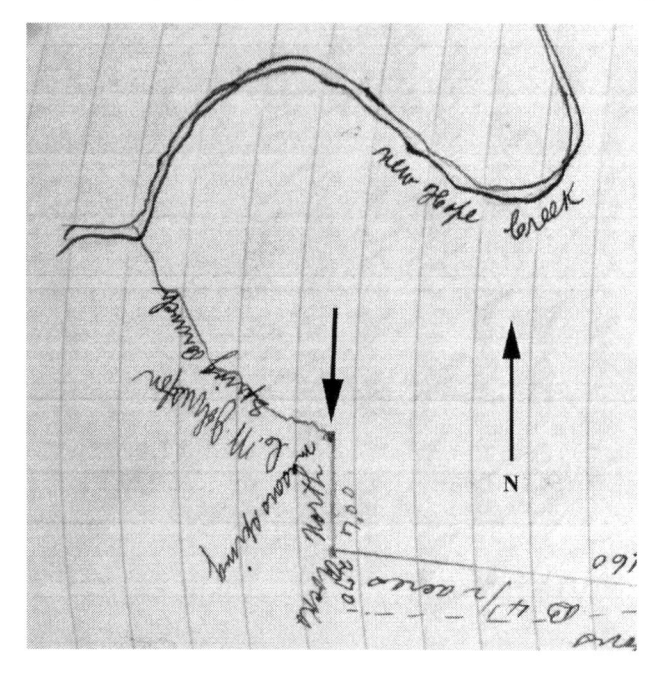

Never the less, locating this spring was important. It was part of the survey, and the boundary of the land. The stream (from the spring) empties into New Hope Creek. At the mouth of this small stream, and New Hope, was the location of the property, following New Hope Creek back to the mill site (actually the edge of the mill pond).

In addition, some of the deed records mentioned Babs Branch, as another land mark on the way to Masons Spring. Thanks to the survey plat being in the deed book, I was able to identify both of these landmarks. Further, a walk in the woods resulted in locating Masons Spring.

In the 20th century, I found references in deed records to this same location under a new name – Marshall's Spring. Also the spring branch was listed as Marshall spring branch. See the Deed Reference Section for more details (deed 72/139). Where did this name (Marshall) come from?

Here is a GIS (Orange County) aerial (2003) map showing the land marks, with my notes added. Wooden Bridge road is the name given by Duke Forest, which is a hiking trail. From there you make a left on West Road (labeled dead end) crossing under the power lines, and then continue another 100 yards. The road looks as if it ends. If you look closely, continuing west, there is a small path that will take you down to the stream bed. You will notice stone walls, used to designate the property line. (Note: the lines for a creek are approx via GIS).

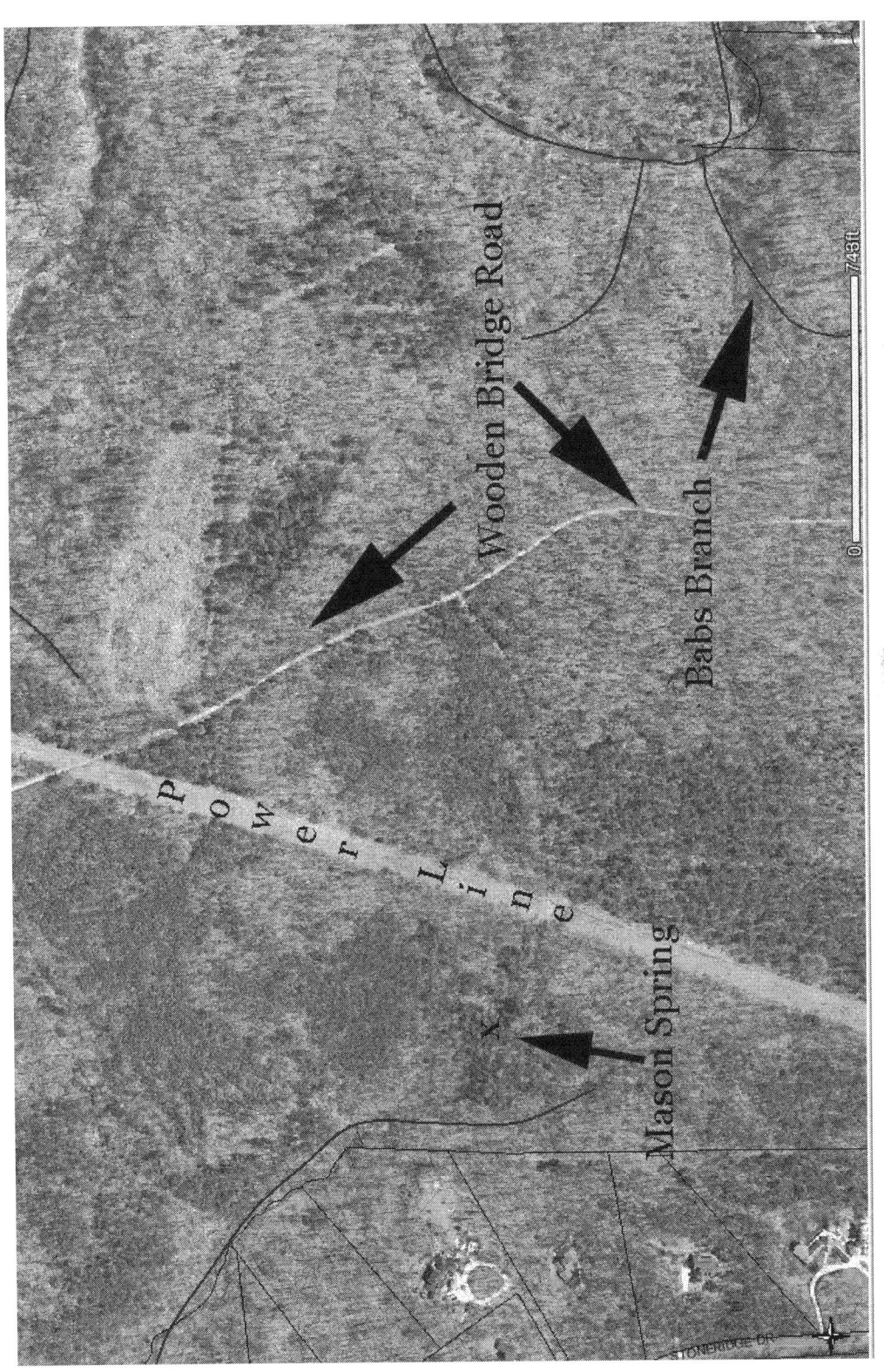

115

Here is a picture of Mason Spring. This spring is more of "seepage" than a flowing spring out of a bank of a hill, and certainly not one "bubbling up" from the ground. Even though we have been in a rainy pattern, the spring was barely flowing.

Below, the image is viewing north or downstream (so to speak) showing the boundary stone wall on the left, and the stream on the right, making its way empting into New Hope Creek. This picture does not show the water very well. However, there was a modest flow present.

The stone walls in this area are impressive. Amazing how pristine they remain despite the years. Still, trees falling across the wall occur, and some uprooting trees have also damaged the wall. As illustrated below, the wall is about 3 feet high in some places, and in others, it can be just above the ground level, and yet, other sections only a foot high. This wall (or stone fence) is on Robson's property line, following along Masons Spring Branch.

Here is a USGS Topo map annotated with the Spring location as I GPS'ed the stream bed, and the dashed lines are the property line from the original metes and bounds. Also you will note the Robson Mill tract.

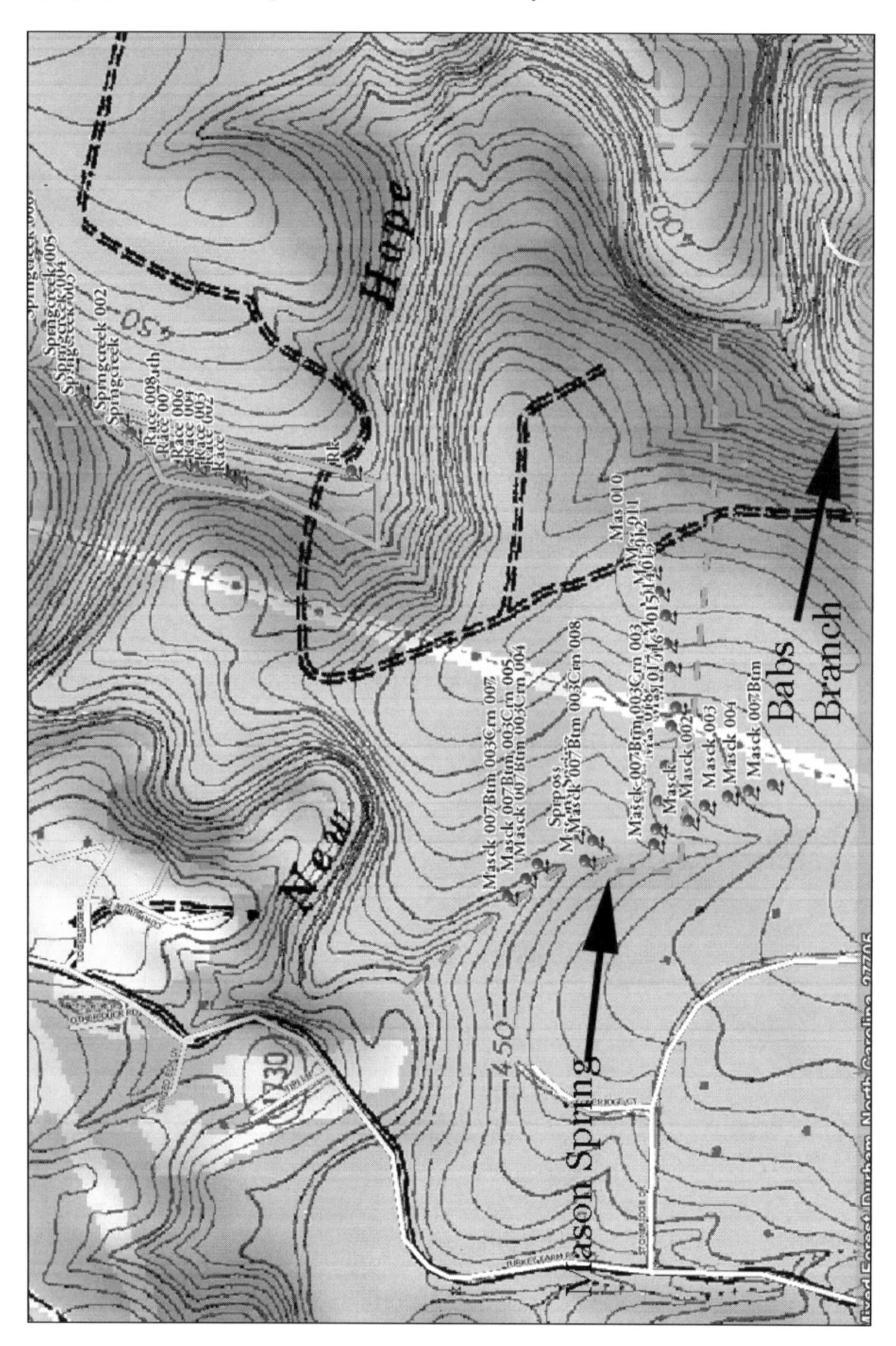

118

Babs Branch

Since this corner, Babs Branch's entrance to New Hope, was so often used, I determined to visit the site. I traversed this small creek, which consists of two separate drains into one creek, and ultimately enters New Hope at a unique location. It's just above a 90 degree bend, or an elbow in the river. This elbow will become the contentious area between Robson and Johnston. All the survey records state, *"Ash on the north bank of Babs Branch on the west side of New Hope"*.

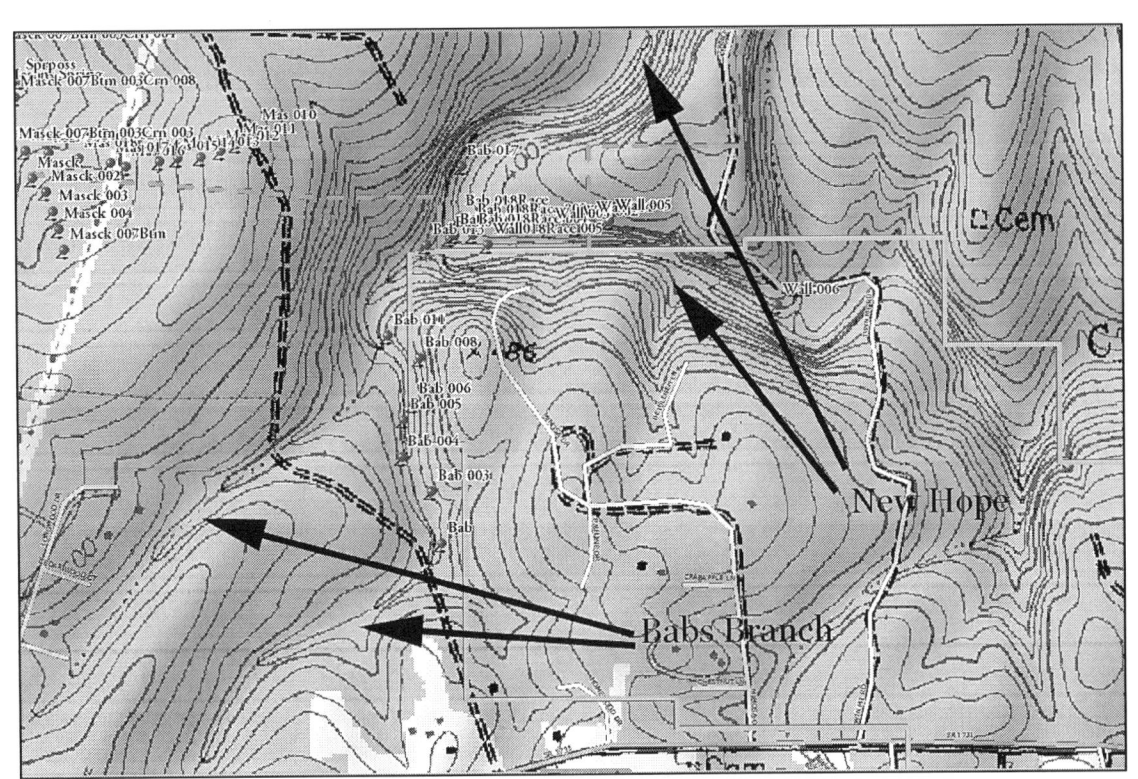

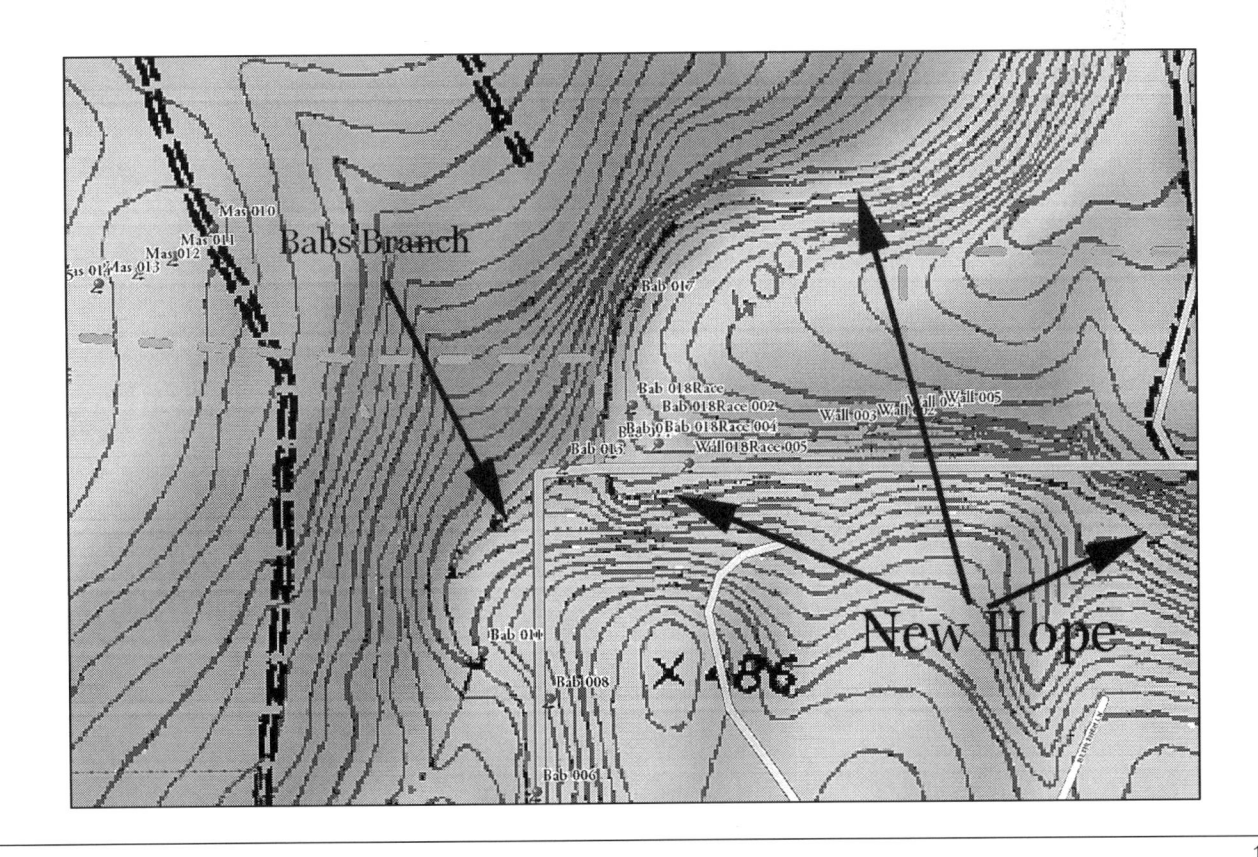

Babs branch begins like so many small creeks, a small meandering stream. The land is rather flat, although the stream continues a slow transition down in elevation. The further down stream you go, the land on either side begins to get steeper. One oddity that I noticed was the reduction of water flow the further down you went, although you are traversing the stream flow – down. Finally when the stream meets another leg at a fork, the combination of the two small streams increased the waters flow, but not by much.

Farther down, after the fork, the terrain becomes rockier, and steeper, on the northwestern sides. Rock bluffs vary from 15-20 feet in height.

Finally, as you get nearer New Hope, the surrounding land starts to flatten out, and New Hope emerges. Below is a view standing at New Hope looking west at Babs Branch. On the left is private property, as the swing shows, and on the right is the corner tree, and Duke Forest land.

Looking northward (New Hope at Babs Branch "mouth"), the river seems flat, and rather wide. In effect, the river was the dividing line between Robson and Johnston land. On the right hand side of this picture would be the Johnston land holdings, extending eastward.

In the other direction, the southern side of New Hope turns into a super-rocky area. This is a view looking due east. My back is at the elbow. On the left is the possible Mill Race.

The southern edge of New Hope is more or less a cliff. The only location for a mill (at this location) is on the north side of the river. The bolder picture below is approximately 8-10 feet in height, and the cliffs on this side are very steep (and rugged).

Here is another view of New Hope, looking due east. On the left (north side) is the possible mill race, and mill seat location. This was Johnston's land.

Below, another view of the bend, after a rain storm.

As shown on the USGS topo map (Babs Branch section – earlier), are some points labeled "Wall" which are shown here. Once again, this is the William Robson signature stone wall. Here, like other sections, the wall just ends. The bottom picture is the most western part of the wall. As with all other areas, this wall is more or less intact. There is a roadbed (clearly worn, albeit with a lot of overgrowth, and spring greenery) in front of the wall, and you can easily follow it towards the elbow. However, as you go east, and at the end of the wall (labeled Wall005) the wall ends, and the road becomes a challenge to follow. Ultimately, a stone cliff blocks all eastward movement as the cliff emerges into New Hope Creek. This circumstance (seems to me) eliminates the "roadbed" as a valid transportation route for a mill location.

125

Adjacent Land

Moving further east, and adjoining the mill land, is B.L. Duke's property. Note the road locations, names, and then compare this to a modern map on the next page.

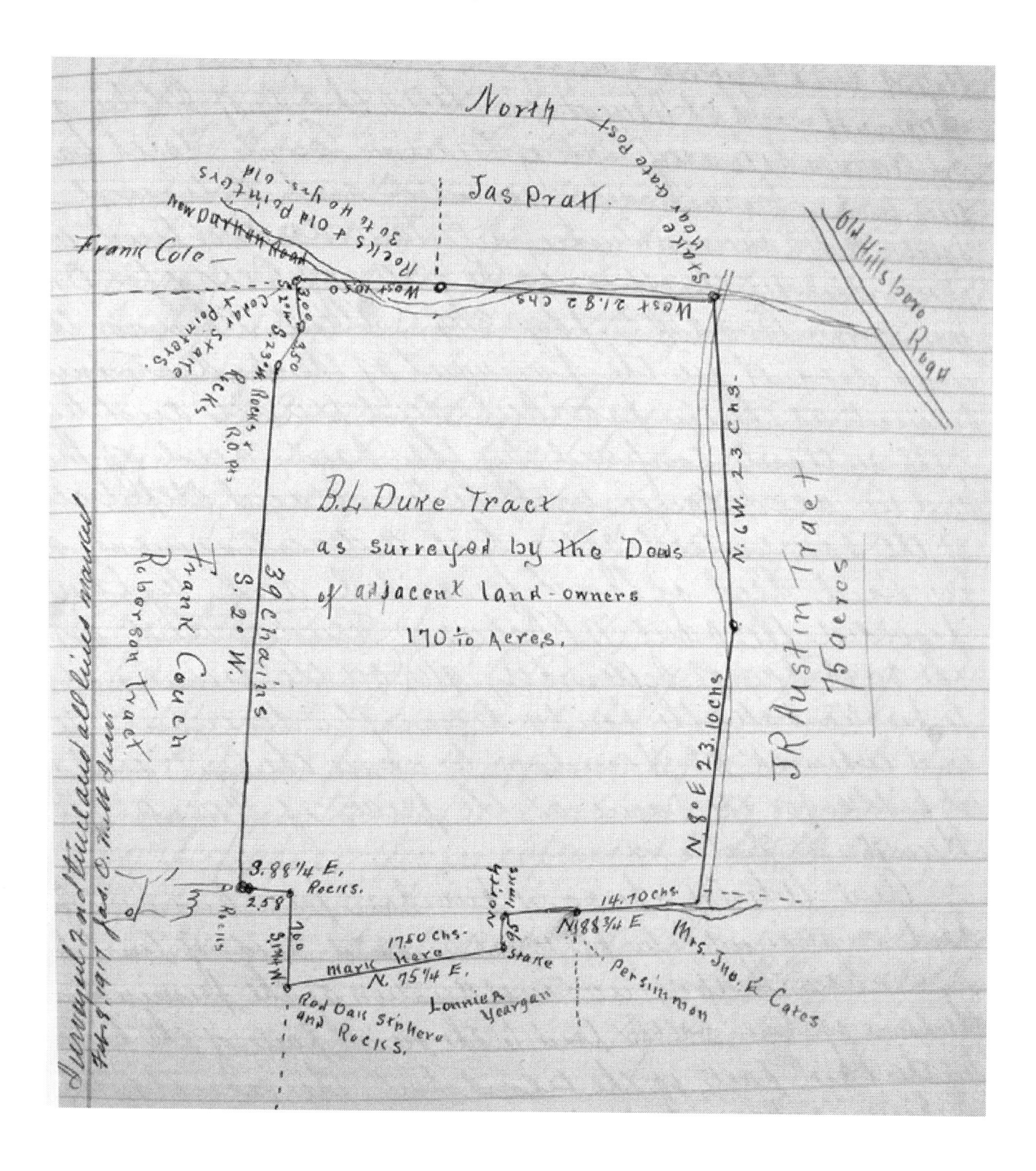

Here is a modern USGS Topo map showing both pieces of land – Robson's and Duke's.

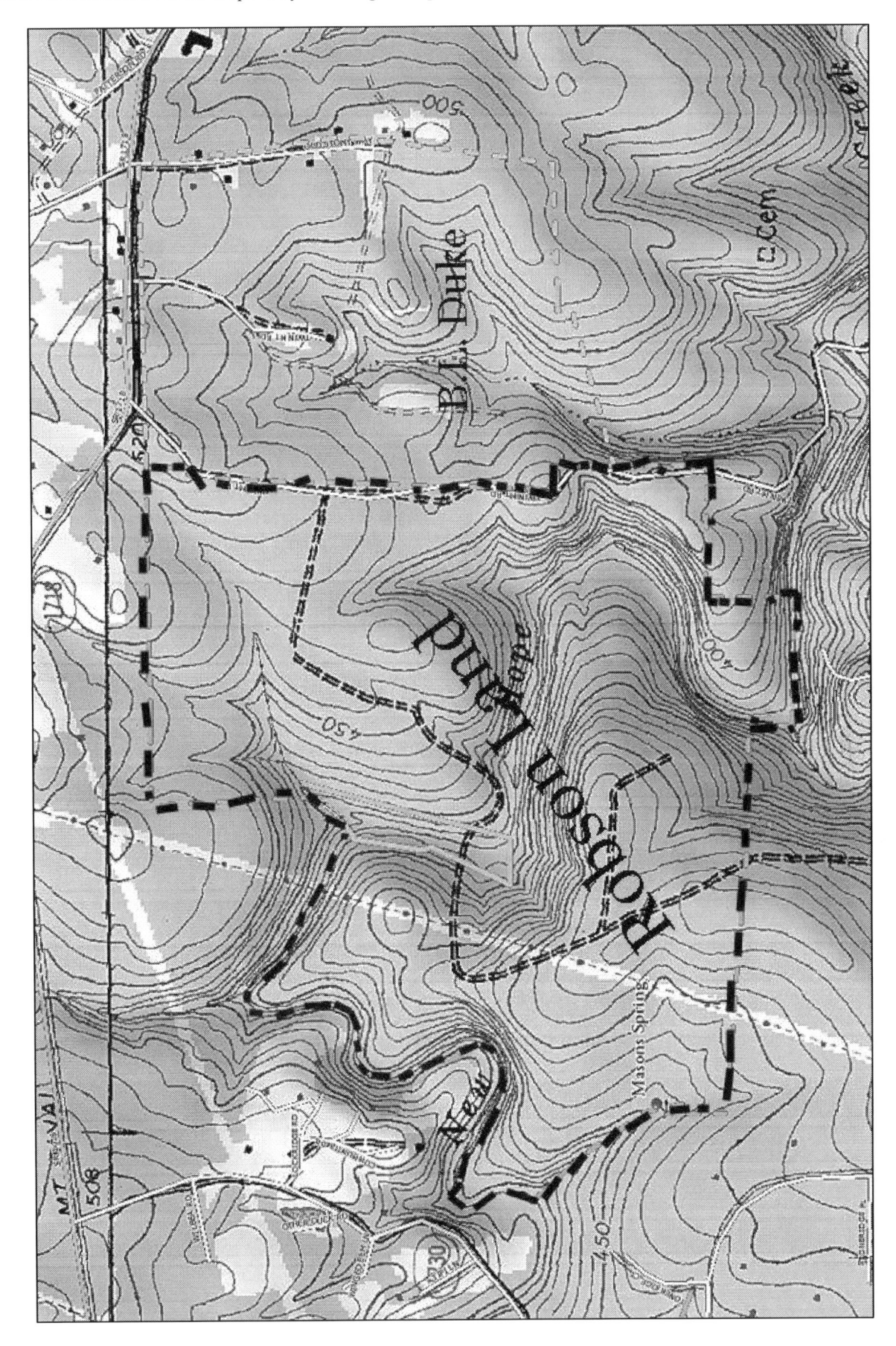

Turkey Farm Road Mill Survey (Charles W. Johnston Mill)

This section of the book will focus on the mill located in the *Triangle Land Conservancy* property – *Johnston Mill Preserve*. This is located just west of Turkey Farm Road. This mill was sold to Charles W. Johnston by his dad, George Johnston (22/269) February 17, 1827. This 17 acre tract of land was another vague land record, as the deed does not mention a mill. However, the Estate Papers of G. Johnston highlighted this sale specifically mentioning the mill. In addition, the deposition stated this was sold with 17 acres to prevent draining of the mill pond (See Appendix B – for the *vivid* details). This $80 acquisition appears to be undervalued when you add in a mill (building, dam, equipment etc.). Due to this record from the estate, it now appears that this mill could very well be the saw mill of the early 1820's, and not a missing mill location on Duke Forest property (although not far downstream).

This mill site is interesting, more from the use of the term "Old Johnston Mill". How old is – old? One insightful map might have the answer. The Tate Map (1891) shows "C. Johnson's Mill", which is Charles W. Johnston. He was the son of George Johnston Sr., and ultimately this land will become property of the Land Conservatory.

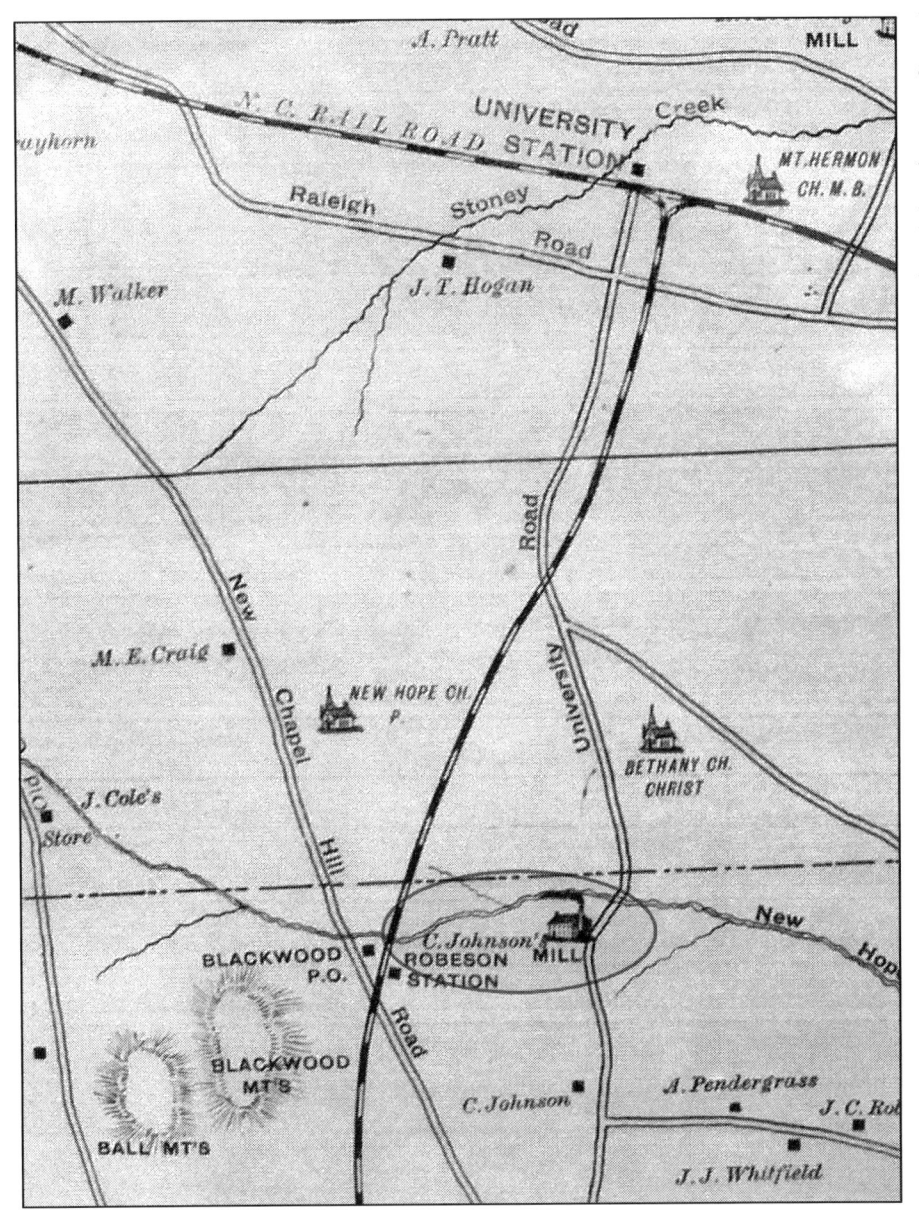

There is *no doubt* that this mill, located right next to the road (now Turkey Farm Road) is *not* George Johnston Sr. old mill (1793). With the discovery of the 17 acre transaction in the estate records, it is assumed that in 1827 this mill was operational. It is very possible this was the saw mill that George and his son were sued over. However, all the Robson land holdings, and maps/drawings in the law suit do not concur with this location. Yet, this additional evidence at least supports the idea as being much more plausible than before.

This location is unique. Not shown on the Tate Map is a stream called Old Field Creek. It enters New Hope near the mill, in fact, just above the mill. One of the original land grants in this area has a corner just across New Hope at the mouth of Old Field Creek in 1756. This would be Richard Caswell's land grant from Lord Granville. Caswell sells this land (640 acres or 1 square mile) to William Blackwood Sr. This corner would be the Northeast corner of that large tract of land. Yet, this still puts the mill up-stream to this corner, but it assists in tracking the location, as land gets sold, and split up then sold into more pieces, to other people! Also note on this map that C. Johnston's house is just south of the mill. This coincides with Charles W. Johnston's purchase (20/129) from George W. Johnston, the home place (known as Green Hill), and surrounding land.

129

The Mill Remnants

Some remnants of this mill exist, although not as much as the Robson mill. The mill location is unique in that it has access to several feeder streams (Old Field Creek, and another small creek called Booth Creek) that are near the mill pond. Old Field Creek traverses the land to the south for many miles. It would provide a lot of drainage water during the rainy season. In fact, the pictures provided in this book were after a heavy rain storm, and the river flow seemed to be as large as New Hope.

The Robson Mill layout seems to be much more of a textbook design. This mill is much different. Yet, we have to take into consideration many years of flooding (and erosion), altering the ground we see today. Also it should be realized that this mill was not a massive mill complex. When reading millwright handbooks (18xx time period), it is easy to fall into the trap of envisioning these rural mills as if they were commercial mill operations, with buildings 100 feet by 50 feet with 3 mill wheels etc. Also these commercial mills (typically) reside on massive rivers that never stop flowing, 100-300 feet across. In this area, these country mills typically resided on modest streams, providing a service for the local neighborhood. Since a number of mills are located throughout the county, there wasn't a need to haul great distances to a single large mill complex. Neither of these mill operations documented in this book were part of the N.C. textile boom.

Damming up New Hope, just below the mouth of the mill race, would provide a fairly large mill pond. The mill race would channel the water required to operate the mill while the general river flow would continue over the dam, and downstream (towards Robson's Mill).

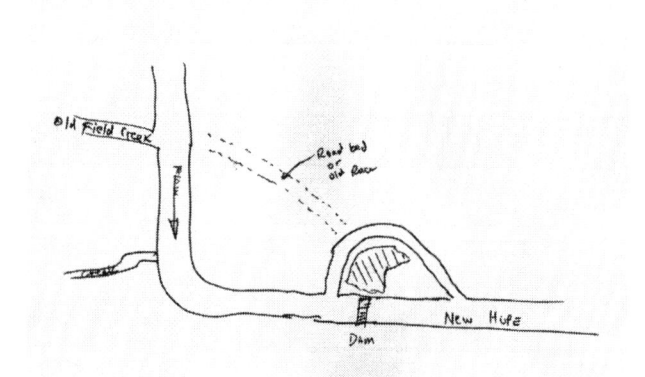

To me, the oddity of this mill seat is it becoming something of an island (drawing on left). Certainly there would be a bridge required to access the mill building, if the foundation area is the mill foundation. Usually the mill race would channel the water to the water wheel on one side of the mill, allowing access to the other side of the building, via adjacent land. (see example below)

Lastly, based on what can be found today, the mill race does not show any significant signs of elevation change. Therefore, it is my assumption that either this was powered by an undershot wheel or a flutter wheel. If this was a saw mill, then a flutter wheel would have (typically) been utilized. Breast and overshot wheels need the water to be elevated, and for a large wheel, this does not seem possible at this location.

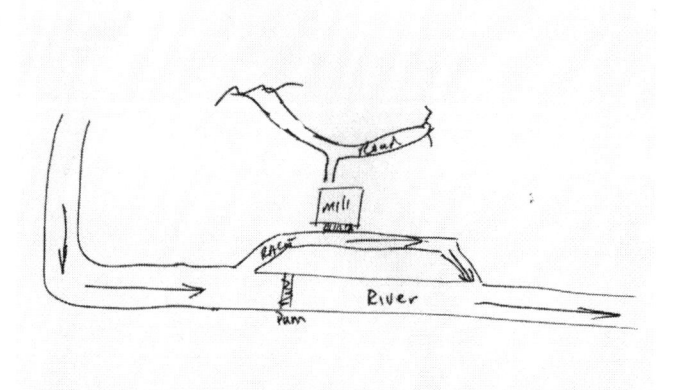

As shown in the earlier example, here is a general layout of the mill seat. From this point forward, I will illustrate the drawing with actual images taken of the site.

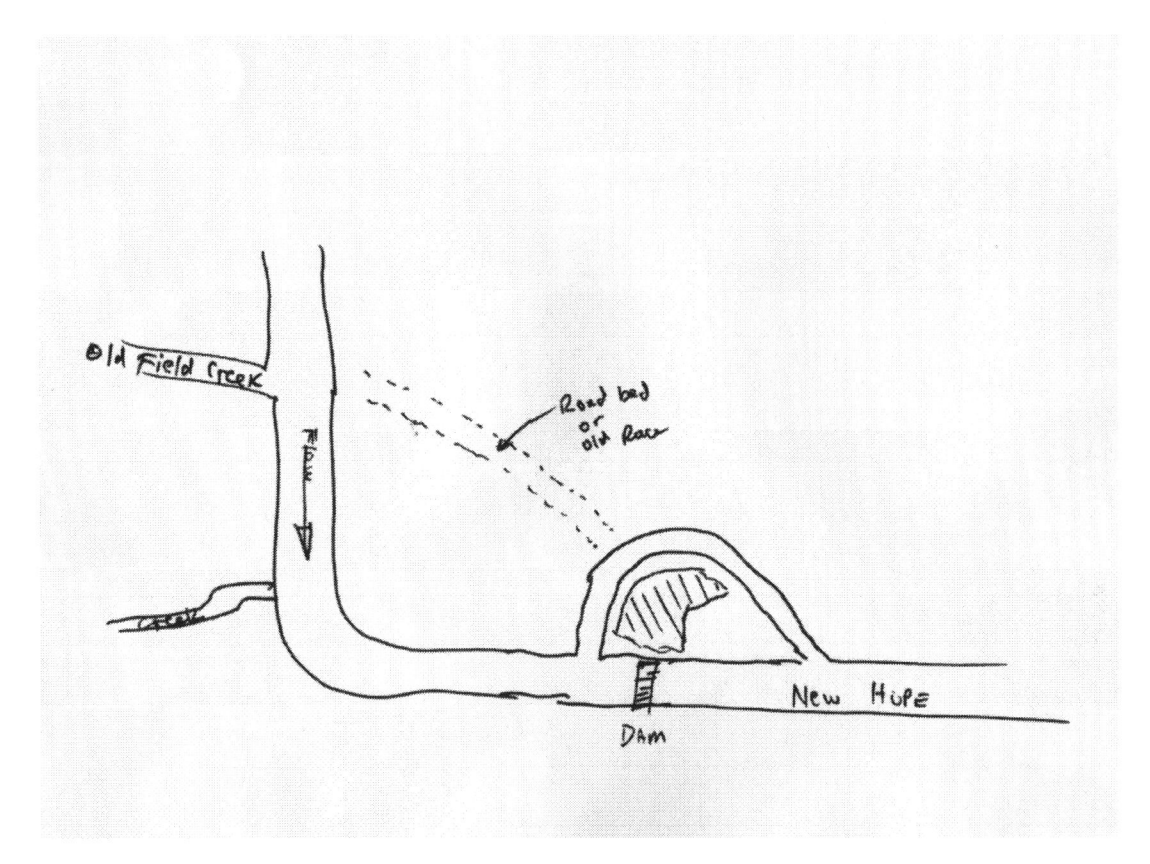

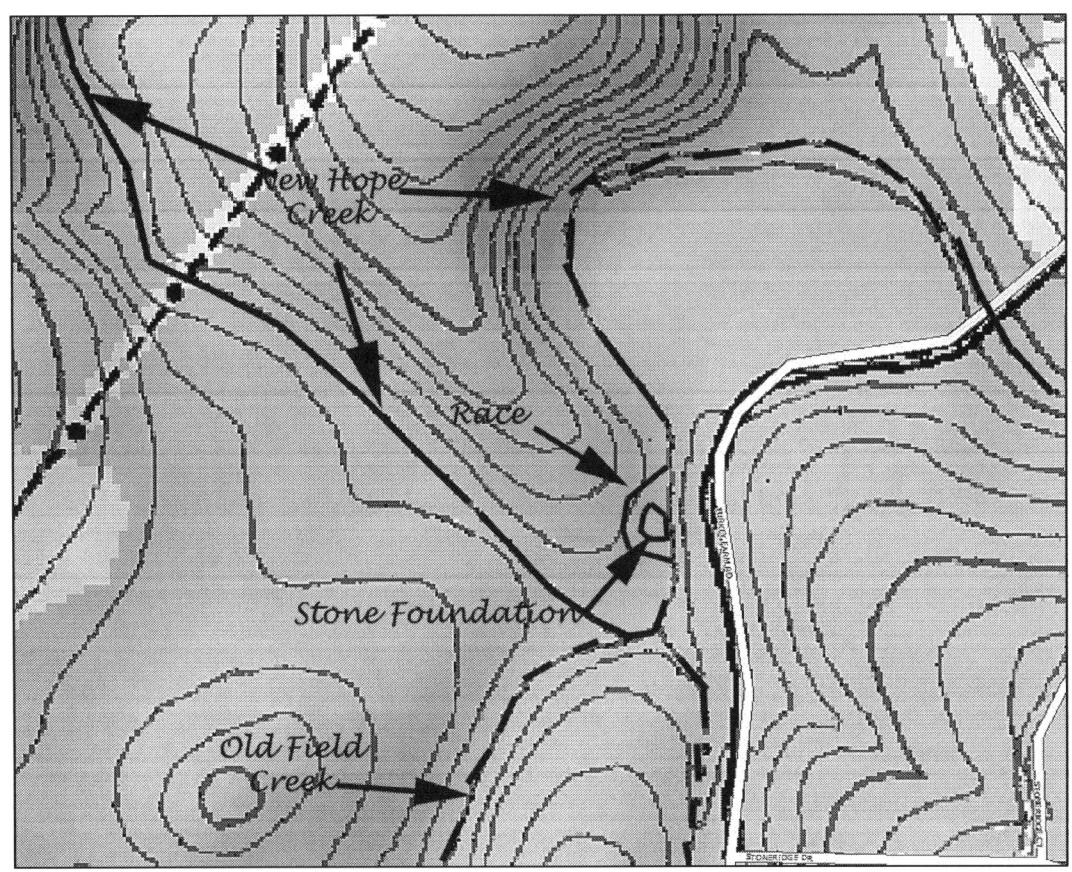

Note: As odd as this may seem, the USGS map has drawn the intersection of Old Field Creek **incorrectly**. It runs straight into New Hope, not the slight bend to the right. *See the County GIS image on the next page.*

131

As stated earlier, the USGS Topo map does not show the proper alignment of Old Field Creek intersecting New Hope. This aerial image proves this. Also note how New Hope runs along Turkey Farm Road, and the mill. Again, the exact location is depicted here properly, as the topo map is very general.

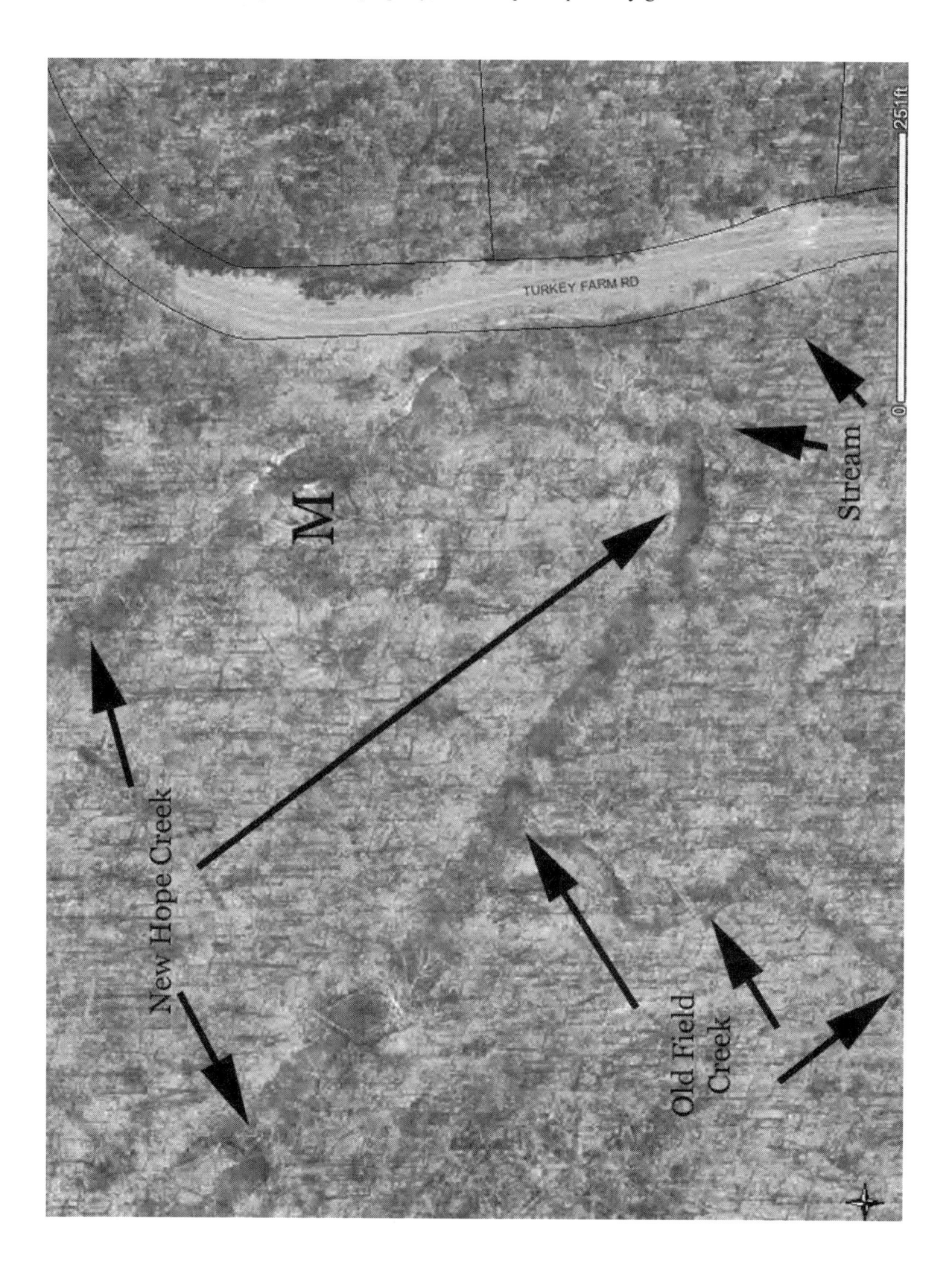

Detailed drawing of the mill foundation area.

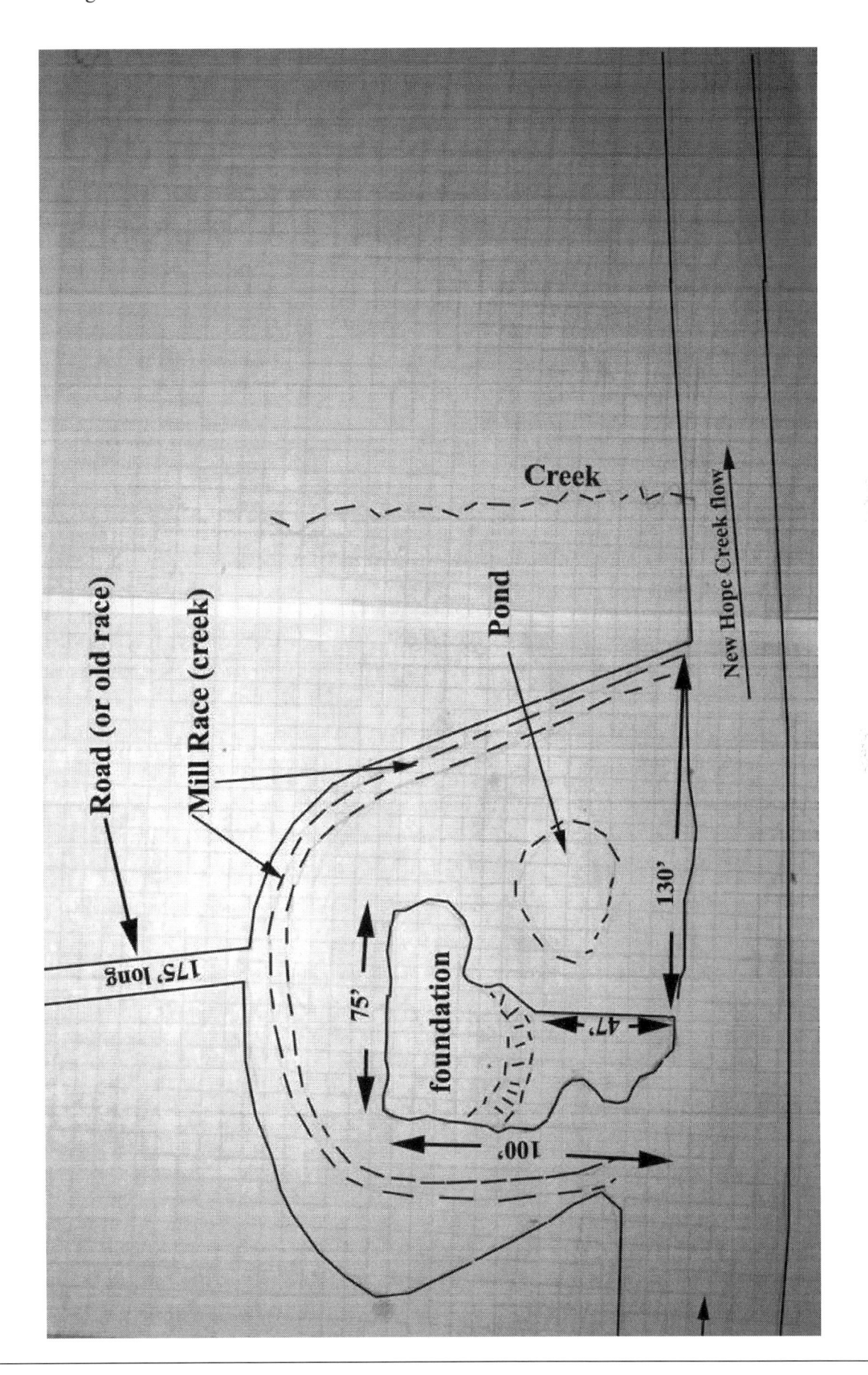

Here is a view (during the winter) of the "island" so to speak. This picture is taken from the east side (Turkey Farm Road) just above the dam.

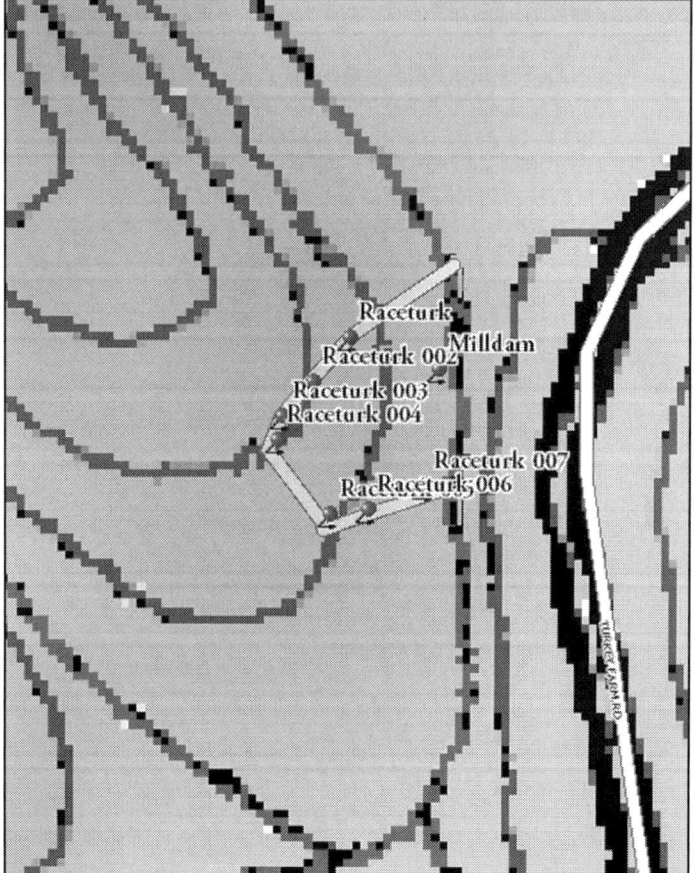

Here is the actual GPS marks as I walked the mill race remnants.

Dam

Only visible during the dry seasons, there is a wooden frame which is probably the dam foundation. Some speculate this is the mill building's foundation. Yet, based on the location, it appears to be the wooden frame for housing stone and earth for a dam. This is not an unusual construction technique. It also adds to a better understanding of the erosion that has occurred over the decades. The picture below is a combination of the actual image with computer graphics to portray the foundation dimensions.

Here is a diagram which shows the location of the wooden structure in relation to the "island" and all of its features. This would highlight the erosion of the "island" near the dam foundation. It also shows the location of what is assumed to be the race all pointing to a dam structure and not the mill building.

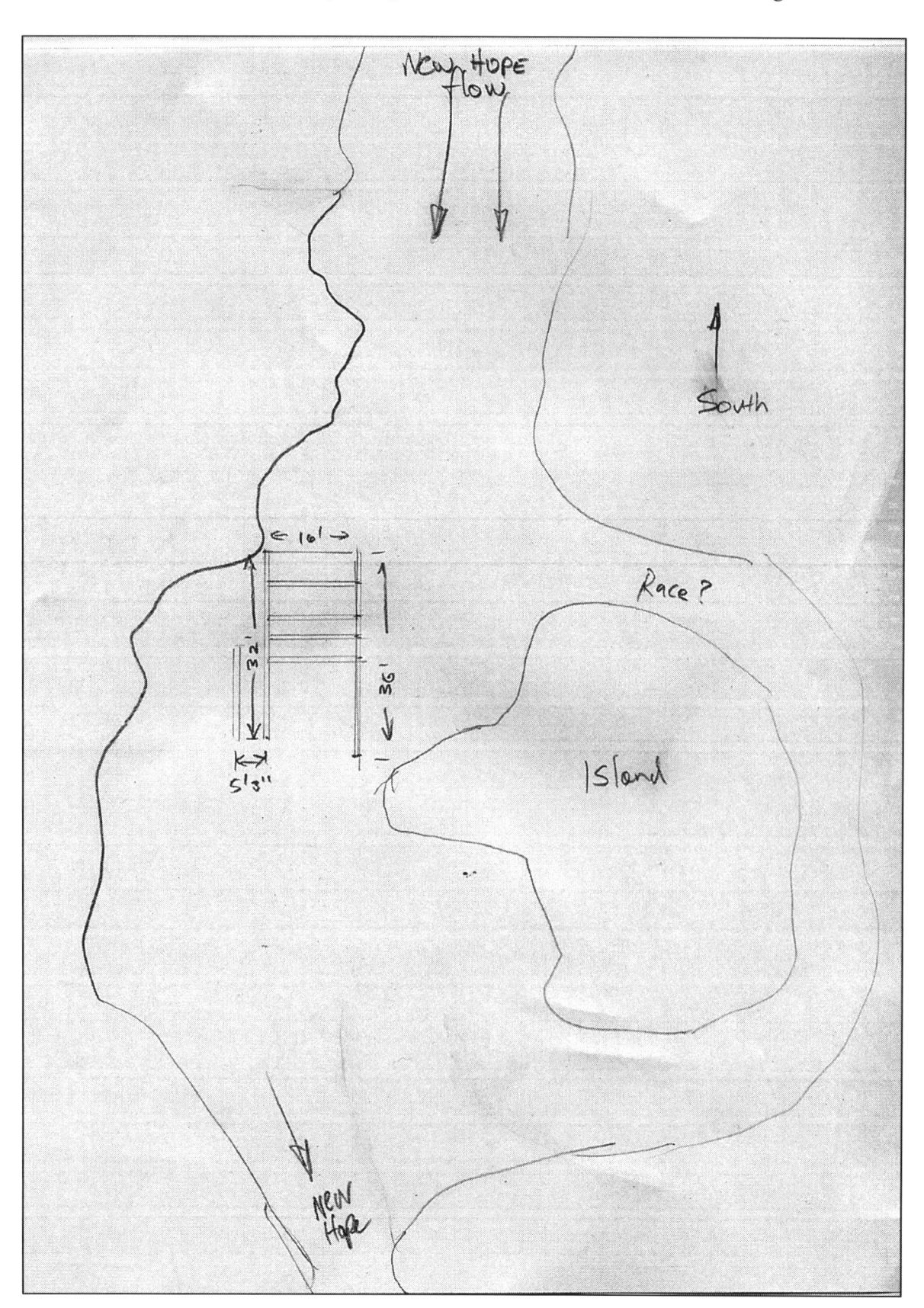

Here is a view looking north as the river continues to flow, showing the unique jog to the beams. Due to the stony river bottom (which could be remnants of the stone dam's content), observing the beams course under the river bottom is very difficult, without excavation.

Here is a view from the very beginning of the wooden structure, still looking downstream (north), with the beginning of the "island" appearing on the left of the image. It would seem plausible that earth/stone was along the immediate left of the beam. This would fill in the island, so to speak, or at least to enlarge its size.

Below is a detailed diagram of the wooden structure, showing the details of the beams locations or distances from the beginning beam.

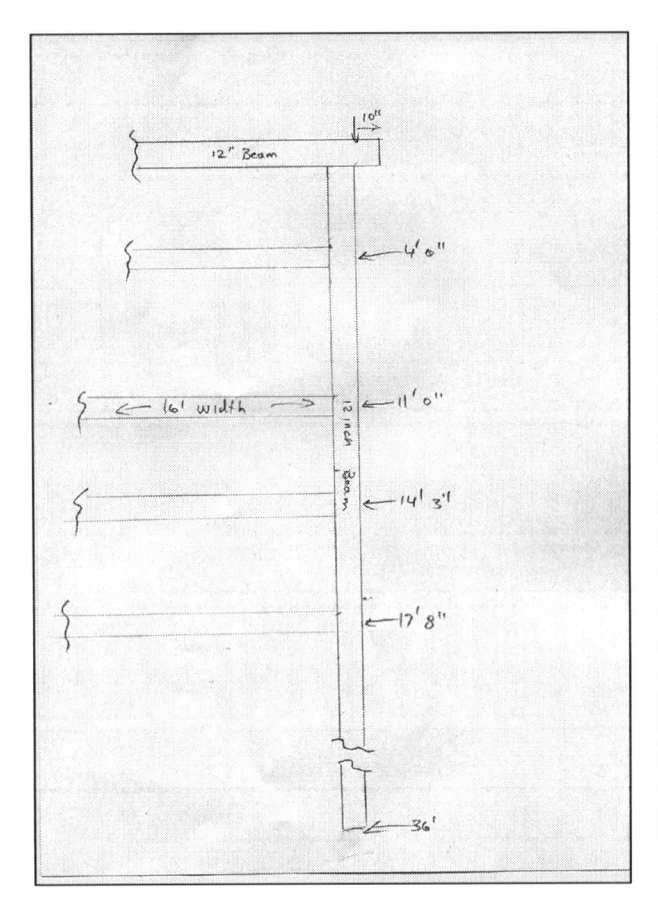

As noted in the above drawing, there is a 10 inch projection of the main beam with its associated connecting beam, which is shown here on the left. This image also shows the unique notches in the center of the beams. These notches are clearly man-made and are "on center" but they are not consistent in location with each other. Neither do they appear on all beams. These notches would be for vertical members.

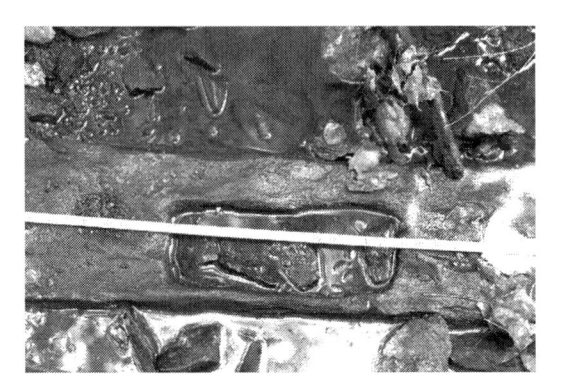

138

More images of the notches found.

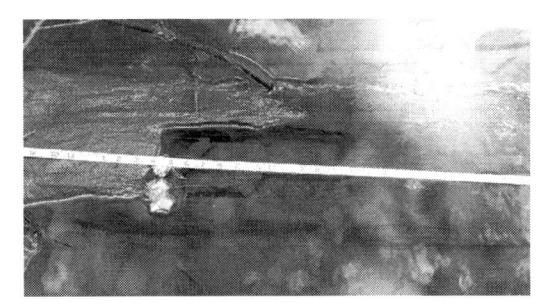

The above image is of the two beams that are along the bank of the river, and are offset by 5feet. This is shown from a different angle below. Here the island is on the right, so this is looking upstream (south).

139

When traversing the mill race, from the north towards the south, on the west side there is this clear "U" shaped entrance. It looks like a roadbed, but could just as well be an old mill race, as it leads directly to the mouth (or intersection) of Old Field Creek and New Hope. If this was a road it went – no where.

Note: off to the western side (left) there is a foundation of some sort, and I marked it with the flag – Foundation. Was this an out building or storage facility for the mill?

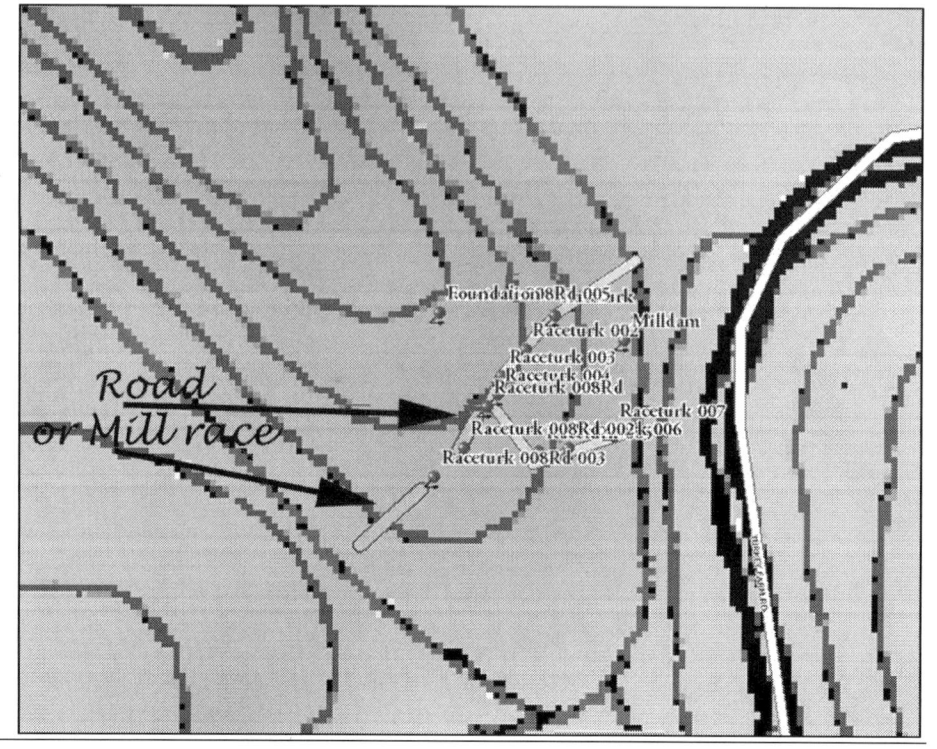

Here is an image of the mouth of Old Field Creek flowing into New Hope. Old Field Creek is in the foreground, and represents a lighter color water, and New Hope appears from the left-hand of the picture flowing to the right.

As stated earlier, these pictures were taken two days after a heavy rain storm. The picture on the right is another view of Old Field Creek looking south (with the twisted old root system of a tree that has been exposed).

In more modern deed records, there are a number of Charles W. Johnston land metes and bounds that follow Old Field Creek as a boundary line. The name Old Field Creek, as near as I can determine – is very old. In fact, the original land grant from Granville to Richard Caswell, references the mouth of Old Field Creek into New Hope. To be clear, this was actually the deed record of Richard Caswell selling his 640 acre tract to William Blackwood in 1756. Never the less, this is very old.

Mill Foundation

When standing on the opposite side of the stream, near the asphalt road (Turkey Farm Rd), you can see the stone wall of the mill foundation. One section of the wall remains in pristine condition. Other parts are missing, and some just altered by weather, and especially trees (roots).

Here is the eastern edge of the foundation, and just outside the picture (left) is New Hope Creek. Then the wall continues a straight westward direction to a bend.

This (almost) 45 degree angle or bend in the wall remains well preserved. This wall area is on the "down stream" flow of the river, and probably the exit area of the race. This wall is varies in height, but runs in the 4 to 4-½ foot tall range.

Once on top of the foundation "mound", looking east towards New Hope, you can get a view of the narrow angle (like a peninsula) of this part of the remnants.

Turning towards the south-west, looking at the westward end of the remnants, you can see another level/layer of stone building upwards. The west side of this area is higher than the river side. Also you can see on the left of this picture, the entrance side of the mill race.

Mill Race

As stated earlier, the mill race, as can be discerned from the remnants, seems to create an island or maybe a mote around the foundation. Erosion was rather extensive, over the years. As you can see New Hope is flowing past the entrance. That is why there is a dam, to raise a mill pond that would be then channeled into the mill race to route the flow to the water wheel.

The image to the left was taken standing in the race-mouth/entrance, looking west. On the far right is the stone foundation. On the left is an eroded section of land that has been removed over the years. All of this area is significantly altered.

Pictured below is in the "mill race" where the water would enter the race. Certainly the stone walls are missing here, and it would be the place that would sustain the most erosion. Over the decades, this part of the mill complex certainly got altered by New Hope's flow. This image is looking north, and New Hope is on the right-hand side.

Although difficult to see in detail, the image below shows the location of the dam. On the left of the river (although this looks like a pond – due to a beaver dam) is a natural stone wall. The dam abuts this location, and is just below the mill race entrance.

As you follow this mill race around (further west then turning northward), on the left is an interesting feature. Either this is a roadbed or this was an earlier mill race, as it heads straight to New Hope at the intersection of Old Field Creek.

Other Features

As you "mill around" the area, you run into other features worth noting. As mentioned before, there is a roadbed or old mill race that runs from the mill area to the other side of New Hope Creek at the intersection (the mouth) of Old Field Creek. As you follow New Hope upstream (North-northwest) 225 feet, a stone wall begins. This wall is *not* like the Robson walls. Although a contiguous line of stone, it seems to be around 18 inches to a maximum of 2 feet in height. It holds a very constant distance away from New Hope Creek. Was this wall to prevent flooding, if the river were to overflow the banks? Certainly this part of the stream is the mill pond for the mill in this discussion. Maybe they built this wall to stop flooding of the land.

Never the less, as you migrate down stream from the mill foundation, you happen upon a very wide roadbed, which (due to rain) looks like a stagnant stream. As you continue down this road, you run into a number of very large trees, and some stone piles that trees are growing amongst. One such tree/stone pile, looks like a corner marker. It is possible that this is the Richard Caswell corner which was north of the Old Field Creek Mouth, just across New Hope. One Red Oak tree (pictured on the left – background) has a diameter of 12 feet 6 inches, measured 4 feet above ground level. This is a very large oak, and the trunk is more or less the same diameter as it towers upwards. Why was this tree left behind for so many years? Was it marking something? It is near the other stone pile/tree.

Here is a view of the roadbed looking eastward. The two trees on the left align with the tree and stone pile which are closely line with the large Red Oak. (is this an old property line or boundary?) Below is a detailed map of the area in discussion.

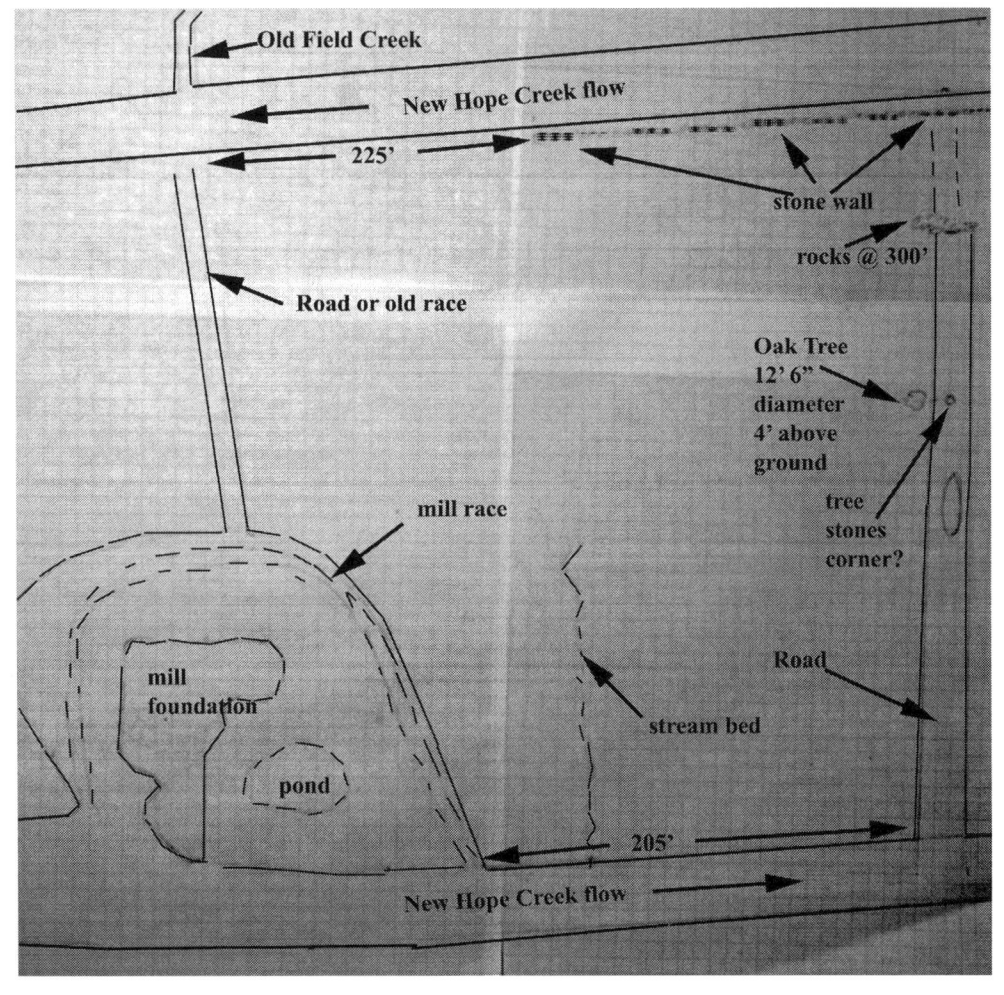

147

The stone wall that runs parallel to New Hope (western side of the mill area) starts abruptly, and ends the same way. It does not make any turns inland, as if to be a perimeter fence around a building. It does not represent a foundation. It is approximately (difficult to measure exactly with the thick underbrush) 525 feet long. The drawing (prior page) does not show the walls "other end". However, it stops very close to where the land suddenly begins to rise up from this flat-low land upwards to a ridge.

The map, and brochure, provided by the Triangle Land Conservancy, annotates an area by the mill as another historical location. They name it "Hogan's Bottom". The Hogan family was in the general area of New Hope, but I have not been able to locate any exact names, dates or land/plats. The wall, and stone piles (all over this area), certainly documents some old activity. Also the 1938 aerial maps show that part of this land bounded by New Hope Creek was farmed. This would have disturbed the ground, and added some other roadbed as well as additional stone interaction. Most farmers create stone piles from plowing their fields. Seventy years later, even the 1938 aerials seem old!

Aerial Images – Transition (1938, 1955, 1975, 2003)

In an attempt to see what changes has occurred over the years, aerial images of the Turkey Farm Road mill site were helpful. However, it seemed (to me) to just add to the list of questions. Never the less, here we go. I attempted to crop each image to the same size in order to keep the image scale the same.

1938 – Note the field (cleared area) which will be visual in the 1955 image 18 years later. Also look at the road that juts off the west side of Turkey Farm Road. This will get altered over time, until it disappears.

1955 – Note the 1938 field is now growing over. Now we have another new object in the area, on the east side looks to be a building. The road/white area that looks like a "Y" is visible.

1965 – Now the field has grown over. The house on the east side is less visible. The "Y" road area on the west side of Turkey Farm Road now has a "circle" look to it. Yet the angle of the road remains the same. The building/area visible in 1955 is grown up in this image.

Today, it is very difficult to see anything that was visible in the prior years. This image assists in locating Old Field Creek and its intersection with New Hope Creek, despite the USGS depiction (incorrect).

Modern and other Johnston Land Transactions

In order to track land for modern day locations, sometimes it is easier to start from today, and work back (as opposed to starting from 1750 forward). The specific land that I wanted to find, deals with the mill site at the land conservatory, next to Turkey Farm Road.

This land (today) is assigned the following partial ID number (PIN) – 9881-44-5704. Orange County deed records reference deed book 1953/580 and 1953/570. Both records reference Plat Book (PB) 83/145 and 83/166. All of this land was donated under "James Martin Johnston Trust for Educational Purposes". This originates from the Will of James Martin Trust dated January 21, 1966.

This land originates from another will, the will of James M. Johnston's father, Charles W. Johnston (Will Book – I, page 582) October 15, 1912.

- He wills the home estate, and 564 acres surrounding it to this wife Agnes. After her death, divides to the sons. (it is much more involved in wording than provided here)

- He then gives 110 acres of land to son, Samuel Coble Johnston who lives on the land called the "tract on Hillsboro road".

- The other 5 sons, Charles Hughes, George A., Joseph Henry, James M. and John Thomas – divide the 1000acres of land remaining. Excluding the 110a to Samuel and 564a to his wife.

- 1.5 acres of burial ground, used by the colored people for their cemetery.

It is interesting to note that "the mill" is not willed specifically, as it was by Charles W. Johnston in his will dated January 23, 1855. This will specifically provides the Mill and Home tract to his wife Lydia and the homestead was to be about 1000 acres.

The table below catalogs all land acquired by C.W. or Charles Johnston. Note that Charles Johnston (George's dad) had a Granville land grant as well.

Buying	Year	Date	Book/pg	Acres	Name (selling)	Notes
C.W. Johnston	1885	4-May	48/480	300	Stepehen Arch	Charles the 3rd
C.W. Johnston	1881	Dec	49/200	41.5	William Burt	Charles the 3rd
C.W. Johnston	1861	26-Feb	50/442	275	David Kerr	Charles the 3rd
Charles Johnston	1776	28-Aug	2/229	220	William Blackwood	This is Geo Sr.'s dad
Charles W. Johnston	1819	28-May	17/279	614	George Johnston	
Charles W. Johnston	1827	17-Feb	22/269	175	George Johnston	
Charles W. Johnston	1827	31-May	22/355	574	George M. Johnston	Home tract purchase from his brother (Geo moved to AL)
Charles W. Johnston	1828	23-Sep	23/412	271	George Johnston	
Charles W. Johnston	1844	13-Jan	30/363	100	John Blackwood	
Charles W. Johnston	1859	31-May	38/453	432	Thomas Blackwood	Charles the 3rd
Charles W. Johnston	1878	26-Feb	49/201	91	David Kerr	Charles the 3rd

Here are the records dealing with their **sales**. Here you can see more "sales" from Charles, than we have for purchases. McNair is also listed as Macnair. I could not locate the sales of Ebenezer's sale of this land he purchased from Charles, another mystery in the old deed world. Most of the other McNair land deals were all lots in downtown Hillsborough, being sold to McCauley.

Selling	Year	Date	Book/pg	Acres	Name (buying)	Notes
Charles Johnston	1776	28-Aug	2/155	570	Ebenzer McNair	Geo Sr. Dad - possible McNair being a relative
Charles Johnston	1779	24-May	2/48	200	John Hart	George Sr. Dad
Charles Johnston	1784	22-Dec	3/70	141	Joseph Kirkland	George Sr. Dad
Charles Johnston	1789	5-Jan	4/231	200	John Freeland	George Sr. Dad
Charles W. Johnston	1853	23-Sep	34/408	65	John Cabe Johnston	
Charles W. Johnston	1853	8-Mar	39/257	252	Jermiah P. Cole	
Charles W. Johnston	1859	1-Apr	36/127	34	Hazel Smith	
Charles W. Johnston			21/482		George M. Johnston	Selling his interest in Cabe Mill to his brother

Miscellaneous Deed Tables

As I read deed records, you find other adjacent property holders that can assist in locating boundaries. Burroughs was one of these names. However, this name is spelled differently, and I have included all their land purchases under both spellings.

Buying	Year	Date	Book/pg	Acres	Name (selling)	Notes
James Boroughs	1833	10-Sep	25/344	201	Thomas Boroughs	New Hope
John Boroughs	1832	4-Feb	26/225		Burton Clark	190a of land no details - orange co.
Reuben Boroughs	1806	3-Feb	12/179		Thomas Couch	Eno River
Reuben Boroughs	1809	14-Apr	13/247		State NC	New Hope Grant#1786
William H. Boroughs	1867	28-Aug	39/360		John Boroughs	New Hope
Zaches Boroughs	1802	24-May	13/183		James Boroughs	New Hope
Lurenda Boroughs	1862	22-Mar	36/434		Francis Atkins	Division of land
John Boroughs	1835	31-Oct	27/14	750	William Cain	New Hope
Thomas Boroughs	1831	19-Sep	29/225		Ilai Davis	Dry Creek
Reuben Burroughs	1802	24-May	11/145	220	James Boroughs	New Hope
Thomas Burroughs	1882	18-Apr	48/46	62	John T. Boroughs	62 acres bounded by CW Johnston and Freeland

For the record, I also traced Blackwood, Duskin, and Mulholland (Mulhollan, Mullholland). The Mulhollen family was related to the Johnston's, and the "M." in their middle name was from this family. It was interesting to see their land acquisitions were primarily land grants. You will find an interesting tract of land called the "burnt cabin" tract that was sold via the Sheriff to pay debt due by the Mulhollans (see 23/412). Hugh Mulhollan was (at one time) Orange County Surveyor.

Another neighbor was the Burch family. They are listed as adjoining lands to the Johnstons, but I did not find their purchases, they primarily were in the Stoney Creek area. Very similar to this was Bevill or John Bevill who acquired land from the Trice (James Trice), and Barbee (Mark and Young Barbee) family on New Hope. Some of this land was on Dry Creek, adjoining Mann Patterson's large estate.

Hogan was an adjoining land owner, and it is a rather old name in Orange County. I didn't find anything in the 18th century in this area. However, as you move forward into the mid to late 19th century the Hogan holdings are more numerous in this part of the county. In particular, one deed (77/283) is included that James M. Johnston bought in 1919 that was listed as their "Old Home Tract". Nearby was the Freeland family. I did not spend time researching the Freelands.

Last but not least, was the Booth (Boothe) family. In fact, one of the small creeks that drains into New Hope by Turkey Farm Road is Booth Creek. I found one deed (5/328) that was next to Johnstons, and it referenced "Cabbin's Old Field". Was this related to the "burnt cabin" place? Was this a name of a person? More research required. The names were John and Daniel Booth, and they owned town lots in Chapel Hill as well as land from Trice and by Mann Patterson.

Deed Transcripts

Here are the deed transcripts from Orange County Deed Office. Note: C=chain (66 feet), P=pole (16.5 feet), BO=Black Oak, RO= Red oak, WO=White oak, BJ = Black Jack, BJO= black jack oak, Hick = hickory.

1/41 – Nov 12, 1754 John Stroud Jr. to William Blackwood. £20 for 325a. Begin Hick on Old Field Creek and waters of New Hope run S65C to BO, E50C to Hick and dogwood, N65C to PO, W50C to begin, land granted from **Granville to Stroud** in 1754.

1/56 – **Granville to Blackwood** – 3/14/1755 – Parish of St. Mathews both side of Buffalo Creek – 480A

1/155 – Richard Caswell of Johnston Co. to William Blackwood £23.15.0 – 640a. Both sides of the forks of New Hope and Old Field Creek begin at WO on the north side of the creek, then south crossing New Hope 80C to WO, W80C to RO, N80C to WO, E80C to begin. May 11, 1756 **Granville to Caswell**. This deed was executed – June 9, 1756.

2/48 – Charles Johnston sells to John Hart, 5/24/1779 – 200 acres part of a tract of land to Michael Waldross via a Granville Grant 2/1/1761 conveyed to Charles Johnston and David Craig by way of a mortgage by John Hart.

2/155 – Charles Johnston and wife Martha – Aug 28, 1776 to Ebenzer McNair £550.0.0 – on New Hope Creek – begin gum on creek, N69C to RO, W50C Hick, S70C to stake, W35C to dogwood in William Blackwood's corner, S crossing the creek S5C to hick in John Youngs corner, along his line 40C to stake his other corner, N43C to creek – 570 acres being two tracts one of which Charles Wilson Johnston purchased from William Cox 2/7/1764 (the Cox piece was 350 acres) and the other, William Blackwood, and Peggy. (See 4/710)

2/229 – William Blackwood and wife Peggy to Charles Johnston (Planter) – Aug 8, 1776, £260.0.0 - Old Field Creek and New Hope. Begin WO in NE corner of the old tract, W40C to dogwood, S55C to Hick in John Young's corner, E40C to stake his other corner, N55C to begin, 220 acres – part of the 640a purchased by William Blackwood from Caswell, deed dates June 9, 1754.

2/379 – James Blackwood to John Strain – 9/7/1782 – 300a – begin at Hick in Old Field Creek, S65C to oak, E30C to sapling, N12.5C to stake, E20C PO, N52C [or N5C] PO, W50C to being, part of the land granted to John Stroud by Granville dated October 23, 1754.

2/380 – 3/14/1780 NC to Abraham Allen – begin Corner oak, S55P to stake E___ degrees S280P to BJ, E144P to WO, N104p to stake, W along line 65P to BO, N along line 132P to WO, W along his line and Alexander Malcolm's line 125P to RO his corner, S28P to RO in Allen's corner, 166P to begin. Both side of New Hope, acreage amount left blank.

3/70 – Charles Johnston sells to Joseph Kirkland, 12/22/1784 - £10, lying on New Hope begin at RO, N106P to BO, W165P to RO, N186P to RO, E70P WO on Charles Johnston's line, then S30P to BJ, E88P to beginning. 141 acres being more or less as by deed from the State to Charles Johnston this being all most one-half.

3/73 – John Young and Robert Agnew 357 acres on New Hope a grant from State to Joseph Young. Begin S100P to PO, W91P to BO, S180P bush, E168P BO, S40P sassafras, E172P BO, N125P RO on Allen line with said line 67P to BJO, N45degW 280P to begin.

3/74 – William Blackwood to John Young Sep 9, 1776. Beg WO SE corner of original tract, W40C dogwood, N20C hick, E40C stake, S25C to first. 100a

4/231 – Charles Johnston to John Freeland 1/5/1789 – lying on the north side of Old Field Creek and part of my own old tract purchased from John Peterson by deed dated Sep 13, 1758. Begin old line where it crosses the said Old Field Creek and running the various courses of the said old line until it strikes the said Old Field Creek again, then up the meanders of the said Old Field Creek to the begin 200a. £20.0.0

4/714 – 5/28/1793 – John Barbee sells to George Johnston, Mann Patterson and Chesley Page Patterson – both sides of New Hope and Ponns Creek. Begin at stake near New Hope west side of the creek W3P to stake, N8P stake, E5P to stake, N9.5°E 44P to WO, N70°W 46P to RO, N1P to bank of New Hope, N87°E across New Hope and Ponns Creek 46P to hickory in the edge of Barbee's new field S9.5°W 10P to WO in the island, N77°E 10P to two hickories, S5°W 18P to BJ, S49.5°W [or North] 12P to RO, S32°W 26P to sycamore, S83°W 11P to beginning containing 10 acres *"…for a mill seat with the privilege of at least one road the best and most direct way for a wagon road from the saw mill seat through John Barbee's land to said Mann Patterson…"*

4/710 – Begin 3 sweet gums on New Hope N69C Ro, W50C hick, S70C to stake, W35C to dogwood in William Blackwood's corner, S crossing the creek 55C to Hick – John Young's corner, along his line E40C to stake at the other corner, N43C to creek, down the meanders to begin – 520a, more or less a grant of 2 tracts to James Lesley assigned to George McLellan Batee Co, first conveyed Thomas Harmenson, agent for Ebinezer McNair…." See 2/155.

5/103 – Samuel Allen to Abraham Allen – 7/19/1794 - £68. Begin WO on a line known as Bollins line, N85C to WO, W45C to RO, south crossing creek 85C to stake in Hardy Morgan's line, formerly called Wilkinson's line, along said line E to begin – 382a.

5/104 – Abraham and Eliz Allen to Andrew Allen – 7/19/1795 - £100 Waters of New Hope. 345a – Begin RO in William Courtney's corner, E128P WO on north side of New Hope, South crossing New Hope 122P to BO in W. Courtney's corner, E6P to stake in the Courtney's line, S104P to two WO, W175P BJ, in Geo Johnstons corner, N40°W 145P to RO/Sassafras on Johnstons line, N155P to hick in Abraham Allen corner, E73P to RO, N28P to begin.

5/104 – Nathaniel King to Abraham Allen – 7/19/1795 £70. On New Hope and Bens Creek, bounded on the south by Hardy Morgan, West by Daniel Booth, East by Abraham Allen where he lives, begin Booths corner RO, N38.5C to PO, E21.5C to hick on Allen's line, S6C to Pine on Morgan's line, W45C to WO, N22.5C to stake in Booths line, E23.5C to begin – 183a.

5/328 – Gray Booth grant #1163 – 267a on New Hope. Begin WO in George Johnstons line, N80P to hick bush Cabbin's old field, E104p RO then N112P Hick, Daniel Booths corner, N12P RO, S224p stake in Davis line, west his line 42P to stake, N224P to begin. 7/6/1795.

5/472 – Grant #1174 – 183a, Water of New Hope bounded by Mann Patterson, Joseph Barbee, William Courtney and John Barbee, begin RO & dogwood Mann Patterson corner, W74P to PO in Joseph Barbee corner, S with his line, 42P to WO at Daniel Booths corner W with his line 142P to PO Gray Booths line, N with his line 128P to PO, W9P to WO, N104P to stake in Courtney's line, E with his line 23P to BO his corner, S106P to BJ, E174P to PO in John Barbee's corner, N140P to stake in Hillsboro Road, E 24P to stake in Patterson's original line, S with his line to begin. As by plat.

5/488 – Samuel Allen to George – Southside of New Hope creek being part of 2 tracts granted to Abraham Allen from the State. Beg WO on the bank of New Hope at corner of George's Mill tract thence S74 deg E 60P, WO near spring, E20P stake in Courtney's line, S144P to RO in Andrew Allen line, W73P to hick in Allen's corner, SW along his line 155P to RO and Sassafras, N45degW 135P to WO, N243P to WO on bank of New Hope, down the meanders to begin. 240 acres.

5/502 – Beg RO E to mill creek, down said creek to the rock then up the south creek to where Jesse Nevel's line crosses then along the said Nevels line to his corner then N then W along said Nevels line to corner RO upon the top of the hill by the said Nevell's Mill then N along marked trees to begin – 200a

6/156 – both sides of New Hope Tract #1) RO in Allen's line E148P RO, N100P to stake, W12P to BJO, N160P to WO, W132P to stake in Halls line, S84P to corner Gum, E6P to stake, S188P to begin. Tract #2) 185a land grant both sides of New Hope WO on Alexander Mebane's line on N side of creek, E23P to his corner stake continuing 97P to hick, S40P beach, E22P WO in William Rhoads line and with his line S22P to Ro, E24P to RO, S200P to WO, W83P to BJO, N106P BO, W83P to BO, N184P to first begin the tract of land whereon said Courtney has had a mill. Tract #3) 142a grant to Mack Patterson and Joseph Cobb May 18, 1789 on waters of New Hope.

6/204 – Feb 27 1797 22a – begin WO E7.25C to post, S crossing New Hope 30.5C RO, W7.25C BO then north crossing New Hope 30.5C to begin. William R. Rhoads to Geo Sr. £10

6/226 – James Patterson – 2/27/1796 – to George Johnston and Samuel Hopkins "…for in consideration of love and goodwill….for my friends.." – Timbering rights.

6/320 – James Patterson (Chatham Co.) to Geo Johnston and Samuel Hopkins - £80.0.0 1/25/1797 – begin Hick on Bolins Creek, W to Benjamin Yeargain's line South crossing the creek to stake on the bank then East to the road then North with the old road to begin with a **saw mill** formerly the property of Hardy Morgan.

6/323 – 1/13/1797 – George Johnston sells to Mathew McCauley £170.0.0 – begin RO then E along a line of marked trees to the Mill Creek then down the creek to the fork, then up the south creek to Jesse Nevill's line to corner RO to the top of the hill by the said Nevill's Mill then North along marked trees to the beginning – 200a.

6/327 – James Patterson (Chatham Co.) to Geo and Samuel Hopkins – Aug 7, 1797 £50.0.0 12.5 acres of land on Bolands Creek – Begin BO Benjamin Yeargain's line near the still house then W with his lime 78P to stake, S26P to stake on the line of the University lands, E with the line 78P to poplar on the head of a branch, then N26P to begin. (See 9/285)

6/333 – George Johnston to Mathew McCauley – 1/13/1797 - £100.0.0 – begin BO in an old field, E30C to stake, N35C to hick, W36C to stake, S46C to RO in Henderson's corner, E6C to Connally line N along the line to beginning – 132a – tract of land made from a grant from the State to Austin Hightower, then to James Blackwood, and from Blackwood to George Johnston.

6/381 – William Burns to Andrew Burns – 1/22/1798 - £50. Begin PO on bank New Hope on James Boroughs line up the creek W to RO 68P, North to stake on John Strayhorns line 233P E along Strayhorn line to James Burroughs corner WO 68P, then south along Burroughs line 233P to begin. 100a.

7/322 Grant #1274 £10 per 100 acres containing 40a on waters of New Hope. Beg at his south west corner Hick of tract of land belonging to John Young E160P along his line to BO, S40P to sassafras Johnston's Corner originally Andrew Patterson W with a line of the same 160P to WO, N40P to begin – Aug 29, 1786.

7/323 Grant #1275 – 51 acres on New Hope begin WO on bank of Cedar Fork, S down creek 53P to WO on John Davis line, W with his line 20P to WO, his corner, then with his line W115P to hick in his corner and with his line N39P to WO on said Johnston line, E with his line 186P to first – Dec 29, 1792 as by the plat.

9/285 – George Sells to Samuel Hopkins – 3/5/1801 - £12.10.0 – sells his half interest in the 12acre tract on Boland Creek. (See 6/327)

10/65 – John Barbee to Geo Sr. 1/12/1800 - £400 – New Hope 218a, begin RO William Carter corner now said Johnston corner, E129P WO, north side of New Hope then S crossing New Hope, 158P to BJ on Courtney line, now said Johnston being Young/Barbees corner W98P to Hick on Henry Burch's line, N47P gum at Henry Burch corner, W ups said branch to said Burch's other corner a gum N40°W 26P to sassafras and RO, N155P to hick called Allen's old corner, now said Johnstons E72P to RO, N28P to begin.

10/105 – Hick on Bolands Creek W to Benjamin Yeargans line South crossing creek to stake on the bank, E to the road, N with the old road to the begin with a saw and grist mill thereto belonging – 10 acres more or less."

10/106 – this was a timber rights to go with the mill above, ½ the pine trees for sawing, then it mentions, "west of Hardy Morgan's wagon path that leads into the road called the Chapel Road…"

11/145 – James Boroughs to son Reuben. – James bought from John Moore. Begin at stake on south side of New Hope 22.39C East down the creek to George Johnstons corner WO, N along his line 83C to his corner PO continue 15.25C to stake, W22.39C to stake, S98.25C to begin. 220a.

11/310 – George Johnston to John Johnson - £500.0.0 4/4/1804 – both sides of McAdams Creek – 251acres including 1 acre for Andrew Murdock's Mill. (See 12/23) (** NOTE: it is possible this is the elder George Johnston, NOT the George Johnston of New Hope. **)

12/23 – George Johnston to Andrew Murdock – 1804 – George Johnston of the Hawfields on one part… Orange County, on McAdams Creek - £5.0.0 for 1 acre of land. Begin on the creek 50L below the wall of said Murdock's Mill Dam running S40L to willow oak, S57°E 3.45C to BO, S65°E 2.5C to stake, N57°E 1.5C to stake, N39°E 4.93C to BO then N52°W to creek, then down the creek to the beginning. (See 11/310)

13/183 – Zacheus son of Reuben Burroughs – New Hope land James bought from John Moore. 219a. Same as (11/145) with these exceptions. …22.39C to William Blackwood's line and Long, the south….N98.25C to John Strayhorns line…"

13/247 – Grant to Rueben Boroughs 105 acres on New Hope. Beg BO Johnston's corner, N20C to Hick in Starlets corner, W50C to BJ, S5C to Stake, W2.5C stake in Borough's corner, S15C to Hick with Johnston's line E42.5C to begin. May 31, 1808. (State Grant #1786)

14/367 – William and Edward Robson - $3500.00 a water grist mill and merchant mill, begin 3 Sweet gum at edge of the mill pond in Hall's corner, E12P to Courtney's old line then S176P with said line to hick, W128P to stake and rocks in an old field, N29P to **Mr. Mason's Spring** down the branch as it meanders to mouth of New Hope, then down the meanders to begin. 143 acres.

15/10 – Edward Robson to William Robson $800.00 selling his half of the mill purchase to William. June 14, 1814.

15/332 – 3/5/1812 – Geo Johnston and Chelsey Page Patterson to Mann Patterson on New Hope and Ponns Creek. 10a. "…east across New Hope and Ponns creek 46P…" – Sold for a mill seat with the privilege of at least 1 road the best and most direct way for a wagon road from the said mill site through the said Mann Patterson land. £20.0.0

16/198 – NC to William Blackwood 6/2/1800 - #1599 grant. New Hope adjacent to John Hogan. Begin Hick in Hunters line, E with his like 78P to stake in old field his corner with his line 80P to WO in Craig's corner, E with his line 180P RO his corner, S100P to stake, W131P to stake, S296P to stake on Shains line, W122P gum and BO on John Hogan corner, N with his line 318P to begin. Entered Nov 6, 1795.

17/279 – May 25, 1819 George to son C.W. Johnston on waters of New Hope adjacent to Blackwood and Freeland. Begin Hick on John Blackwood's line E8.5C to stone pile, S16°E 29.75C (129.75C?) to WO on Ezekiel Trice line, W45.25C PO Alex Gattis line, N51.75C to Hick, N85°W 22C BJ, N19.5C WO in Kirkland corner, W29.5C to Hick John Strains line, N33.5C Old Field Creek down meanders 64C to stake, S50C RO, E14.75C to begin. 614.75A.

18/155 – William Sr, to son William Jr. begin stake in William Blackwood's Sr. old field W22.5C to WO on John Freeland line, N68.5C RO on South bank of New Hope, down meanders to Hick on Andres Burns corner, S59C BO, E1.25C Hick, S14.5C to being. 148a.

20/124 – Geo Sr. to daughter Mary, land adjacent to George M. Johnston and William Robson. Part of the land George Sr. lives on. Begin stone pile in William Robson corner, S85°W 30C to Hick in Robsons corner, E10.5C to haw bush on the bank of New Hope, down the creek South passing Ash at the mouth of a branch [* is this Babs Branch? It always is referenced as an Ash at mouth of Babs branch.] 25C to hick, E5C stone pile in small old field, S24C to PO in Bevills line, W2C stake in Burch's line, N20°W 11.75C to gum on a branch, Burch's corner then up the meanders thereof to a gum another corner, S45°E 27.5C to BJ Corner in said Burch's and George Seniors, W34.5C to RO on line of George M. Johnston [Geo Jr.] with his line N51C to PO, W3C PO, N25C to begin 255a. 10/2/1821

20/129 – Geo Sr. to Geo Jr. 10/30.1821 – New Hope adjacent Burroughs being what Geo Sr now lives on. Begin Stake/stone pile Burroughs line S90C crossing creek three times and running with his yard fence to the NW corner of a stone ???, E with said stone fence 1.5C to persimmon, S passing through said garden 4C30L stake, W5C to stake, to center of a spring, S52.25C hick, line of a tract south end of Johnston Jr. land then with said line E43.5C to pointers, N91C to PO, W3C PO, N25C stone pile in corner of William Robson the same course continued to WO said Robson Corner, 6.5C by a spring, down the meanders of spring branch 14C, N16°E 7.5C, N30°W 9.5C to said creek up meanders to PO of Thomas Johnstons, E1C to stone pile in Burroughs, W15C to begin 574.25 acres. (see 22/355)

20/246 – William Blackwood Sr. to William Robson - $55.00 Begin maple on the bank of New Hope N 32P to beach on Burrows line W on said line 12 P to sweet gum, S12°E 32 P to W.O. E4P to begin 1.5 acres and 16 poles. (** This is the land that Robson sued Johnston for flooding **).

21/301 – Aug 5, 1824 Geo Sr to William Duskin and wife Mary $1338. "Water of New Hope adjacent to the late Ruben Borough and others being part of the seat or body of land the said Geo Sr. now lives on. Beg stake or stone pile corner of the said Boroughs near said creek W1C PO on north bank of creek, down the meanders to the mill dam of William Robson, N66C to W.O and dogwood on the north side of an old road, W55C to dead hick corner of said Borough with his line S75.5C to begin 373a.

21/482 – Charles W. to George M., Merchant grist mill on Eno River formerly John Cabe Mill.

21/546 – 10/8/1825 – This is an interesting deed. It was to be a piece of land given to his son-in-law Gray Huckabee and his wife (Geo. Sr. daughter) Martha. But it looks that William Robson wanted to buy it. The deed stated, "…I designed giving to my said son in law…". Robson pays Gray Huckabee $500 and yet, Geo. Sr. is the grantor of the property. "Beg at a hickory in Robson corner with his line N43C to state, W1.5C to sweet gum on Robson Mill pond, N with the line of William Duskin [Geo Johnston Sr. son in law] 23.5C to stake in Couch's corner with his line E37C PO, S45C B.J. E3C stake, S26.25C Stake where a red oak was, continue 1 C dogwood, W29C ash at the mouth of Babs branch on west bank of New Hope up said creek 5C to a haw bush W 10.5C to begin 261.75A.

22/269 – Geo Jr. to son C.W. $80, begin stake and stone pile said Charles W. corner on Burroughs line running with said line W16.5C to rock near where a dogwood stood and near W. Robson corner with his lime S6C to sake in center of New Hope down meanders to sake in center of creek on Charles line with his line N to begin 17.5a. Feb 17, 1827

22/355 - $3500 George M. sells to C.W. Johnston – reference deed from Geo Sr. Oct 13, 1821 and registered Feb 26, 1823. begin stake and stone pile on Burroughs corner, S90C crossing creek three times and running with his yard fence to the new corner of stone garden, East with said fence 1.5C to persimmon, South passing through said garden 4.3C to stake, W5.5C to the center of George Johnston spring, S52.5C to Hick, E43.5C to corner William Duskin, North with his line 91C to PO, W3C PO, N25C to stone pile corner William Robson, the same course continued 6.5C WO (by a spring) down meanders of the spring branch 14C, N16°E 7.5C, N30°W 9.5C to said creek, up the meanders to PO of said Duskin E1C to stone pile corner of Burroughs, W15C to begin 574.25A. (See 20/129)

22/439 – Oct 30, 1821 – George Johnston Sr, to Elizabeth Johnston (minor – his daughter) - Beginning at an Ash on mouth of Babs Branch at the west bank of New Hope running with the creek some distance with Huckabee's line now William Robson, E29C to dogwood, N1C to stake, E19.75 C to hick in William Jenkins corner, S10.75C willow oak E11.25C W.O., S 11.25C B.O. E7.25C R.O., S52.5C W.O. in Mann Patterson's corner with his line W21.75C BJ, N27.5C BO, W22.25C BO, N3.5C to BJ, W20C PO in Mary Johnston's corner N24C to stake and stone pile in a small old field, W5C to hick, N20C to beg – 333a. (See 26/123)

23/17 – 7/22/1826 – Johnston Blackwood (Son of William Sr.) buys land from James Blackwood for $500. Begin persimmon and gum in George Johnston, W21.8C to dogwood, west side of Back Branch, N29.1C to Rock pile, E27.8C to dogwood, S29.1C to begin – 62a. See (26/349 then to 33/348).

23/27 – "…undivided 3rd part of a certain tract of land including a merchant and grist mill on Eno River formerly the property of John Cabe deceased whereon he ??? previous to his death and since his decease has been laid off and allotted to Lydia daughter of said John Cabe deceased now the wife of Charles W. Johnston and by the said Charles and Lydia conveyed to George M. Johnston by deed bearing date June 1, 1825 and by the said George M. Johnston conveyed to George Johnston Sr. by deed January 21 last. Viz the 1/3 part the other 2/3 part to Mary wife of Mann Patterson and Margaret wife of John W. Caldwell daughters of the said John Cabe deceased by commissioners appointed for that purpose by order of court. Adjacent the land of Abraham Nelson lying on both sides of Eno River, beginning stake S43C PO, E6C BO, S46C PO, E38C PO, N40C WO, W5C WO, N40C to Spanish Oak, W39C to beginning. Contains 304 acres in the whole three parts be the same more or less…"(Sep 21, 1826 – Geo Sr. to Mary Duskin wife of William Duskin and Geo Sr. daughter).

23/32 – William to Johnston Blackwood – 12/10/1826 – dogwood on George Johnston line W24.55C, N10.4C to stake, W2.25C to Hick, N17.25C WO, E22.5C to gum, S9°E 8.2C WO, S21.12C to begin. 70A.

23/50 – Aug 25, 1824 George Johnston to Sarah B. Johnston – "love and affection" daughter of George, 300 acres of Haywood County, TN land on Big Hatchee River. Being a piece of 2500 acres of land Johnston bough May 9, 1789.

23/51 – Aug 25, 1824 George Johnston to Elizabeth Johnston – "love and affection" daughter of George, 300 acres of Haywood County, TN land on Big Hatchee River. Being a piece of 2500 acres of land Johnston bough May 9, 1789.

23/223 – Sep 14, 1822 – Thomas Watts – Sheriff selling land to the highest bidder – Ezekiel Trice's land was being sold to pay debt owed to National Bank of NC. Aug 27, 1822 George Johnston was the highest bidder at $1850.00. This purchased, 16a of Chapel Hill town land, around Lot #4, 450a on Bollings Creek, plus two adjoining pieces, 29a and 16a. ** MY guess – this was a transaction of George Jr. ** This is difficult to figure out. Even further, I could not tract this land being sold off or given as inheritance. See the next deed.

23/412 – Burnt Cabin Tract – this was a deed from sheriff selling the land of John Mulholland, Henry Mulholland, Geo Johnston to the highest bidder to pay off debt of $715.90 to NC Bank. The deed said (John Mulholland did not have any goods or chattels). The deed stated that George Johnston lives on this land. See the prior deed. Was this George Jr?

24/464 – 3/1/1831 – John Blackwood to son William C. Blackwood – 79a – no mention of a creek or neighbors.

25/89 – Waters of New Hope – begin RO on south bank of New Hope said Blackwood Jr. own corner, S36.45C to gum, W20.32C to Spanish oak in William Robson line, N8.75C to ash and box elder on bank of New Hope, down the meanders to begin. 47.5A.

25/187 – Gray Huckabee my son in law and Martha his wife by William Robson New Hope adjacent William Robson and Thomas Couch, begin at Hick in William Robson corner with his line N43C to stake, W 1.5C sweet gum in said Robson's mill pond, N with his line William Duskin 23.5C to stake, E 37C to P.O. then S 45C to B.J.O. then E 3C to a then South 26C and 25L to stake, then 1 more C to dogwood, W 29C to ash at the mouth of Babs Branch on the west bank of New Hope up said creek N5C to bush, W10.5C to begin, 261.75acres.

25/344 – James brother of Thomas Borough – stake in Geo Johnston line 21.85C to WO, N91.53C to BO, W23.5C to RO, S91.5C to being – 201a. Heirs at law of Reuben Borough deceased.

25/360 – 12/29/1829 on waters of New Hope – William Robson to Mary Flintoff - $325.00 part of tract Robson bought of Zachias Borroughs from his dad James Borroughs – stake on north side of Strayhorns line running east 23.39C to corner, S on Borroughs line 32C to WO, W22.39C to stake in Andrew Burns, North to begin – 21 acres. Tract #2 – Begin on New Hope Creek, North on Robson line 38C to rock pile and stake, E20C to stake in James Boroughs line, S49C to stake in corner in Charles Johnston's line, W10.6C to beach corner, N5.5C to beach on the bank of New Hope, running with said creek to begin 80a.

26/349 – 11/20/1834 ($195) William Burns buys the 65 acres from Johnston Blackwood. (see 33/348)

26/123 – Oct 23, 1833 – Thomas King and wife Elizabeth to William Robson. Elizabeth is the daughter of Geo Johnston Sr. begin Ash on mouth of Babs Branch at the west end of New Hope running with the creek some distance with Huckabees line now William Robson, E29C to dogwood, N1C to stake, E19.75 C to hick in

William Jenkins corner, S10.75C willow oak E11.25C W.O., S 11.25C B.O. E7.25C R.O., S52.5C W.O. in Mann Patterson's corner with his line W21.75C BJ, N27.5C BO, W22.25C BO, N3.5C to BJ, W20C PO in Mary Johnstons corner now William Duskins corner N24C to stake and stone pile in a small old field, W5C to hick, N20C to beg – 333a. (See 22/439)

27/14 – begin stake where Hick on bank of New Hope corner of Mann Patterson house, E3.5C to stake where a Spanish oak stood, N15.5C to Hick, E51.25C Hick, S10C Ro, E14.75C stake in a field, S73.9C stake, E13.7C to iron wood on east bank of Bakers on First Creek down meanders to Ash on William Trice's corner, E with his line 11.75C stake, S44.25C RO, W10C to 2-elms on bank of New Hope up the meanders to begin – 750a. Land willed to William Cain by his deceased father and 2 others bought from Eleanor Patterson and another from Zechariah Trice.

28/174 - $249. William buys from John Burroughs - New Hope adjacent to Duskin. Begin WO Duskins line, N8.5°W 47.74C to stake, S81.5°W [or S8.5] 5.35C to pointers, N8.5°W 9.5C to WO, N70°W 4.1C to willow oak, S76.5°W 21.78C to Hick, S15°E 8.9C to Hick, S5.15°W 6.65C to persimmon, S24°E 75C to willow oak in the edge of a pond, S17C to pointers, E33.4C to begin. 172 – 4/5 acres. 7//4/1838

30/363 – begin BO corner of Geo Johnston deceased, then East with his line (now C.W. Johnston) 133P BO, N14.5P Ash, E33P to Hick, N86P to gum, W166 WO on west bank of Old Field Creek line of John Freeland deceased, S100P to begin. Conveyed by old William Blackwood to son John 1/25/1813 in which said Blackwood died.

31/145 – 5/11/1843 – William Robson to Charles King - $273.50 – 99.5 acres on Morgan Creek known as the Cautler Tract, Morgan Creek is on the east of the property.

33/348 – Charles W. Johnston buys from William Burns – 11/11/1848 - $57.00 – on New Hope Creek adjacent to William Robson and Mary Flintoff beginning at Hick on south side of New Hope, Andrew Burn's corner formerly Thomas Hogan's, S26.92C to stake A. Burn's corner, W18.6C to stake, what was formerly Johnston Blackwood line, North dividing line between William Burns and Samuel Burns to WO on the south bend of New Hope, with the meanders of the same to the beginning 65A. Also one other beginning at 2 WO formerly William Blackwood's corner, N36C to hick on bank of New Hope, down meander to Sourwood and WO formerly Burroughs line now William Robson, then South along the same 40C to WO, W9.25C to begin 34 ¼ acres.

34/408 - 9/23/1853 - CW to son John Cabe Johnston 65a on New Hope adjacent to William Robson, and Thomas Hogan.

36/127 – 4/1/1859 Charles W. Johnston to Hazel P. Smith. Adjacent to Robson and Flintoff – Beg Hick south of New Hope (Andrew Burn's corner and Thomas Hogan) S36C 92L to stake (Burns corner) W18C 60L to stake what was Johnston Blackwood line, North a dividing line between William Burns and Samuel Burns WO on south bank of New Hope with meanders to begin. 65A. the other tract, two WO and BO formerly Blackwood's corner, N36C to Hick on Bank of New Hope down meanders to sour wood and WO formerly Burroughs line now William Robson, S along the same 40C to WO, W9.25C to begin. 34.25 acres.

37/410 – 1/1/1867 – William Robson to son William G. Robson adjacent to Blacknall and Craig Freeland. Beg Ash and elder in south bank of New Hope, N8°E 15C, N50°E 14C, N6.5C, N55°E 9C to mouth of the great branch N45°W 10C then 6.5C, N31°W 13C, N20°W 6.5C to an ash on said branch W22C to hick , S47C PO

W5.25 C to PO, S49C PO, to Freelands line, then 22.5C to dead PO corner, N41C to the beg 281 acres also the adjacent tract on the public road purchased of Charles Jordan 9.5a.

38/348 – William Burns to Charles Johnston – New Hope adjacent to William Robson and Mary Flintoff and others. $57. Begin Hick south side of New Hope Andrew Burns corner, formerly Thomas Hogan's S36.92C to stake in Burns corner, W18.6C to a stake on what was formerly Johnston and Blackwood's line, thence N dividing line between William and Samuel Burn to WO on south bend of New Hope then with the meanders of the same to being. Contains 65a. THE SCOND TRACT – adjacent to Robson and Samuel Burns – begin WO and Bo formerly William Blackwood corner N36C hick on bank of New Hope down meanders of creek to sour wood and WO formerly Burroughs line now William Robson, South along same 40C to WO, W9.5C to being. 34.25acres. Both tracts adjoining and containing 99.25 acres.

38/452 - 5/24/1858 – John C Johnston deceased adjacent William Hogan stake in Chapel Hill Rd at a gate run with the road N80.75°E29C70L to stake a corner for lot #10, S15°E 27C90L to pointer in west side of new road, S58°W 23C stake in the middle of Chapel Hill Rd then north on road to begin 91 acre – lot number 8.

38/453 Thomas Johnston to Charles W. 5/31/1859 ($2500) – Stone pile Robson corner S85°E 31C to hick, E 11.5C [or 10.5C] haw bush on the bank of New Hope, S25C to hick, E5C to stone pile, S24C to PO, W2C per deed to stake, N20°W 12.15C to gum on branch, up branch to gum, S [or north] 45°E 27.4C to BJ, E16.5C BJ, S29C RO, W26C hick, S11C to stake, W26C to pointers, N90C PO, W3C PO, N25C to begin 432a.

39/257 – Charles W. to Jeremiah Pendleton Cole – 3/8/1853 - New Hope, formerly known as the Petty Road (formerly Samuel Craig) sold by Sheriff Turrentine for $700.00. Begin – fallen BO east side of creek near Isaac Craig's corner N26.1C to pointers, W18C to stake formerly a dogwood, N27.8C to stake where a BO stood, W24.4C to high stump stone pile and pointers, South crossing creek 41C to stake, West crossing creek twice 26.7C to Chapel Hill Road and Hillsborough Road, Southward with the road 20.75C to stake Walson's corner, E9.25C, S3.25C, E14.25C, N2.5C, E20C, N26.5°E 3.5C, E10.5C, N51°E 11.1C to the beginning. Contains 252 ¼ acres.

39/364 – East side of New Hope adjacent to William Trice land and Vickers and Mann Patterson. 171a

40/329 – 4/6/1862 - to my son J.W. Robson tract of land I purchased from Geo Johnston and Huckabee on New Hope, beg gums on north side of mill pond, running N23.5C WO in Duskin Corner, E37C PO Duskins corner, S45C BJO, E 3C rock pile in Jenkins corner, S26C65L stake in Jenkins corner, E19C75L to Lytle Jenkins corner, S10C75L to a Willow on the bank of New Hope, E11C25L continuing 7C25L to Hick in Jenkins Corner, to South bank of New Hope at the **old mill seat** following the south bank of New Hope to an ash on the mouth of Babs Branch where it enters into New Hope Creek then N5C to a stake, W10C50L continuing W32C to rock pile in Johnston's Corner, N7C to **Mason's Spring** then follow meanders of spring branch to New Hope and down the meanders of New Hope to begin, 430 acres.

40/330 – 4/20/1863 - to my son J.W. Robson a certain tract of land J. Boughs [Boroughs?] of Thomas King and George Johnston give to his wife Elizabeth adjacent to lands of Mann Patterson, Jenkins and others – 300a – mentions Babs Branch… "beg stake on south bank of New Hope on Copley's old Mill seat, south 5C to the top of the hill at a large RO marked for a corner, S52.5C to WO in Patterson corner, W21.75C BJ, N27.5C RO, W22C to Hephen's corner, N3.5C to BJ, W20C to Jenkins Corner, N24C to rock pile, W5C stake, N20C to an ash at the mouth of Babs Branch on the south side of New Hope down south side to beginning …300acres…"

42/17 – 9/6/1873 – Robert H. Sharp and John L. Tate - $800 - On waters of New Hope Creek adjoining the lands of J.W. Robson, Johnston and others, known as **Robson Lower Mill Tract**. Beginning at WO along race on the south side of the mill pond S9°W 8C to peach tree then S20°E 90 links to corner of a rock fence near the mill then S20°W 9C to rock pile thence E5C 62L to a rock in the middle of the creek, N15°E 24C to Spanish oak on a small branch, down said branch as it meanders to the mill pond and across said pond to beginning 12 acres…includes mill home fixtures and all the appurtenances thereunto belonging together ….with all the necessary privileges of said mill seat and ….privilege to raise the mill dam two feet higher then present standing without further charge for damages…"

44/122 – Mary 4, 1874 – J.W. Robson was part of a bankruptcy hearing – James Whitted bankruptcy and the sheriff sold part of Lot #6 to J.W.

44/123 – 10/19/1875 – J.W. Robson and Mary C. $1270.00 part of lot #6 in downtown Hillsboro upon which now stands Tobacco Factory lately by E. Pogue.

44/385 – Nov 30, 1875 J.W. Robson buys part of lot #25 for $1000.00 – 23/100 acre.

44/545 – J.W. and M.C. Robson $371 for 44.5 acres sold to H.P. Smith on Oxford Road and adjoins H.P. Smith's land.

45/173 – 5/11/1877 – Mary C. Robson, W.G. Robson, Louisa Borrough, and Matilda W. Hogan to Alice Burton – 1 store house and lot in Hillsboro bounded by the south by King St., west by alley east of store house of James Webb Jr., on east by the old tin shop on north lot of John W. Graham… (see 44/385) * NOTE *: I believe these are the other sisters, as Matilda was certainly one sister, and Louisa Borroughs the other. Was Alice Burton the third and final sister?

45/258 – William G. Robson, Louisa E. Borrough, Matilda Hogan, Franklin X. Burton and wife Alice Burton to Mary C. Robson - $1000 – Beg Ash Babs branch on W bank of New Hope with creek some distance east (love that measurement!) with J. W. Robson's line 29C to dogwood, N1C stake, E19.75C to Hick in Ashley Jenkins corner, S10.75C to willow oak, E11.25C to WO, S11.25C to BO, E7.25C to RO, S to the public mill road Nash Booths corner on said road, W21.75C on said road to a BO, said Booths corner, W22.25C to BO, N3.5C to BJ, W20C to PO in Alston Pendergrass line, N24C to stake and stone pile in small old field, W5C to Hick, N20C to begin. 275a same tract deeded to J.W. Robson to Mary C. Robson Sep 10, 1876. (* This was per the agreement to remove their rights from the home estate*).

48/22 – 10/3/1883 - begin at gum on North side of mill pond N 23 c 50 l to take formerly Duskin corner, E37C PO Couch's corner, S45C to BJO, E3C rock pile formerly Jenkins corner S26C 25L to stake formerly Jenkins corner, S1C to dogwood, W29C to Babs Branch on the west side of New Hope creek N5C to stake, W10C 50L stake the same west 32C to rock pile in Johnson's corner, N7C to **Masons Spring** follow meanders of branch to New Hope down meanders of New Hope to first station, 403 acres. That was conveyed to the late J.W. Robson by his father William Robson. Known as the Robson Homestead Place and conveyed to Mary C. Robson by W.G. Robson and others

48/51 - 2/15/1876 J.W. and M.C. Robson $457.00 – 58 acres of land on Borlins Creek near the village of Chapel Hill.

48/197 – 12/19/1884 – M.C. Robson on Durham County $2250 part of lot #25 – 23/100 of an acre.

48/485 – 3/15/1876 – J.W. and M.C. Robson to Nash Booth, $275.00 – begin BO on south side of the public mill road leading to Patterson's Mill south with Silas Carden's line 28C to BJ then E21.75C to WO in Patterson's corner, N27C to aforesaid road along said road to begin 55a.

49/200 – C.W. Johnston buys from William T. Burt – Dec 1881 - New Hope adjacent to William Hogan and Johnson Johnston – begin East side of Chapel Hill road about 2.18C North from W.J. Hogan's corner on the road, E26.5C to pointers, N45°W 23C pointers, S8°W 28.35C to stake in road at the corner of field then South with Chapel Hill road to begin. 41.5a. ($100).

49/201 – Waters of New Hope, adjacent to William J. Hogan, begin stake in Chapel Hill road at a gate with road 80.75°E 29.7C to stake in corner of Lot #10, S15.5°E 27.9C to pointers west side of University Road, S58°W 23.35C to stake in the center of the chapel hill road, north with the road to begin. 91A. Lot #8 of lands late of John C. Johnston conveyed to late Lydia Johnston by Webb. May 24, 1858.

49/275 – 12/31/1874 – Robert H. Sharp to George W. Tate - $580.00 – "…half of a certain tract of land…adjacent lands of Wesley Robson [J.W. Robson] and known as Robson Lower Mill Tract…consisting of 12 acres more or less including the Robson Mill…" ** It is interesting to note some small, but helpful, changes to the metes and bounds. *"…begin at a white oak above the mill race on the south side of the mill pond, then S9°W 8C to a peach tree…"* then it follows all other descriptions as before, except the following ending statements, *"…down the spring branch as it meanders to the mill pond and across said pond to the beginning…"*. Typically it states New Hope Creek and not the pond. This helps to locate the mill race entrance, since it is across from the creek. And this confirms the spring branch that I followed up stream to be the "spring branch" listed in the deeds. **

49/491 – 3/4/1882 – W.G. Robson to William Lloyd and Morris King $800.00 on New Hope. Begin rock where the Rail Road crosses County road, then with the Rail Road to the branch 166 yards, with the branch to New Hope Creek 50 yards with the creek to the bridge 75 yards, thence with the county road to begin 195 yards. Contains 3 acres and also ½ interest in and to a certain stream saw and grist mill thereon including all the fixtures, implements, structures…"

50/442 – C.W. buys from David Kerr – 2/26/1861 - stake in Chapel Hill road at gate then N80.75°E 29.7C to stake on South side of road, S15°E 27.9C to pointers, west of the new road, N58°E 5C to pointers, N15°W 18.35C to stake then E4.75C to stake, S11°W 14.6C to rock in the lane on the east side of Moccosin Meadow, N50C to apple tree, N57°W 1.25C stake, N21.25°W 1.9C to mulberry, N2.5°W 6.5c TO sweet gum, N12°W 5C to stake on line of the Blackwood tract East with same 4.5C to stake, N3.75C to stake, E8.25C stake, N21.75C black gum on Robson Corner, W40C to stake on the west bank of Old Field Creek on Freelands old line with his line S4.75C to stake on bank of creek up creek to Chapel Hill road and southward with road to begin. The same being lot #10 of J.C. Johnston – deceased. 275A ($1095)

50/464 – 11/4/1881 – W.G. Robson to America L. Robson to Mary C. Robson - $90.00 – Waters of New Hope adjacent to George Freeland and others. Begin stake in Hillsboro Road South to gum on Hillsboro Road, 26 rods to stake, E56 Rods to stake, N26 Road to WO, E56 Rods to begin – contains 8a.

59/584 – 5/6/1905 - begin at gum on North side of mill pond N 23 c 50 l to take formerly Duskin corner, E37C PO Couch's corner, S45C to BJO, E3C rock pile formerly Jenkins corner S26C 25L to stake formerly Jenkins corner, S1C to dogwood, W29C to Babs Branch on the west side of New Hope creek N5C to stake, W10C 50L stake the same west 32C to rock pile in Johnson's corner, N7C to **Masons Spring** follow meanders of branch to New Hope down meanders of New Hope to first station, 403 acres.

72/139 – begin rock in the NE corner of Lot 1 with lit 1 line W54.9C to rocks in NW Corner of Lot 1, line of T. Burroughs with his line N27.22C to corner of Burroughs and Thomas Hogan and with Hogan's like N4°E crossing New Hope Creek 13.5C to rocks in Hogan's corner with his line E8.5C to rocks his and Kirkland's corner, with Kirkland's line E20.85C to PO on New Hope Creek as it meanders to the mouth of Marshals spring branch Frank Couch line up said branch as it meanders to Marshall's Spring S30C to rocks in Frank Couch's corner and corner of Lot #6 with line of #6 S10C to begin – 185 1/3 acres.

72/144 – begin with Black gum E side of Hillsboro Road Perkins corner with his line E17.2C to University Rd the SW corner of Lot #3, North with said road as it meanders 37.75C 5to WO on the left side of road to corner of Lot #1, thence with the line of Lot 1, S85°W 10.64C to rocks a corner of Lot 1 with line of Lot 1 N11.93C to rocks in an old road, SE corner of Lot #5 with the old road S81°W 31.5C to center of Hillsboro Road at SW corner of Lot #5 with said road S47.58C to begin, 123.5A.

72/147 – begin center of Durham road south bank of road NW Corner of Lot#2 with line of lot 2 S41.45C to rock in Weaver tract, SW corner of Lot 2, with weaver line W46C to rock in Lloyds corner with his line S16°E 1.8C to rock in Perkins corner with his line W9.3C to center of University Road with said road as it meanders N37.75C to WO west side of road corner of Lot #4 and the home tract continued NE to said road 20.55C to the intersection of Durham Road East with said road 32.82C to begin – 220.7a.

72/150 – begin center of Durham rd rock places on south side of road at NE corner of Lot #3 then with line of Lot 3, S41.45C to rock SE corner of Lot 3 on the Weaver line with like and Clarks line E35.5C to rocks in fork of the road, Clarks corner with his line N11C to rocks, N89°27C to rock and RO Clark Corner and Burroughs line N29C to WO east side of a country road, Burroughs, Whitteds and Yeargans corner, with Yeargans line N89°W 17.4C RO, N45°W 14C to center of Durham Road on SE corner of Lot #1, westward with said road as it meanders 38.58C to begin. 241.7a.

72/154 - begin center of Hillsboro Road rock at the mouth of an old road the NW corner of Lot #4 with line lot 4 and an old road N81°E 31.5C to rock in NE corner of Lot 4 on line of lot 1N24.7C rock a corner of Lot 1, with lot 1 N17°W 23C to rocks in Burroughs line his and Freelands line W16.76C to pointers in Old Field Creek, down creek to pointer at the corner of Kirkland's on the west side of creek, then S12C to pointers on Creek thence up said creek as it meanders to Hillsboro Rd and with said road southward 38.97C to begin 155.5a

77/283 – begin at Willow Oak SW corner of the tract with the line of Cates S68°871' to stake in Walkers line, N21°E 1008' BO Walkers corner, S87°[no direction] 627' to Sallie Johnston corner, N20°627' to rock on Johnstons corner, N2°E 361' to rock in Stroud's line, N87°W Blackwood's line 900' to stake Blackwood's corner N2°1762' stake in Caroline Andrews line S88°W with Andrews line 950' to stake in Kirkland's line, S2°W 2095' to stake, S2°W 1450' to begin 175a. $100. Known as the Alexander Hogan Home Tract – 12/27/1919. James M. Johnston buying.

83/622 – 2/2/1925 – iron and pointers in line Gaston Lockhart's at his SW corner with W.D. Wilkens, S2.5°E 23.35C to branch along meanders 5.79c intersection of two branches thence with the E prong 1.16C to pointers S15°W 24c to center of New Hope Creek, S87°W 5.62c to rocks, N20°E 9c to stake, N20°W 90links to stake, N9°E 8C to stump N44°E 1.18c to center of New Hope Creek then along and with New Hope as it meanders to a point where Mason Spring Branch enters said creek in the corner of C.W. Johnston then in a SE direction along and with said spring branch to **Masons Spring** then S7C to rocks in corner of C.W. Johnston then with his line S85°E 31.60c to rock and pointers in the line of C.W. Johnston, E along line 10.90 c to pointer in the corner then S5C to Babs Branch then S89°E 14.2 c to corner of Levi Carden, N1°E 9.86c to rocks and pointer in Levi's corner then N88.75°E 14.63c to dogwood pointers, N1.75°E 17.40 c to rock in corner of B.L. Duke tract, N88.25°W 2.58c to rocks in Duke corner, N2°E 23c to the corner of a 125 acre tract cut off for Major Trice then N62.5°E along the northern border line of said Major Trice tract 38.32c to pointers and the road, N4.19C to stake near gate post in the corner of James Pratt, W crossing the New Durham Road along the line of Pratt 21.82C to rock and old pointers, W along Frank Cole line 10.5c to cedar stake in Cole's line, W along Cole's line 10.20 c to pointers in Cole's line, west along Cole's line 10.55c to stake on a branch in the corner of Cole and W.D. Wilkens, S88.5°W with Wilkins line 17.6c to iron at begin, 365acre being land purchased from J.R. Blacknall (59/584) and land purchased by Duke land Co (72/245). See Divorce (82/133)

84/59 – 3/17/1913 – J.L. Tate & others, devisees of George W. Tate deceased against Mamie Lynch and Others, sold to highest bidder on Court house steps – Robert M. Dickson - $150.00. Begin at the WO stump above the mill race and on the edge of the old mill pond S9°W 8C to stake where a peach tree stood, S20°E 90L…

86/181 – 6/3/1926 – 13 tracts of land. **Erwin Cotton Mill Inc to Duke Land Company ($100)**
   14) New Hope Creek – high bluff near Blacknall's corner, 60A (74/84)
   15) 31acres (74/83)
   16) Sinai Baptist (colored) Church near 2.4a (78/400)
   17) Upper Mill (83/622)
   18) Late C.W. Johnston and Frank Couch corner – Allen's Branch to Yearagins line, mouth of Allen branch and New Hope creek – 180.61a (73/341)
   19) Willow Spring, near Levi Carden and Couch property 35.5a (74/409)
   20) New Hope and the mouth of Willow Spring Branch – 31a (79/473)
   21) 0.83a (85/8)
   22) New Hope – 15a (85/70)
   23) 4a (85/70)
   24) New Hope, spring branch in Carden's corner, old Whitfield line – 88.8a (82/108 & 85/75)
   25) North side of New Hope – 13.5a (85/75)
   26) Lower Robson Mill Tract – 11.5a (84/59 and 85/71 which points to 42/17) – "begin WO stump along mill race and in the edge of the old mill pond S9°W 8c stake (peach tree in the old deed) S20°E 90 links on the east side of an old rock fence with fence S20°W 9c to rocks, E5.62C rock in middle of New Hope then N15°E 24C to Spanish oak on spring branch down branch as it meanders to said creek then across said creek S44.75°W to begin 11.50acres, known as the Lower Robson Mill Tract.

This deed had one exception – Crawford Stake and Handle Company has timber rights to land #11 and #12. (82/108)

Modern Deed Info

The Land Conservatory that owns the "old Johnston Mill" is PIN – 9881-44-5704.

This references the Deeds – 1953/570 and 1953/580

1953/570 – 6/28/1999 from the Trustees of the James Martin Johnston Trust. Per the will of James Martin Johnston, 1/21/1966. Plat Book 83/145 describes the land. However, this plat represents general property boundary, and does not include creek and stream positions, nor reference a mill site.

1953/580 – looks to be a subdivision of the same land and references PB 83/166

The plats do NOT reference the deed books for the Johnston property nor does the 1953/570 entry. However, surrounding land owners are shown and reference their deed books:

To the north – Kirkland 193/410 (I checked this deed and the one below and did not find any creek or association to Johnston property nor any mill)

To the west – Freeland – 614/172, 297/312, 292/313 (see above comment)

James M. Johnston is the son of Charles W. Johnston (1839-1916). I found two older deed records associated with James M. It looks to originate from the death of C.W. Johnston in 1916. There is a series of deeds dividing the land into lots. I found five of them (72/139, 144, 147, 150, and 154). This deed (72/150) states the land was subdivided per the Will in Book – I, page 582. It also states that James Webb surveyed the division August 29, 1916. Charles M. was receiving lot #1 and the home tract, totaling 241a.

Then James M. buys the Alexander Hogan home tract of 175 acres in 1919 (77/283). Then he moves these two pieces of land into a corporation registered in D.C. (100/59 and 100/60). Then later on, these same two pieces get moved into a corporation registered in DE (109/206).

Plats related to the Deed Transcripts

This section contains my hand drawn plats that coincide with the deed transcripts previously provided. This helps locate relationships and ultimately to find locations. When you draw the first location of a stream, or a road, you begin to introduce (to some degree – based on age of the deed) errors. Never the less, here they are.

Caswell Grant, to Blackwood to Johnston.

As with all land, it will become divided and combined, over time. The further forward in time, the more convoluted this becomes. Here is a great beginning deed to reference. It is actually the Granville Grant to Richard Caswell, then months later to William Blackwood, who then subdivides, and Charles Johnston then combines.

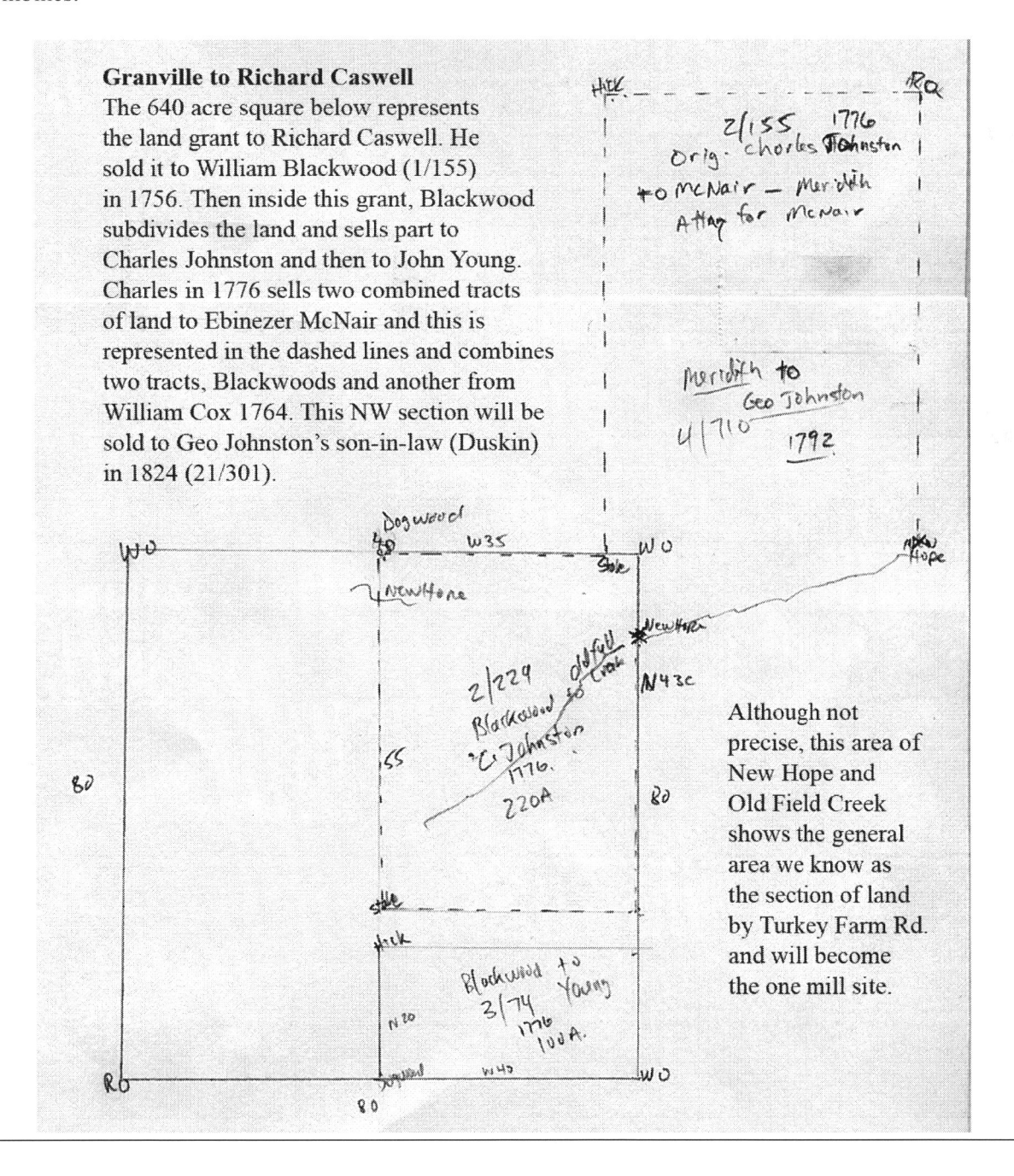

Granville to Richard Caswell
The 640 acre square below represents the land grant to Richard Caswell. He sold it to William Blackwood (1/155) in 1756. Then inside this grant, Blackwood subdivides the land and sells part to Charles Johnston and then to John Young. Charles in 1776 sells two combined tracts of land to Ebinezer McNair and this is represented in the dashed lines and combines two tracts, Blackwoods and another from William Cox 1764. This NW section will be sold to Geo Johnston's son-in-law (Duskin) in 1824 (21/301).

Although not precise, this area of New Hope and Old Field Creek shows the general area we know as the section of land by Turkey Farm Rd. and will become the one mill site.

Here is a cropped image of the greater combination of the George Johnston estate. Now the land has Duskin, Robson and others being divided out of the larger estate.

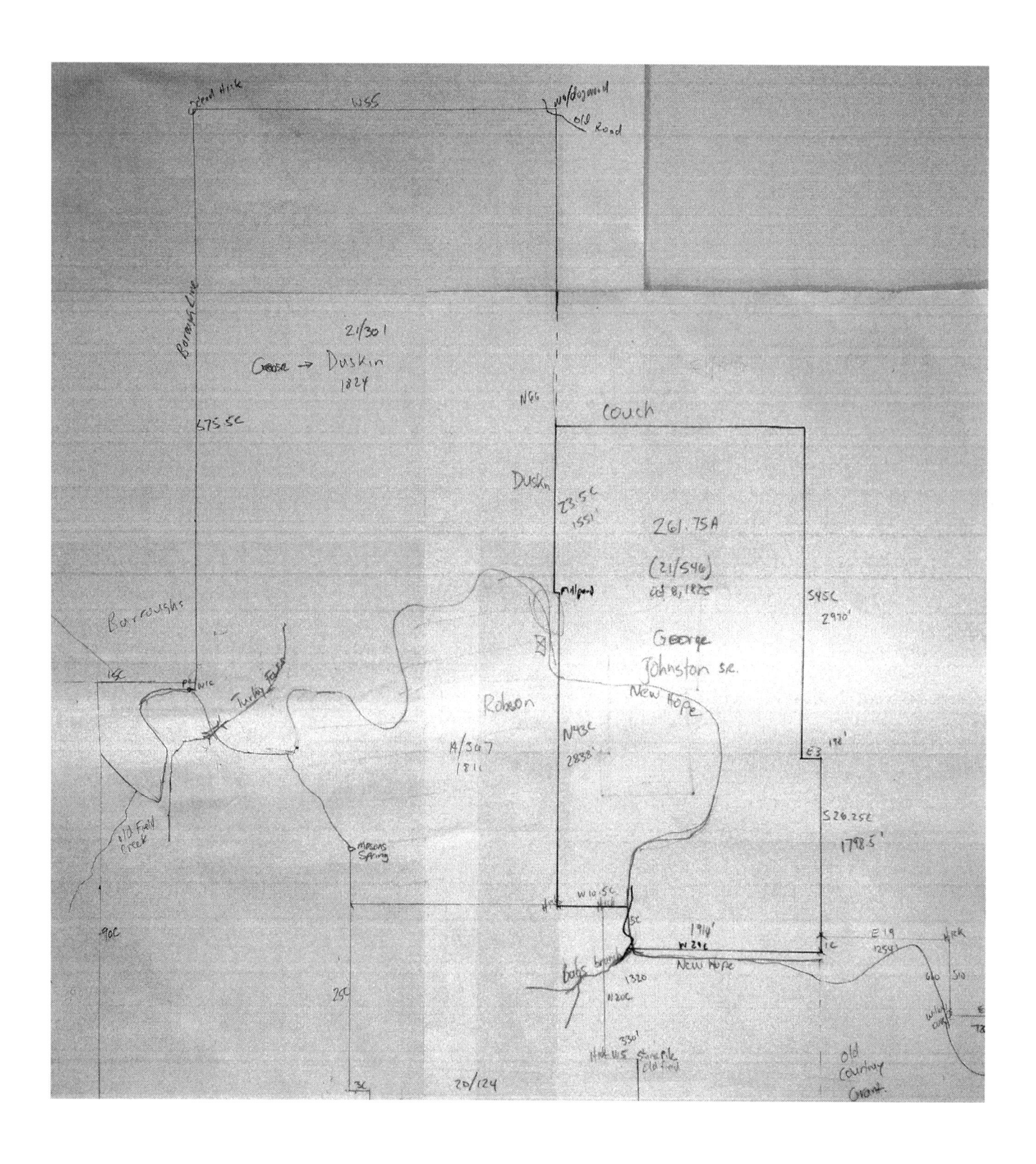

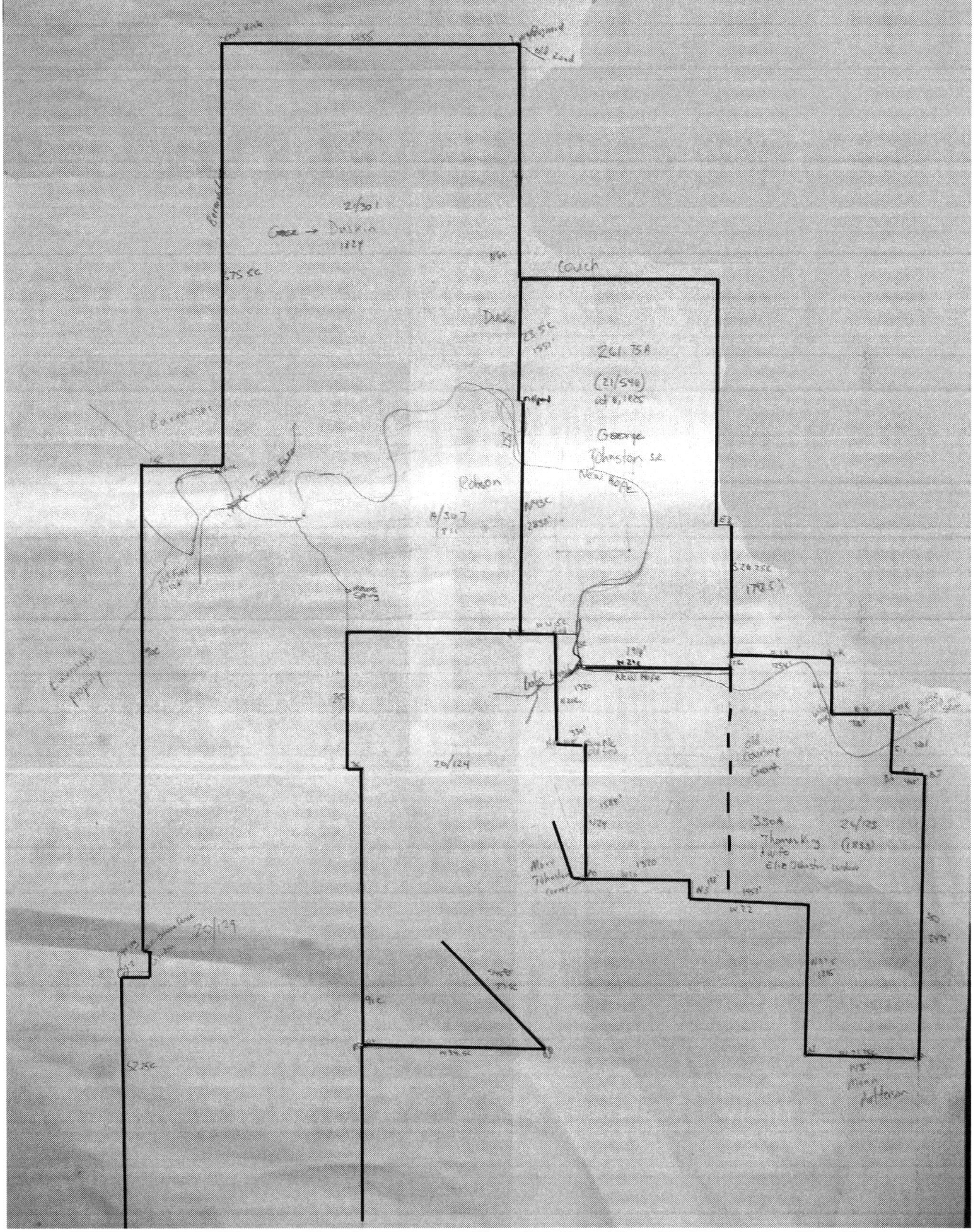
21/301
Gose → Duskin
1824
Couch
Duskin
261.75A
(21/540)
George
Johnston sr.
New Hope
Robson
New Hope
20/124
330A
24/125
Thomas King
& wife
Eavenson's property

Plat 3/73

This plat works its way back to a state land grant.

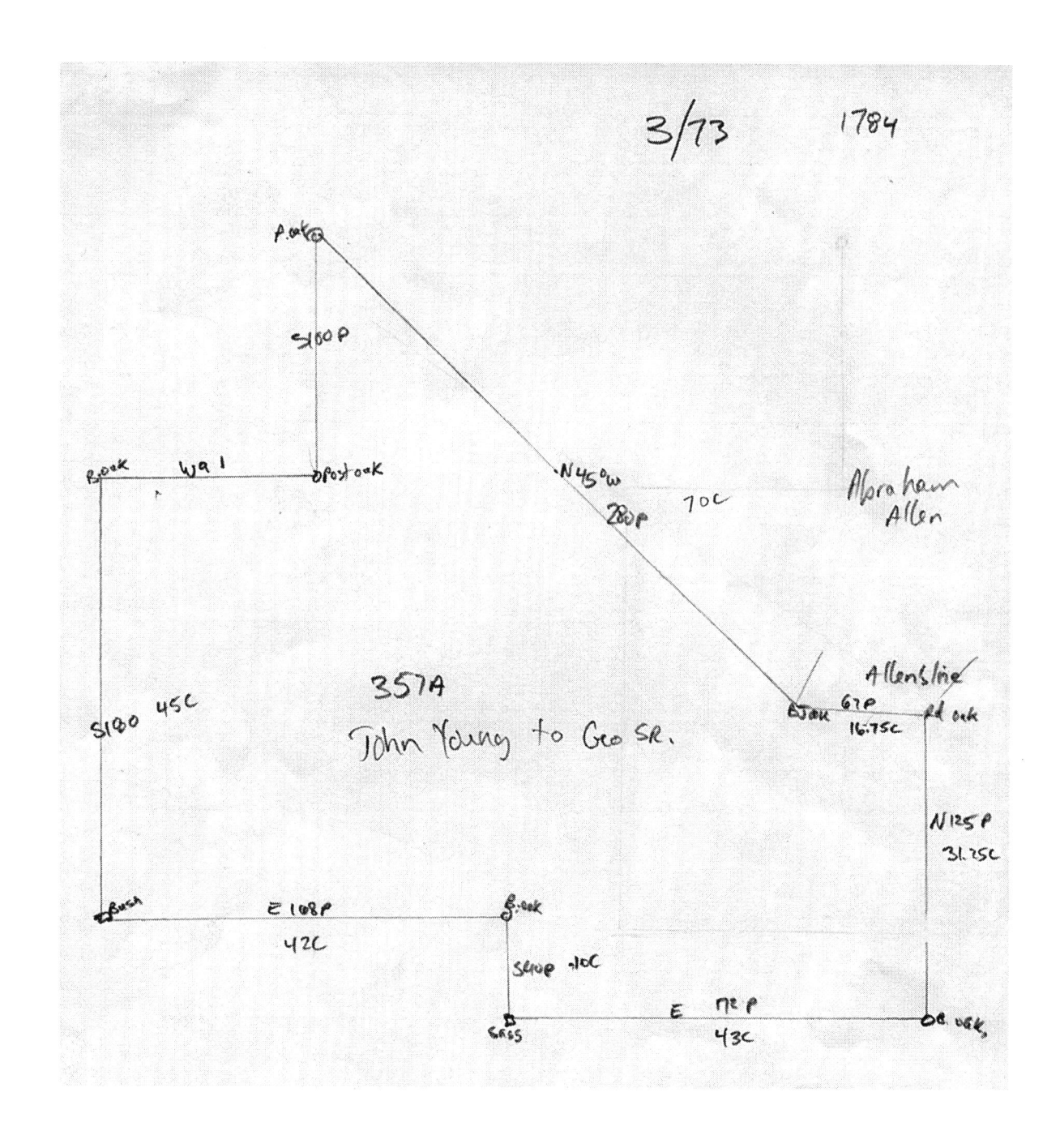

Plat 5/472

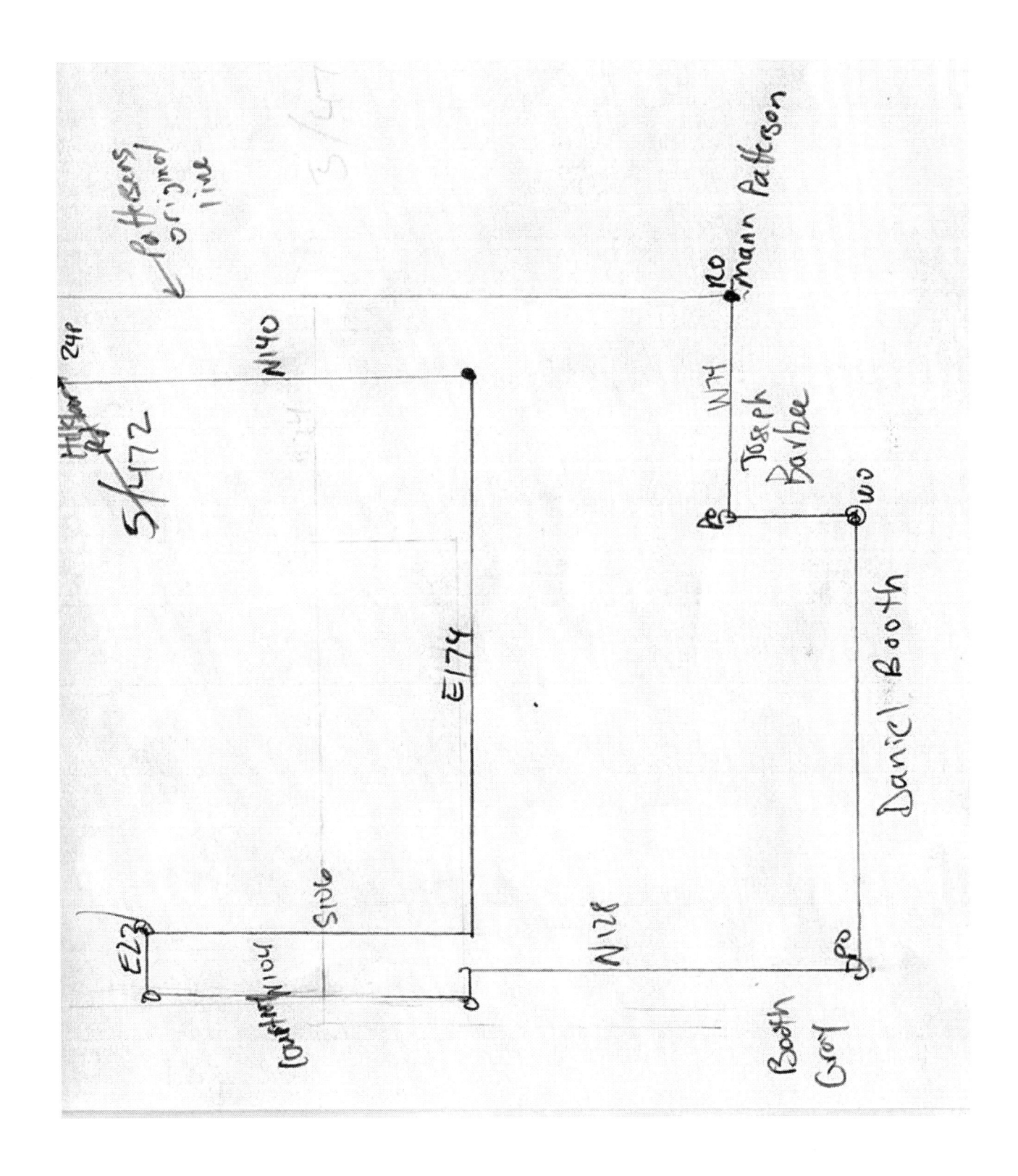

Plat 10/65

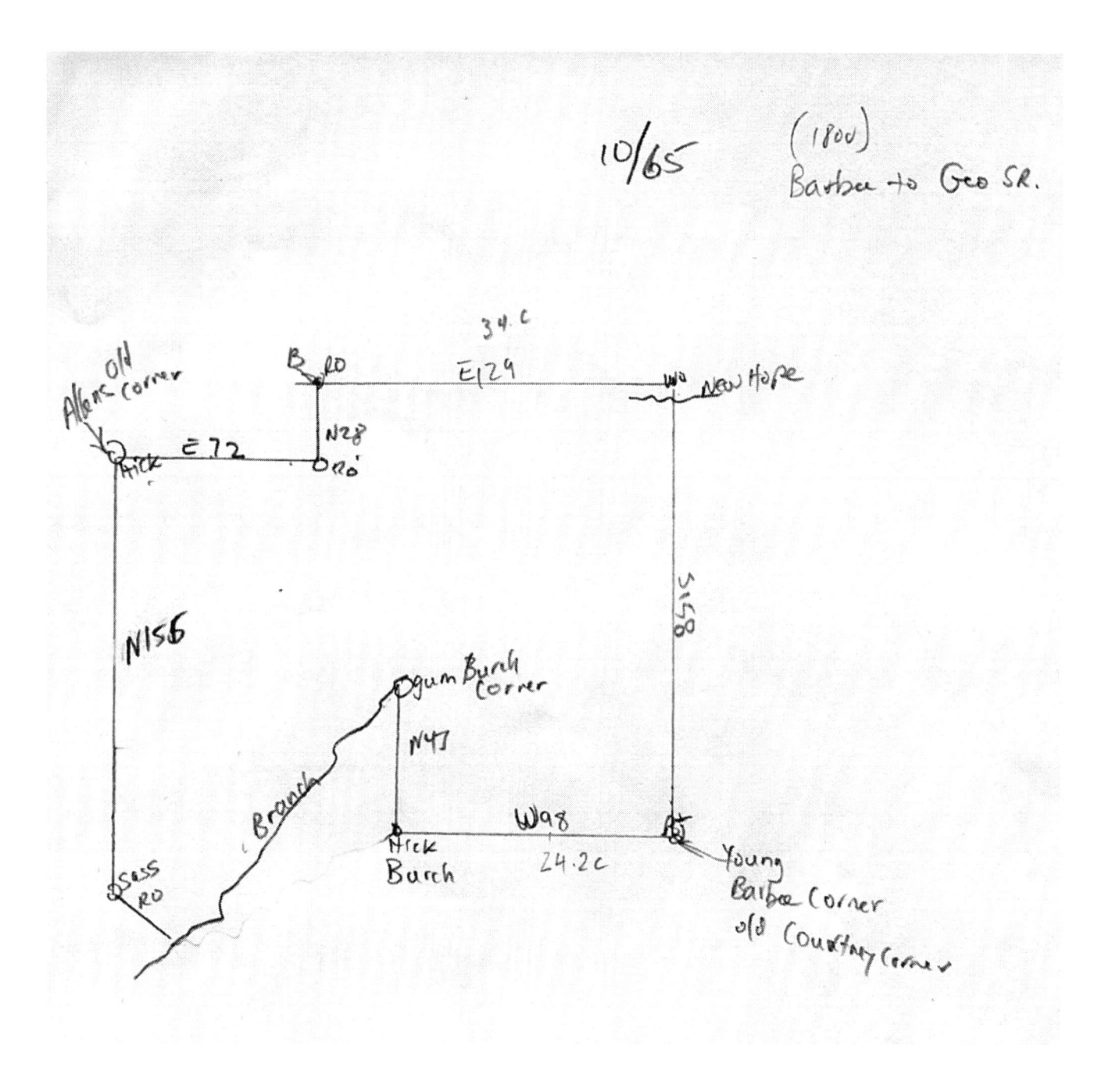

10/65

(1800)
Barbee to Geo SR.

Allens Old Corner — Hick — E72 — B RO — 34.c — E129 — WO New Hope
N28
O RO

N156

S158

Branch

gum Bush Corner
N47
Hick Burch — W98 — 24.2c — Young Barbee Corner old Courtney Corner

Sass RO

Plat 6/156

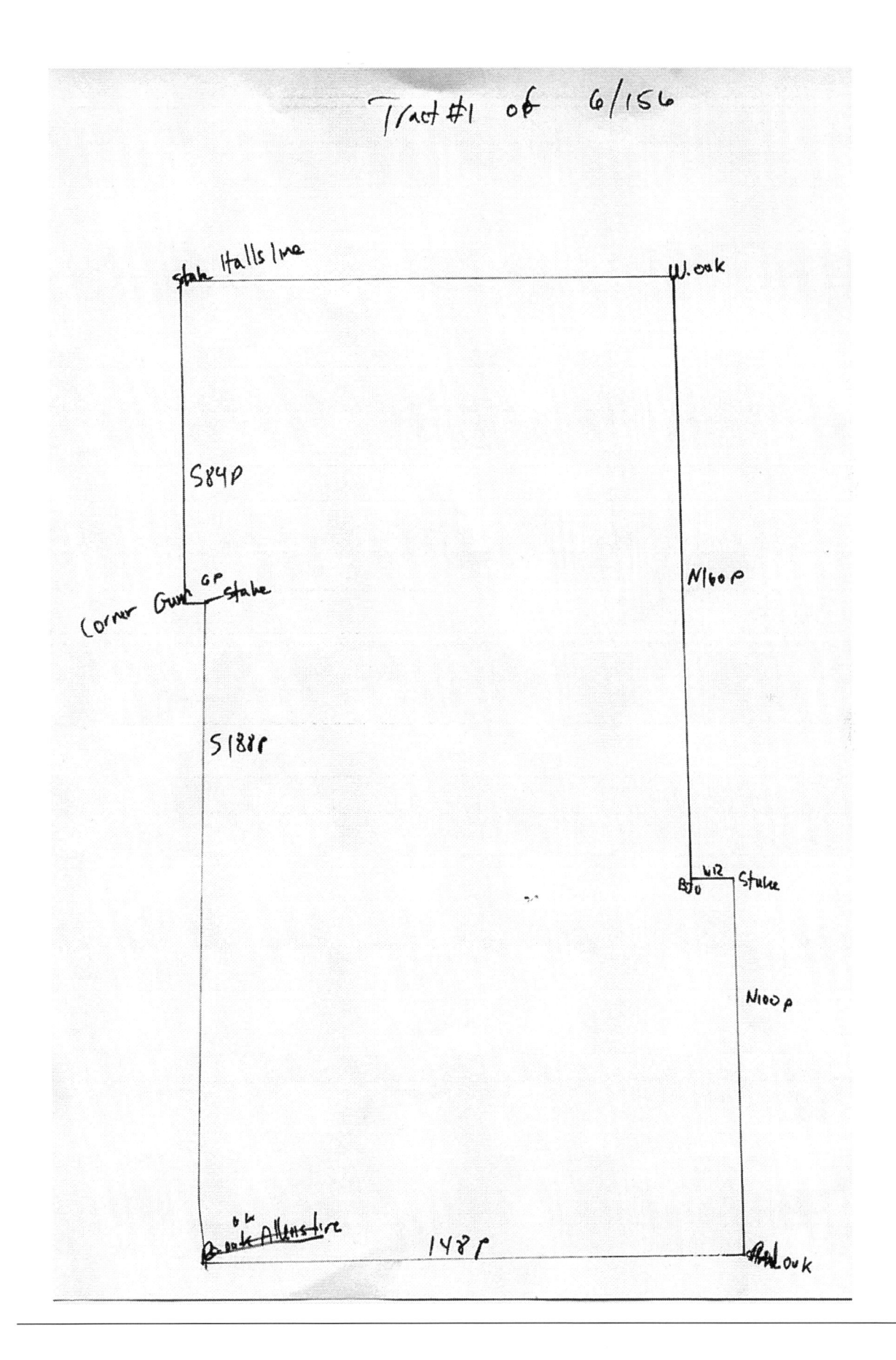

Tract #1 of 6/156

- Stake Halls line
- W. oak
- S84p
- Corner Gum GP Stake
- N160p
- S188p
- BJO W2 Stake
- N100p
- Book Allenstine
- 148p
- oak

Plat 5/488

Due to streams and exact locations, this plat was incomplete. When you run into metes and bounds that state, up or down the meanders, it becomes difficult to draw this, without a precise map.

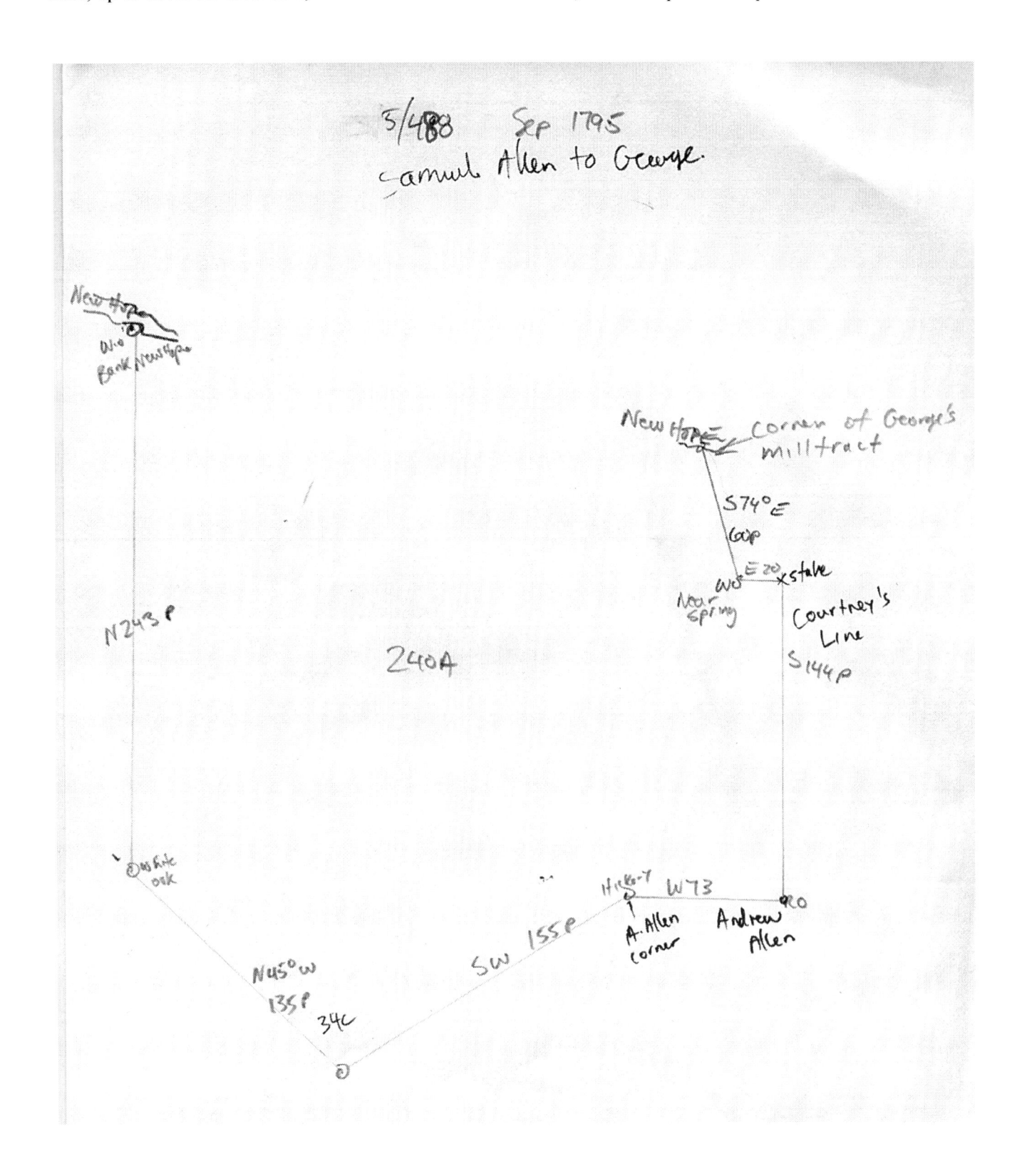

Plat Book – 3/37 - 1940

Here is a plat (8/26/1940) that shows the Johnston estate (150 acres) that borders SR #86 and Old Field Creek. The next page has a cropped section of the plat showing the alteration to the #86 as noted on the plat.

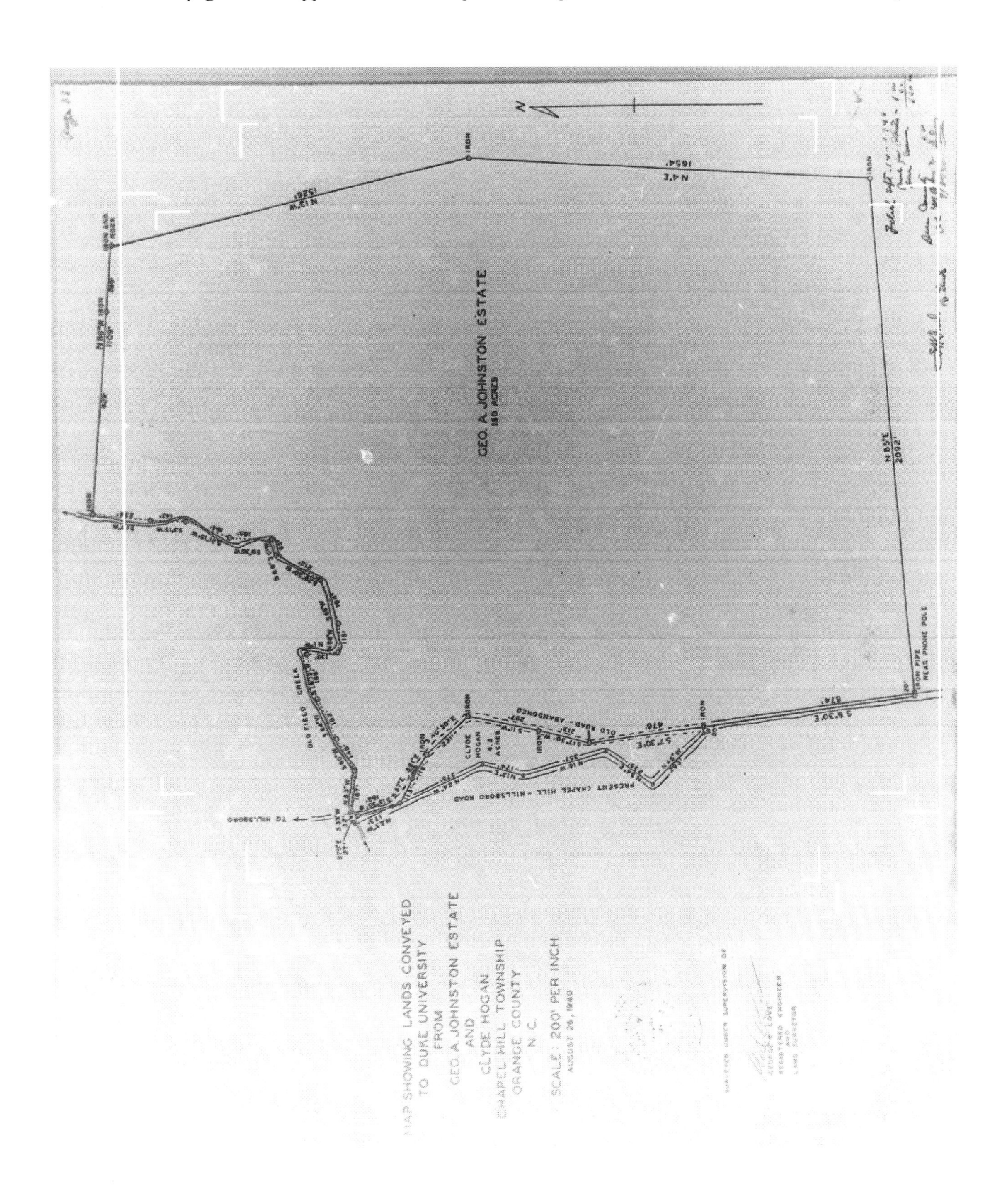

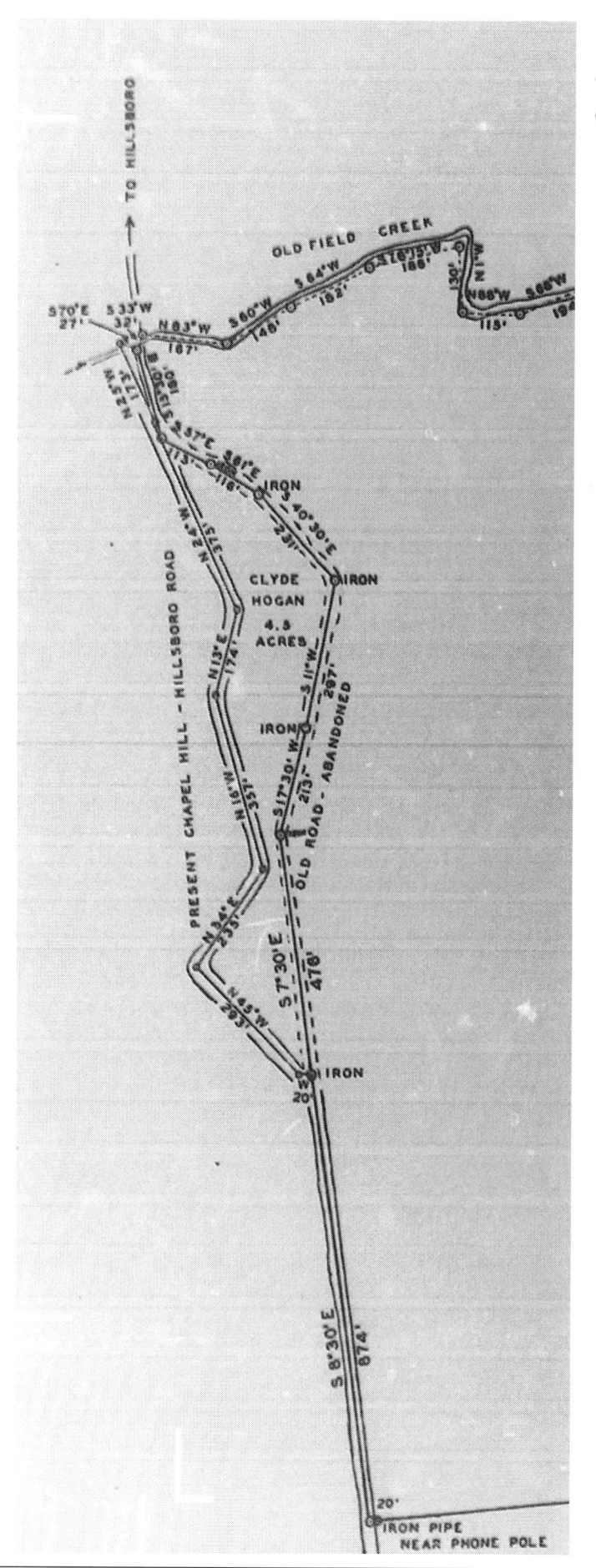

This interesting drawing illustrates the changes to SR #86 and its name.

Plat Book - 83/145

This plat documents the land that surrounds the Turkey Farm Road mill site. Unfortunately, the surveyors did not include any metes and bounds of any creeks. They show where New Hope enters the land at the bridge and that is it. This plat is referenced by (1953/570)

Plat Book – 83/166

This plat documents a subdivision of the surrounding land. See (1953/580).

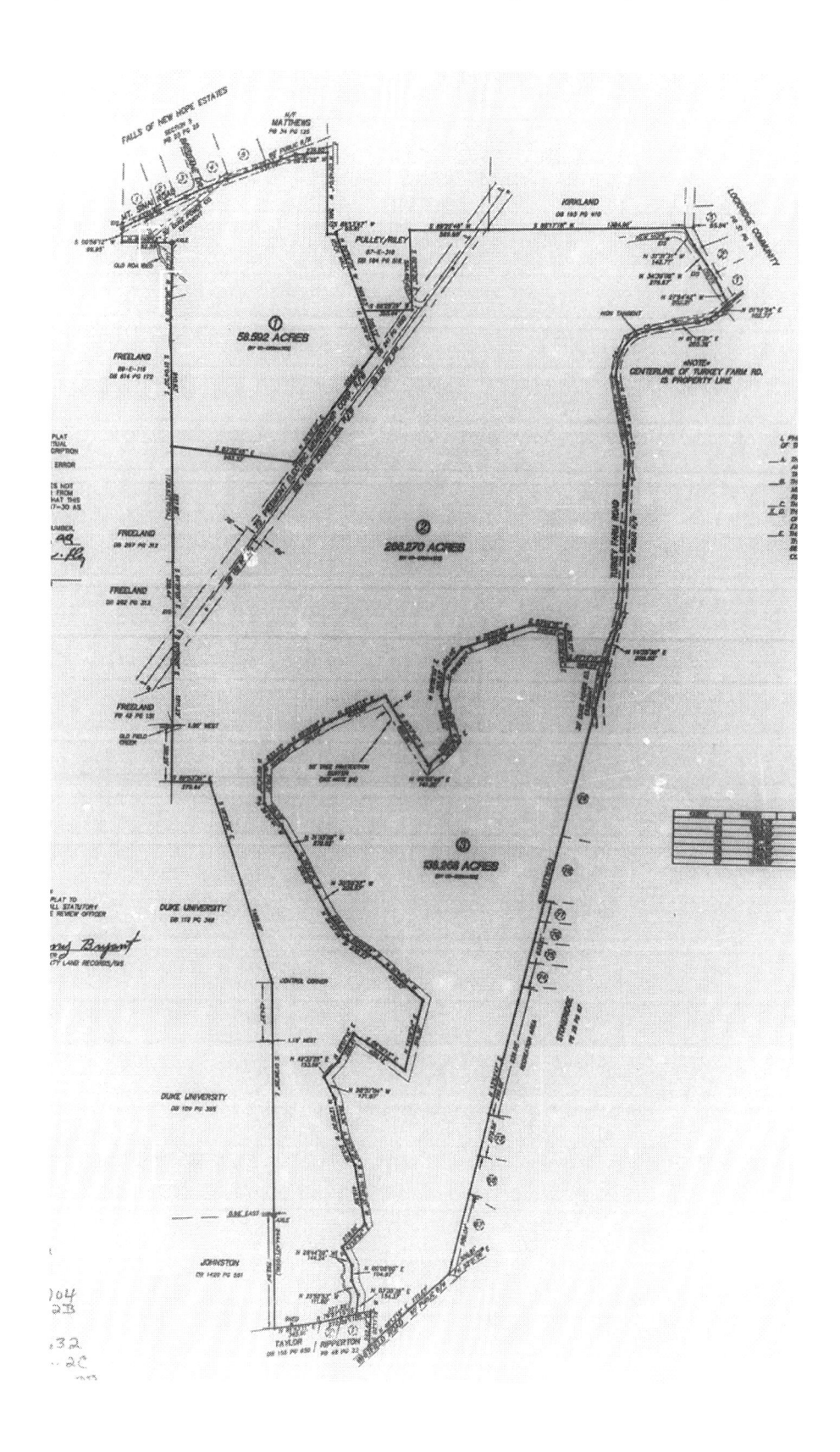

Here is a close up of the bridge on Turkey Farm Road and New Hope Creek.

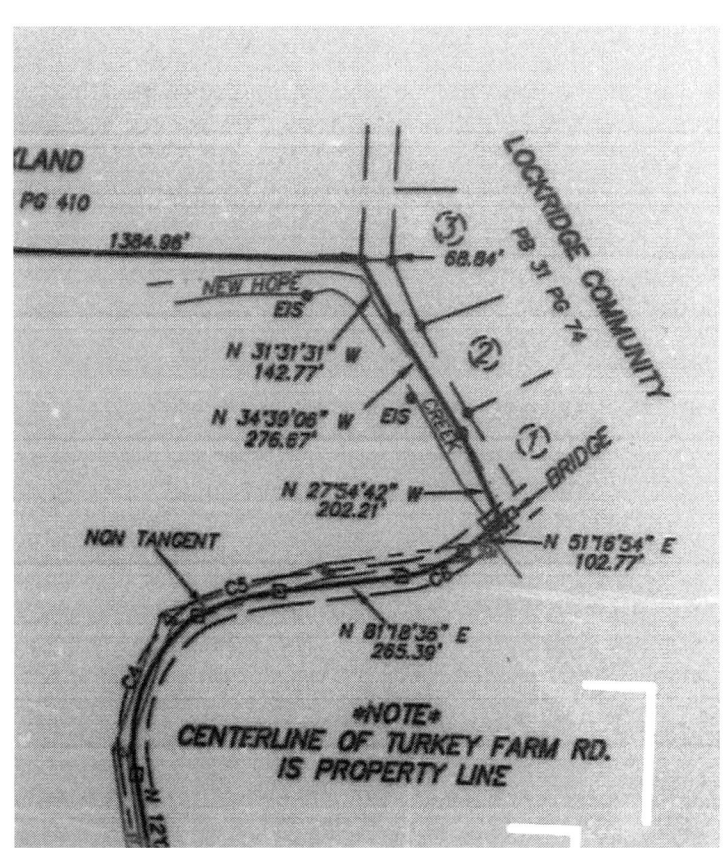

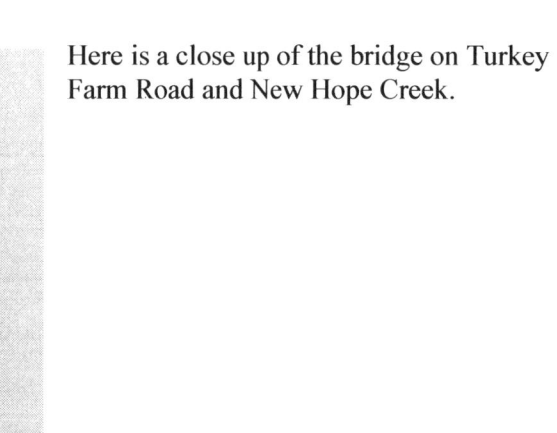

Below is a close up of the southern part of the land, showing the land intersecting with Whitfield Road.

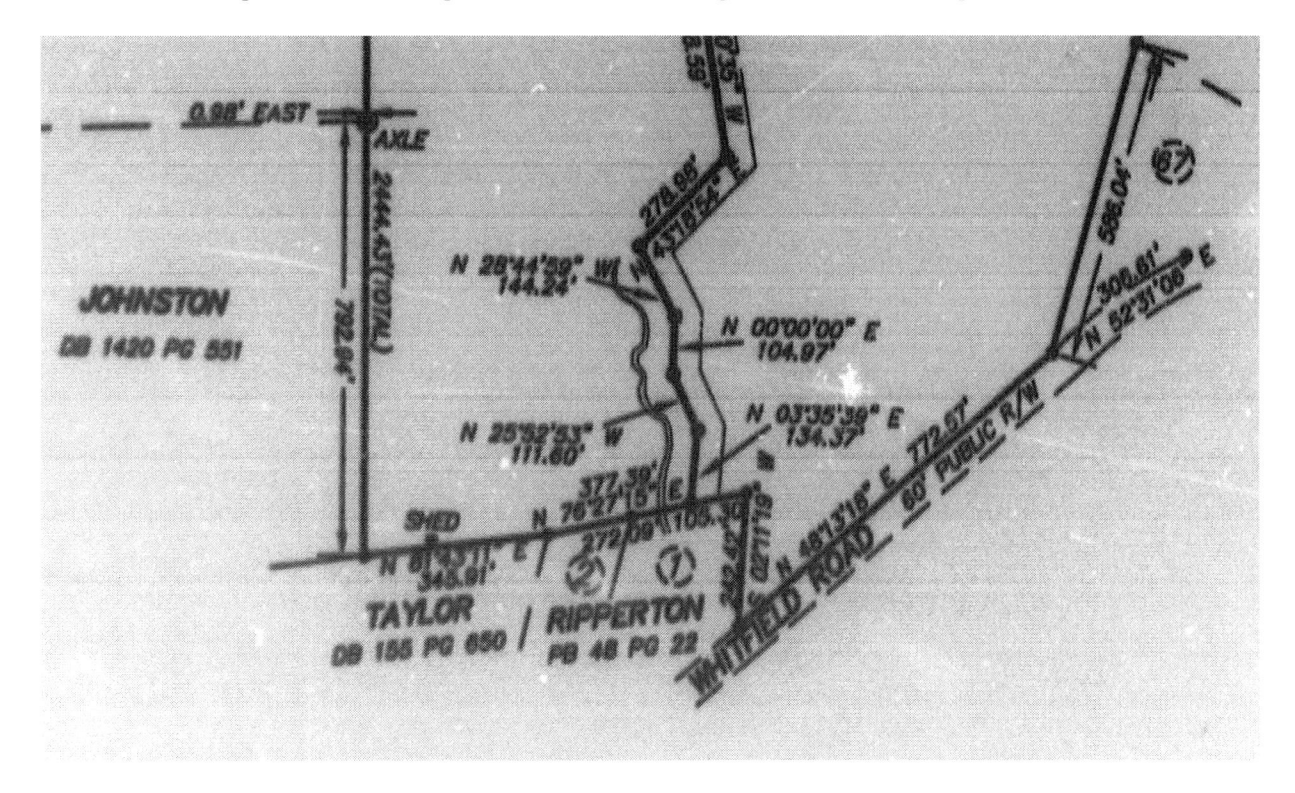

183

Last close-up. Here is the northern (NW) part of the tract, showing surrounding landowners.

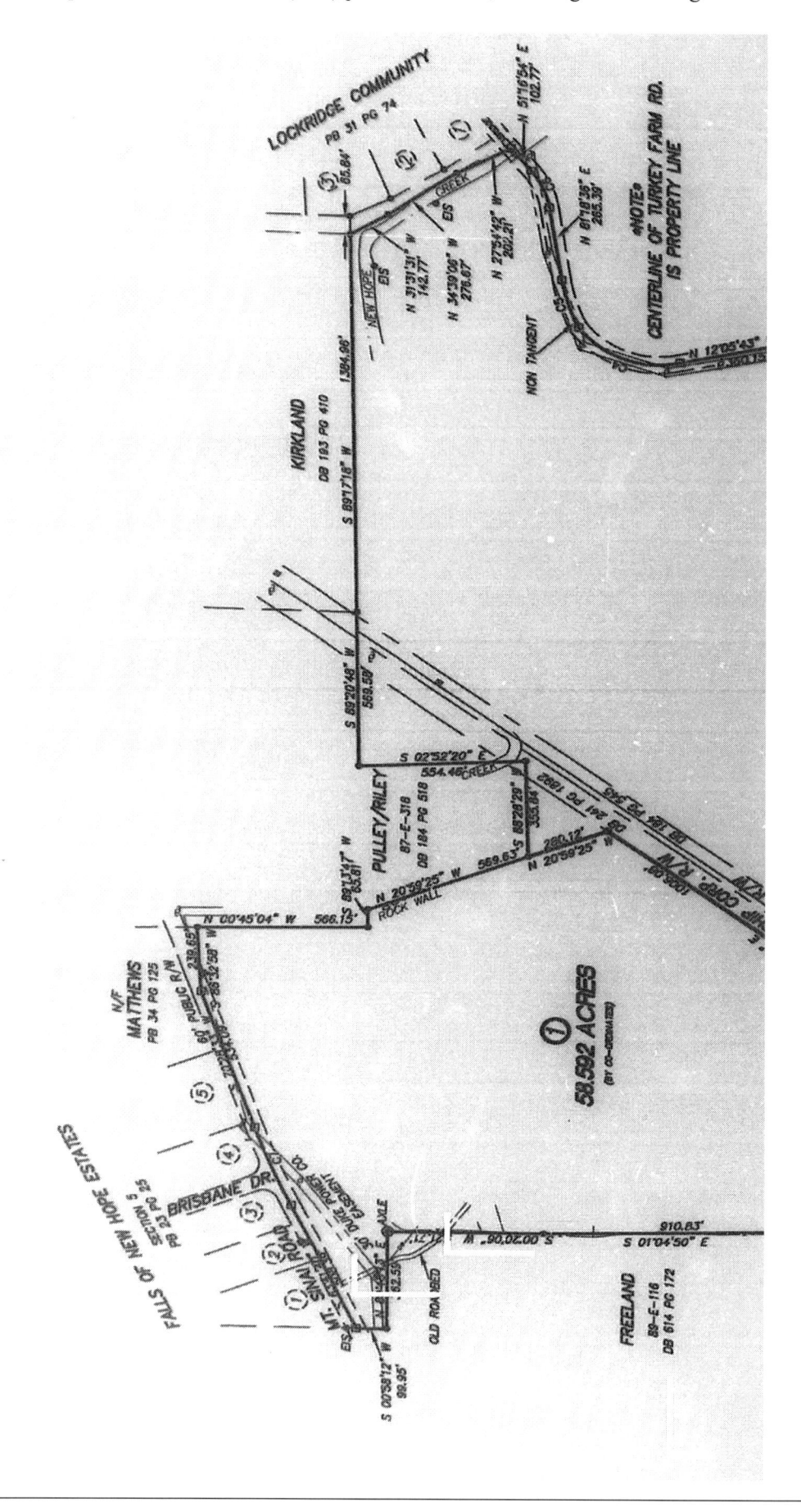

Allen Plat (Land grant) on New Hope Creek.

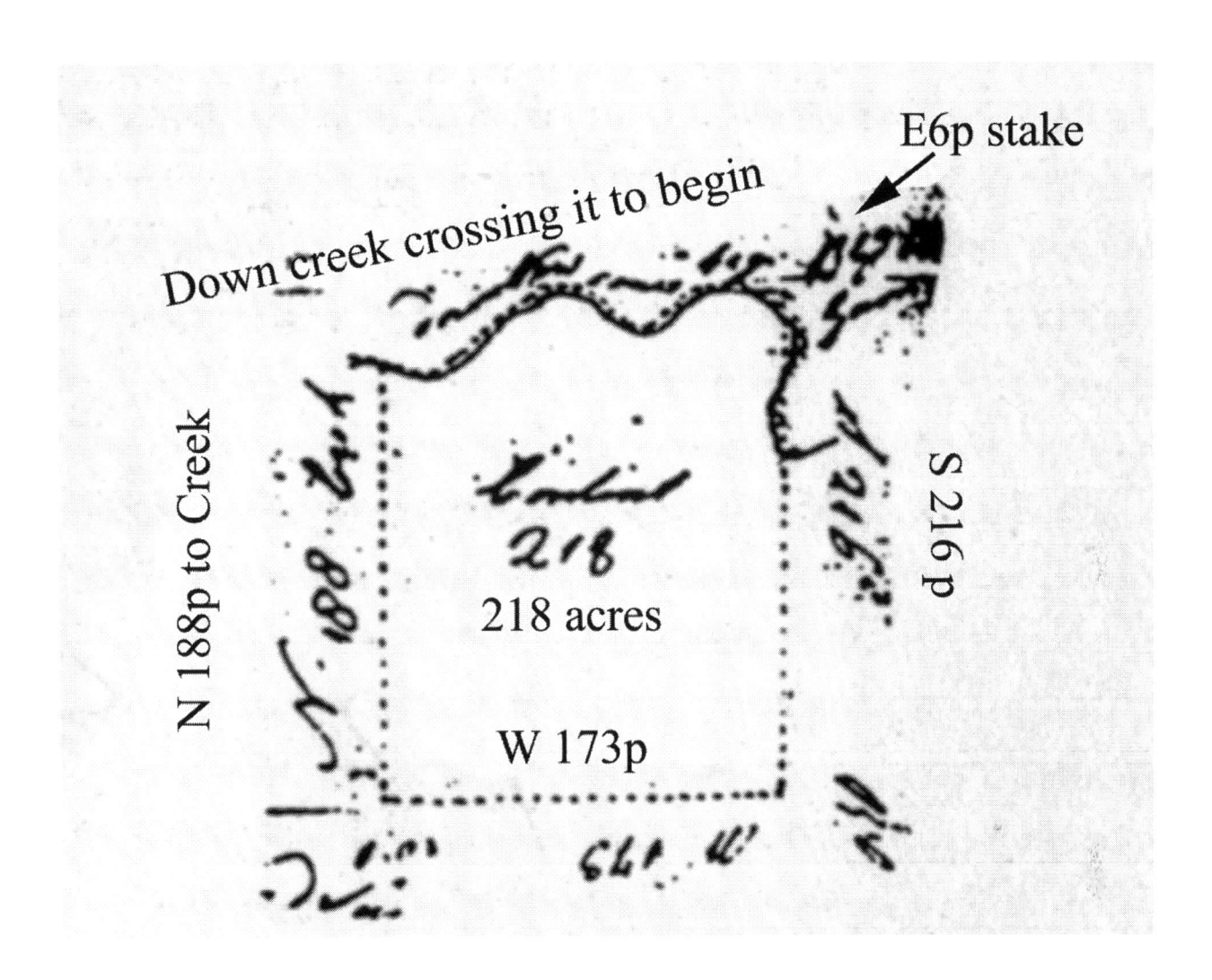

Down creek crossing it to begin

E6p stake

N 188p to Creek

S 216p

218 acres

W 173p

Allen Plat (Land grant) on New Hope Creek.

Courtney Plat (New Hope Creek)

It mentions in the text – Saw mill and Paper Mill. The plat shows "Saw mill".

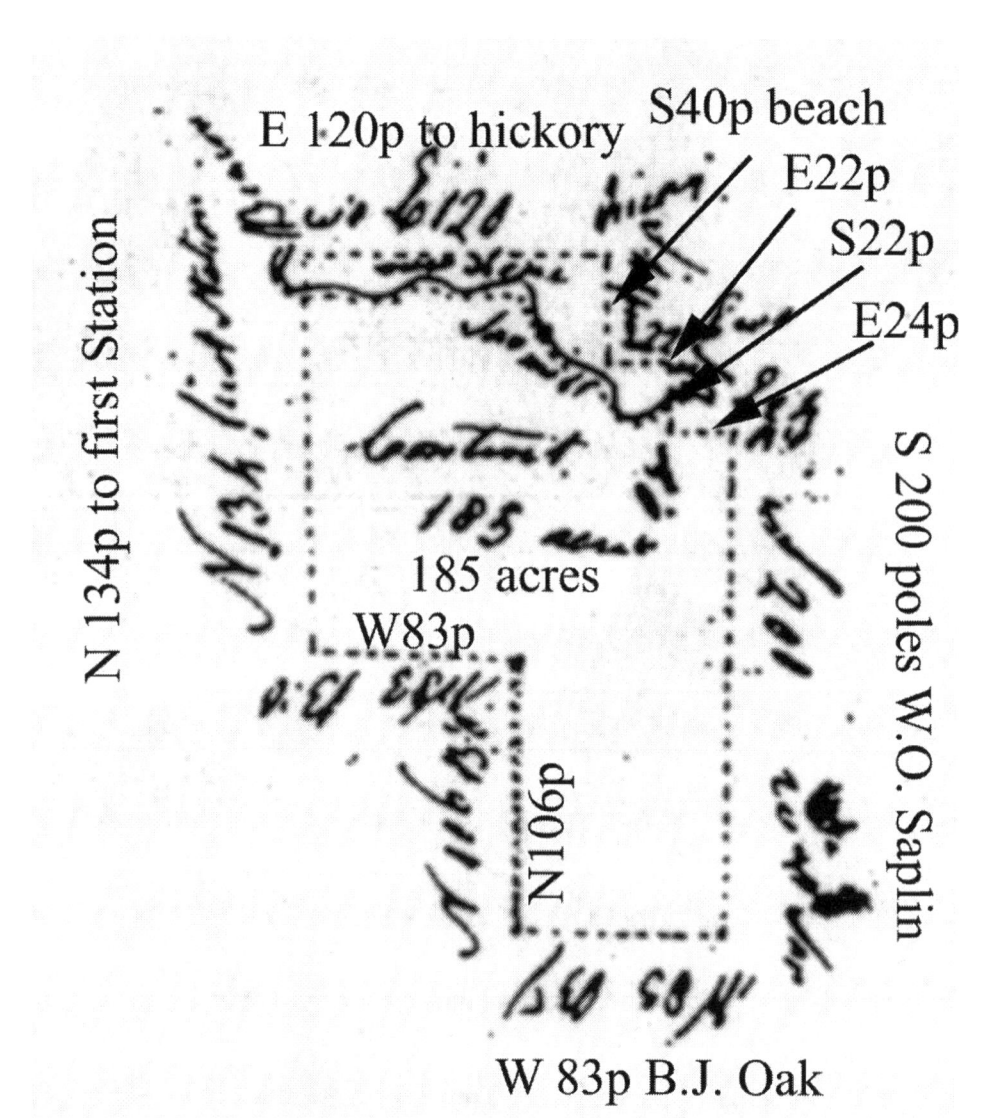

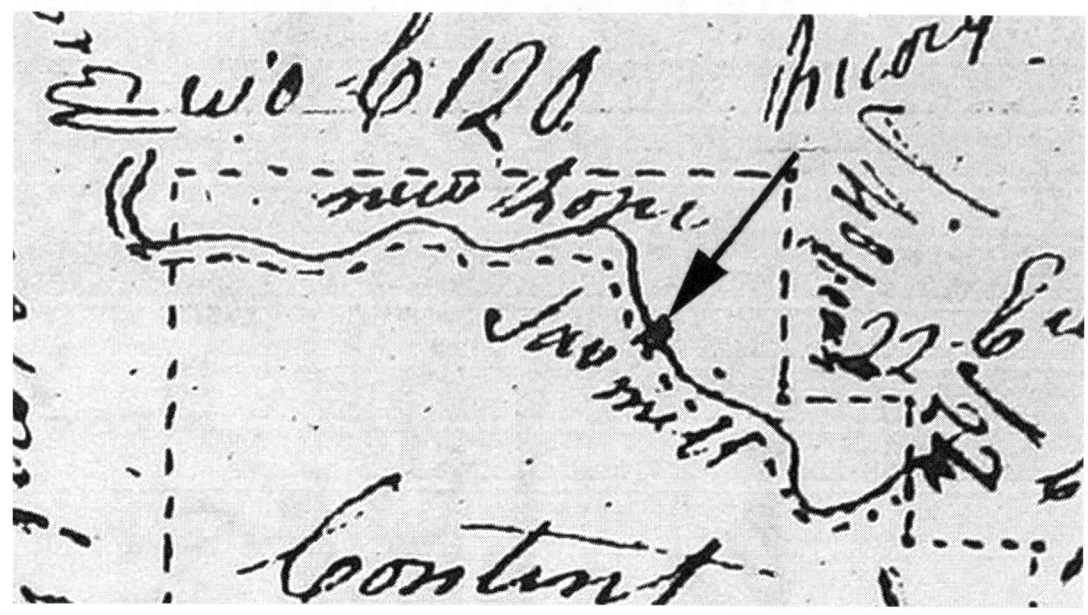

From the NC State Archives

STATE of NORTH-CAROLINA.   No. 150

JOHN BUTLER,
Entry Officer of Claims for Lands in the County of Orange

To the SURVEYOR of the said County, Greeting.

YOU are hereby required, as soon as may be, to lay off and survey, for *William Courtney* a Tract or Parcel of Land, containing *two Hundred* Acres, lying in the County aforesaid; *on both sides of Newhope Bounded by land of Bernard Bowling on the North, on the East by Lands of William Rhodes and John Barker and on the south by a conditional line between him and Abraham Allen including his sawmill and paper mill.*

Observing the Directions of the Act of Assembly in such Case made and provided for running out Lands. Two just and fair Plans of such Survey, with a proper Certificate annexed to each, you are to transmit, with this Warrant the Secretary's Office without Delay.

GIVEN under my Hand at *Mount Pleasant* the *fifteenth* Day of *June* Anno Dom. 177*8*

John Butler

From the NC Archives.

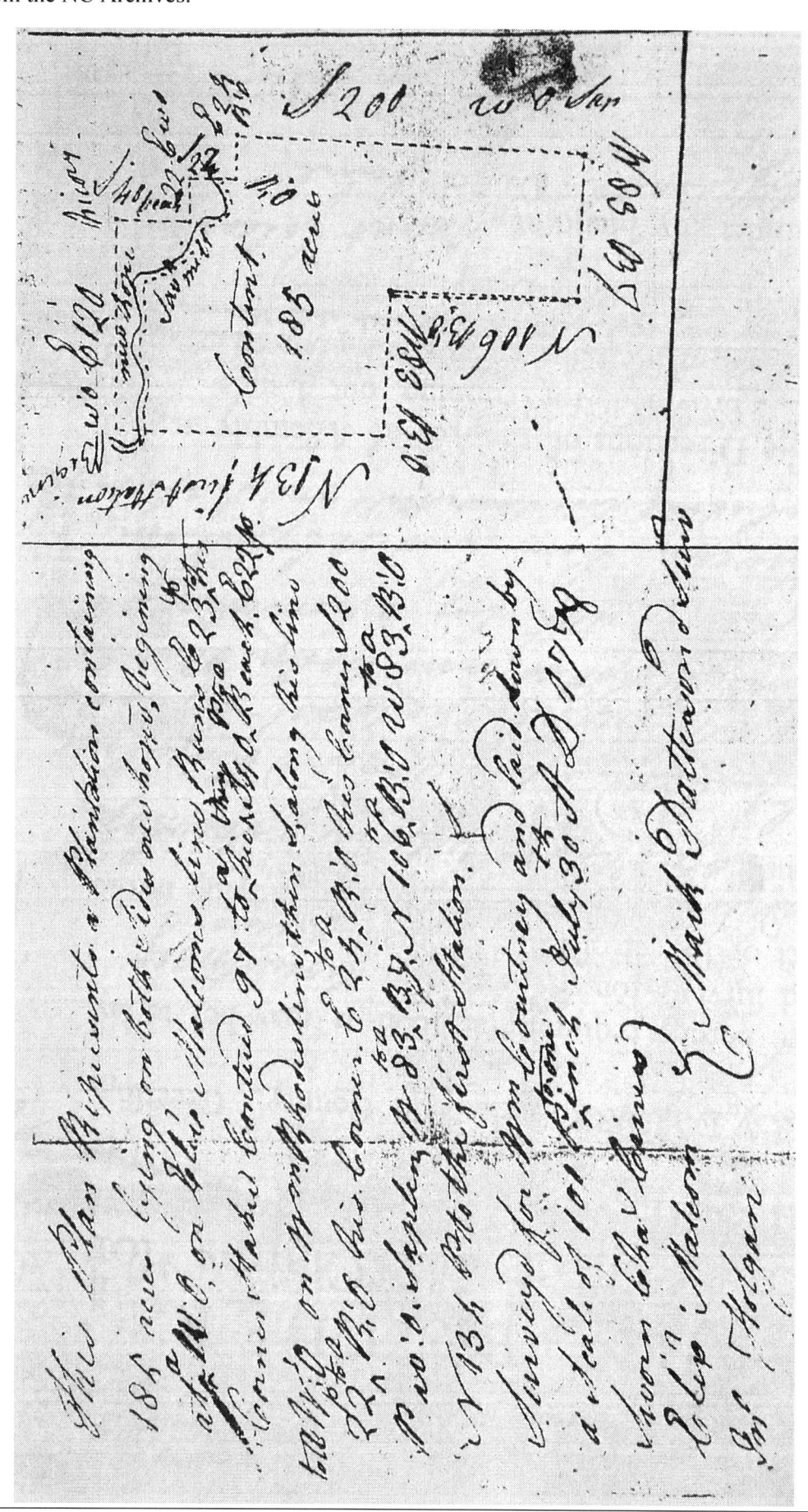

This Plan Represents a Plantation containing 185 acres lying on both sides of New Hope, beginning at a W.O. on Blue Malcoms line, thence N 62 3/4 E 96 po to a Stake & pointers, thence S 28 E 229 po to a Stake & pointers corner Mabel Couches, S 8 W to twenty A Branch 62 po to W.O. on Mary Shoddings then along his line to S 25 B.O. his corner, to S 25 B.O. thence S 200 to a S.O. W.O. F.B.O. N 106 B.O. N 83 B.O. 22 po S.O. his corner, to S 25 B.O., F.B.O. N 106 B.O. N 83 B.O. N W.O. Hickory W 83 B.O. N 106 B.O. N 83 B.O. N 134 po to the first Station.

Survey for Wm Courtney and Peter Lowry on a scale of 10 p. inch. July 30th 1754.

Sworn Chain Carriers
Elip. Malcom
Jno. Morgan

Mark Patterson, deft

Courtney Survey – and plat

In my search up and down New Hope Creek, I only found a couple of locations that could have been "something" as remnants. What I initially found was a long row of stones, not a wall, but a foundation or embankment. This was located in the woods. I GPS the location and found that this was near the "stair step" of the Courtney Plat boundaries that I platted on my map/GPS software. Although the site did not match exactly, it was close enough to take a second look.

Upon my revisit, I scoured the land for other signs. Mainly I was looking for a roadbed or other foundations. There are some interesting aspects towards the "concrete bridge road", which could be additional ground alterations (flattening) and some peculiar stone work. As all of this is near the "concrete bridge road" (roadbed term via Duke Forest), it is possible that was the "old roadbed".

The last interesting coincidence was across the stone foundation/embankment, was a possible raceway. After dragging a tape measure around the "island" it looks to be much more uniform than just a creation of the river. The land is (more or less) uniform for some distance, and the channel is much more exact, as opposed to a random (or wandering) stream.

I have to say, the overall difficulty to this research is one of age (200 years) and erosion. Toss in the lack of documentation and here is my best guess.

Here is a picture of the entrance or split from New Hope Creek into the possible raceway. Arrows are illustrating the flow direction.

Here is what I call the "island" with the raceway to the right and New Hope Creek on the left (not visible).

Turning (south) to the right, you look up into the woods and the stone foundation/embankment is in the woods.

STONE WALL/FOUNDATION

Here is a panorama, standing in the "fork" looking east, New Hope on the left, the raceway on the right.

Here is my drawing, from measurements that I took with my 300 foot tape measure.

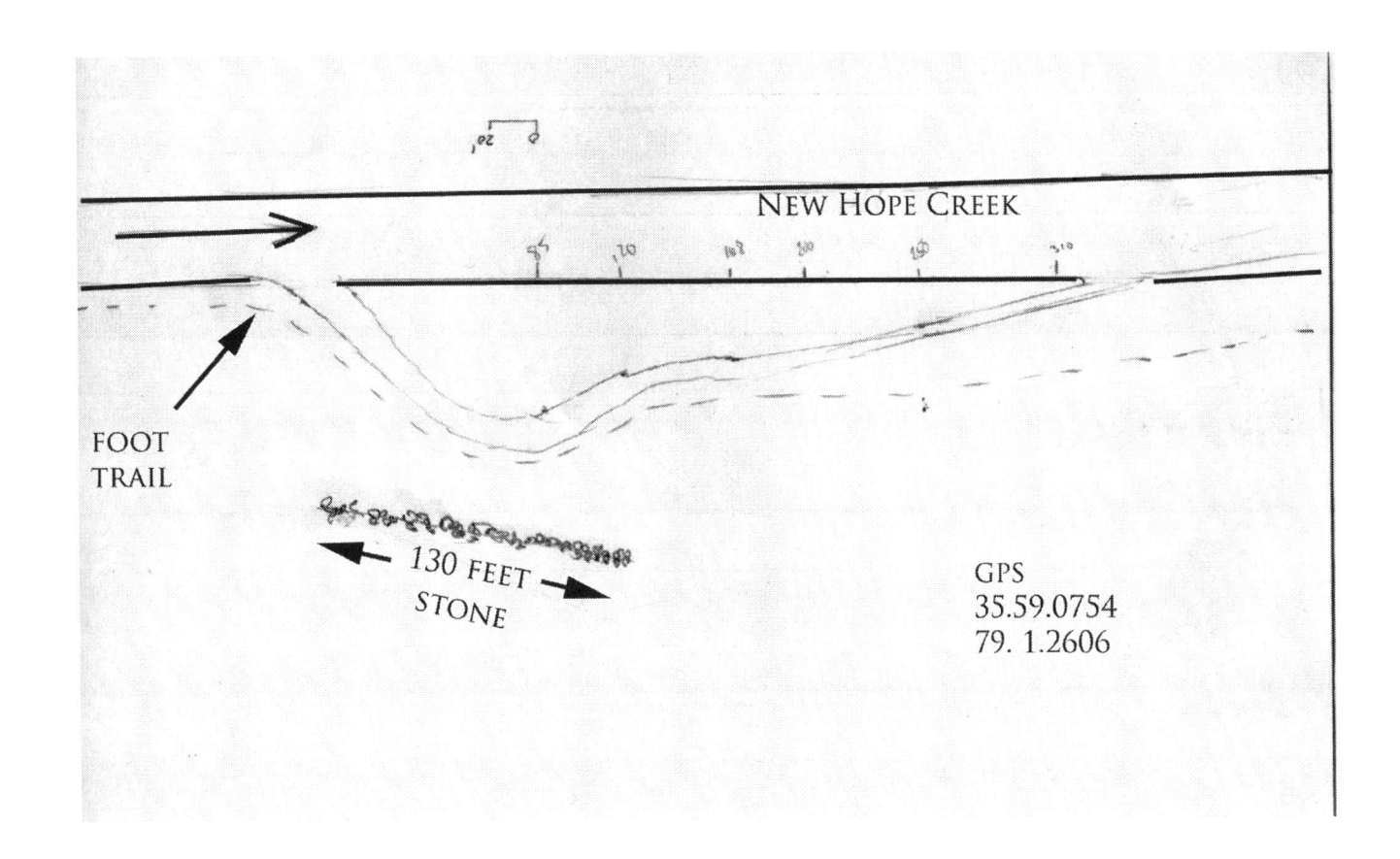

NEW HOPE CREEK

FOOT TRAIL

← 130 FEET → STONE

GPS
35.59.0754
79. 1.2606

Richard Caswell Deed – Plat

Here is a copy of the Richard Caswell Deed (Granville Land Grant) and the plat. See Deed References (1/155) when Caswell sells this square mile of land to William Blackwood.

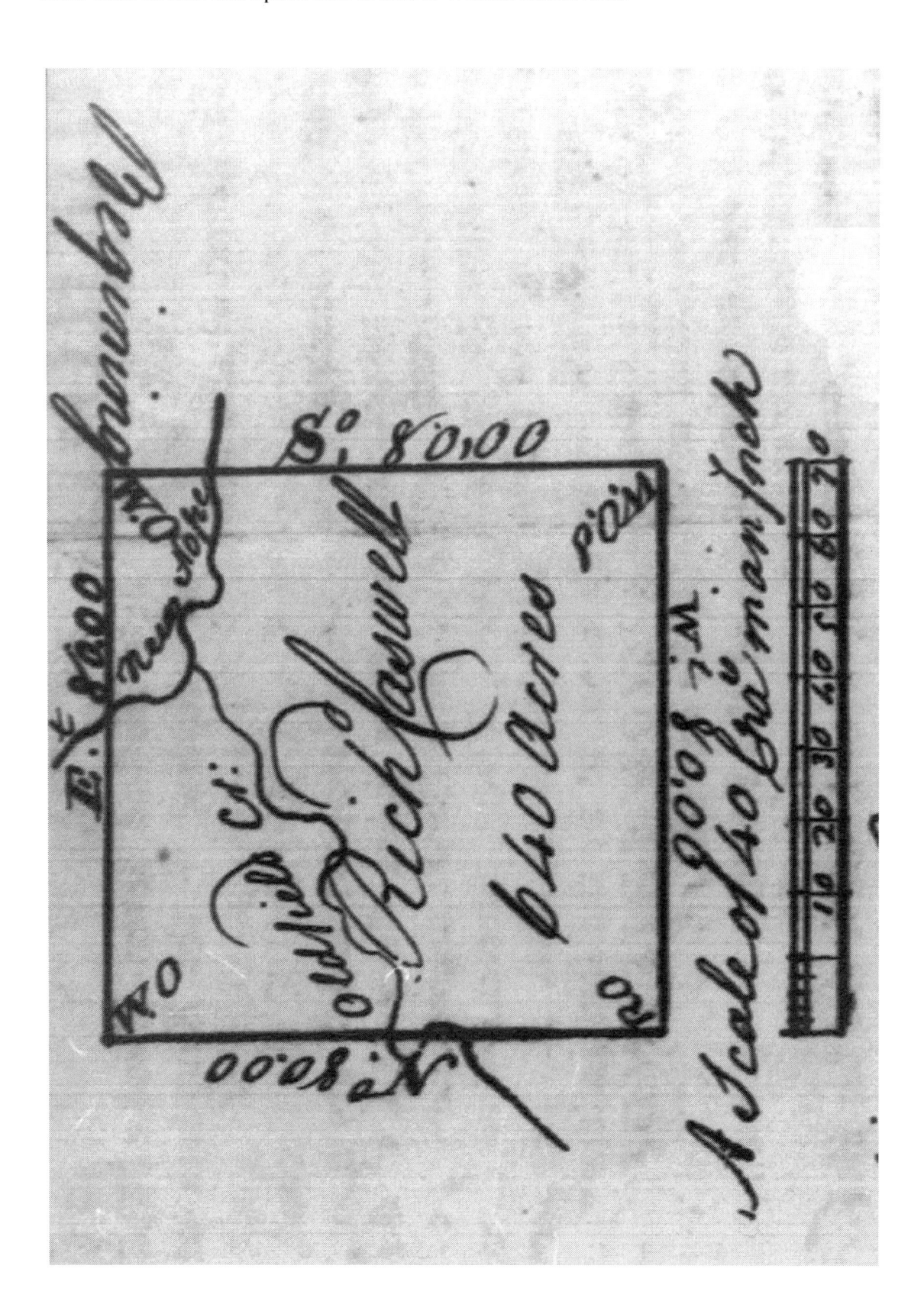

The complete plat with the survey metes and bounds.

North Carolina } This Plan represents a tract of Land
Orange County } Surveyed for Richard Caswell lying on
both Sides the Fork of New Hope and Old Field
Creek, Beginning at a White Oak, then South Side the Creek, then cross:
:g crossing New Hope 80 ch: to a White Oak, then West 80 ch: to a
Red Oak, thence North 80 ch: to a White Oak, then East 80 ch: to the
first Station containing Six hundred and Forty Acres. ———
Surveyed the 19th Day of August 1735.

Sworn Chain } John Rhodes
              William Pickett   Wm Churton

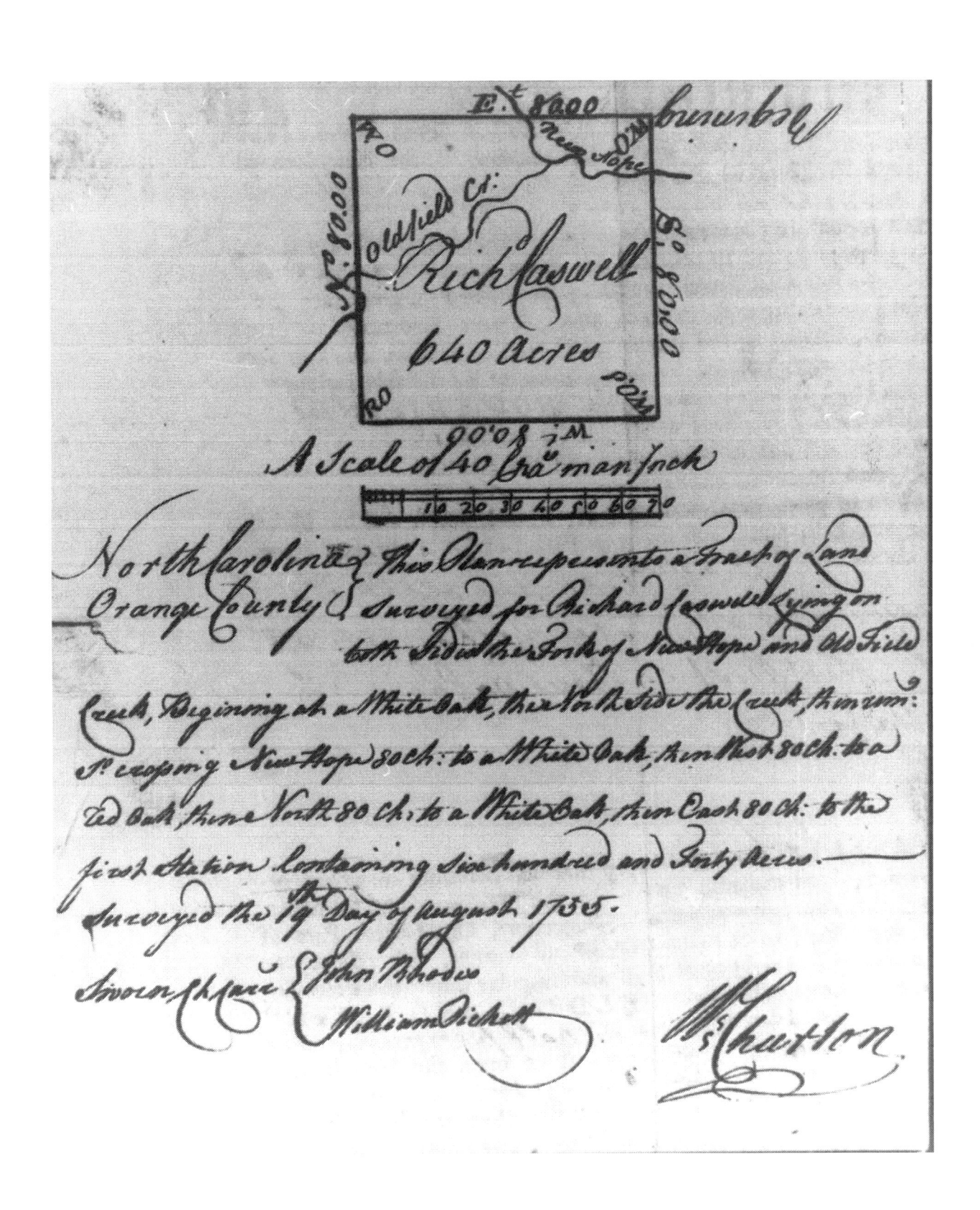

Here is an image of the original Granville Land Grant to Richard Caswell in 1755.

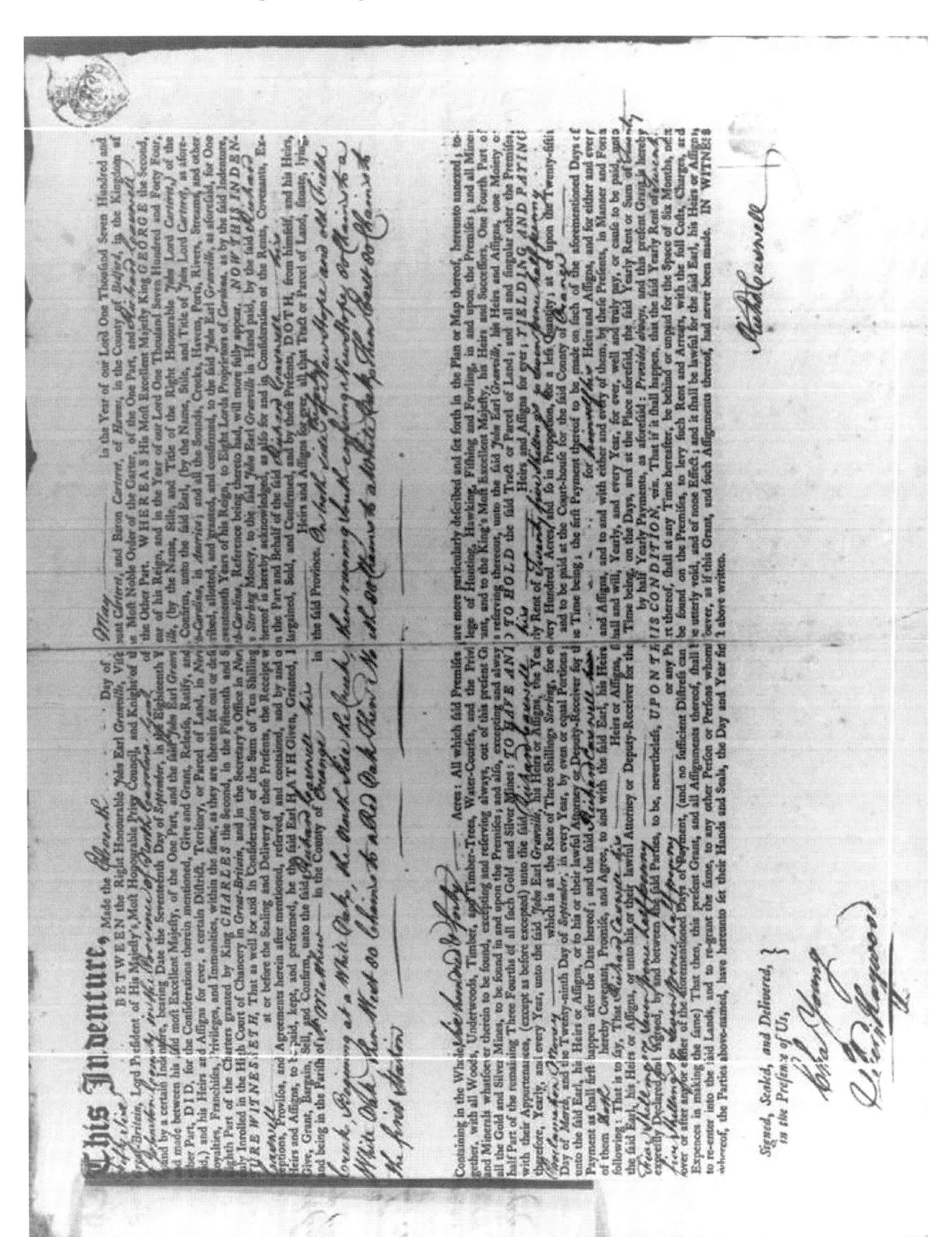

William Blackwood – Granville Grant – Buffalo Creek – 1754

Here is an interesting grant, for 480 acres in Orange County on Buffalo Creek. In 1754, Orange County included (western boundary) part of what we know today as Guilford County. Buffalo Creek branches and flows into the Reedy Fork, which flows into (headwaters) of the Haw River. This was ALL in Orange County.

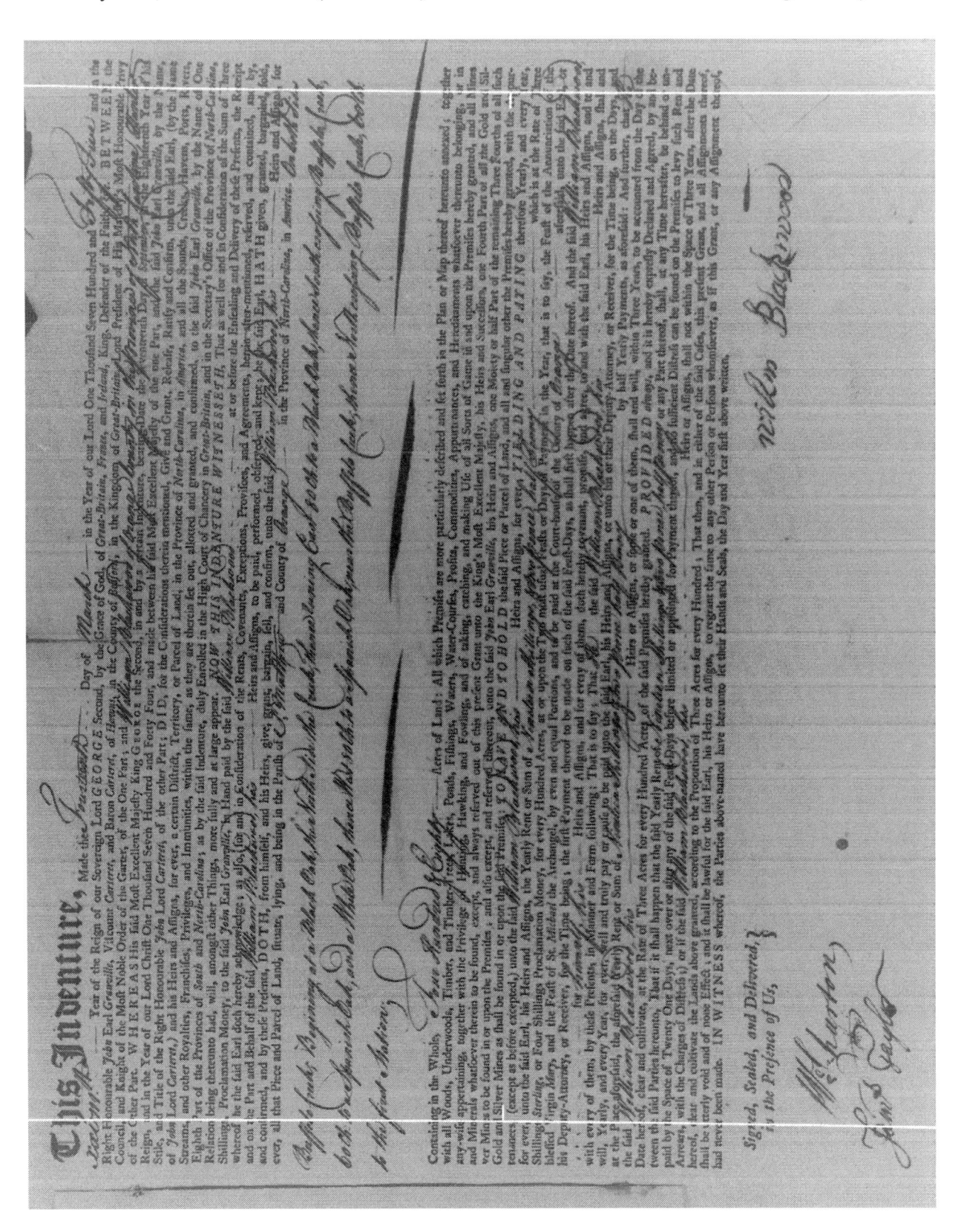

North Carolina
Orange County } This Plan Represents a tract of Land Surveyed for William Blackwood Laying on Both sides of Buffalo Creek: Begining at a Black Oke the North Side the Creek thence Runing East Eighty Chains to a Black Oke thence South Crossing Buffalo Creek Sixty Chains to a Spanish and a White Oke thence West Eighty Chains to a Spanish Oke Near the Buffalo Creek thence North Crossing Buffalo Creek Sixty Chains to the first Station Containing Four Hundred and Eighty Acres Surveyd the 8th Day of November 1754

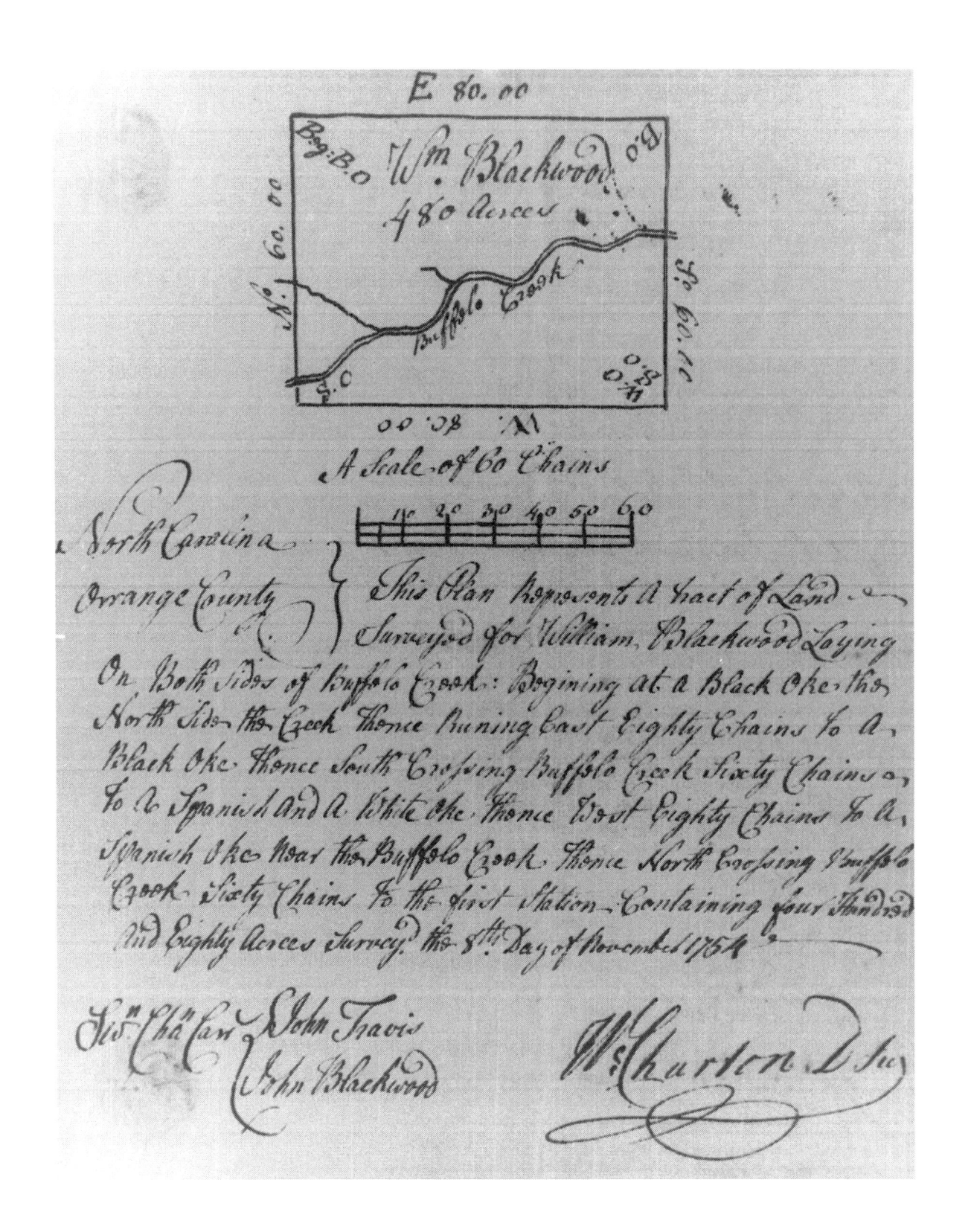

Jno. Chatam   John Travis
           John Blackwood   Wm Churton D Sur

I do not mean to imply that this is an *exact* location of this land grant, but the dashed lines are a general outline of the Buffalo Creek that *seem* to align to the drawing shown on the Granville plat.

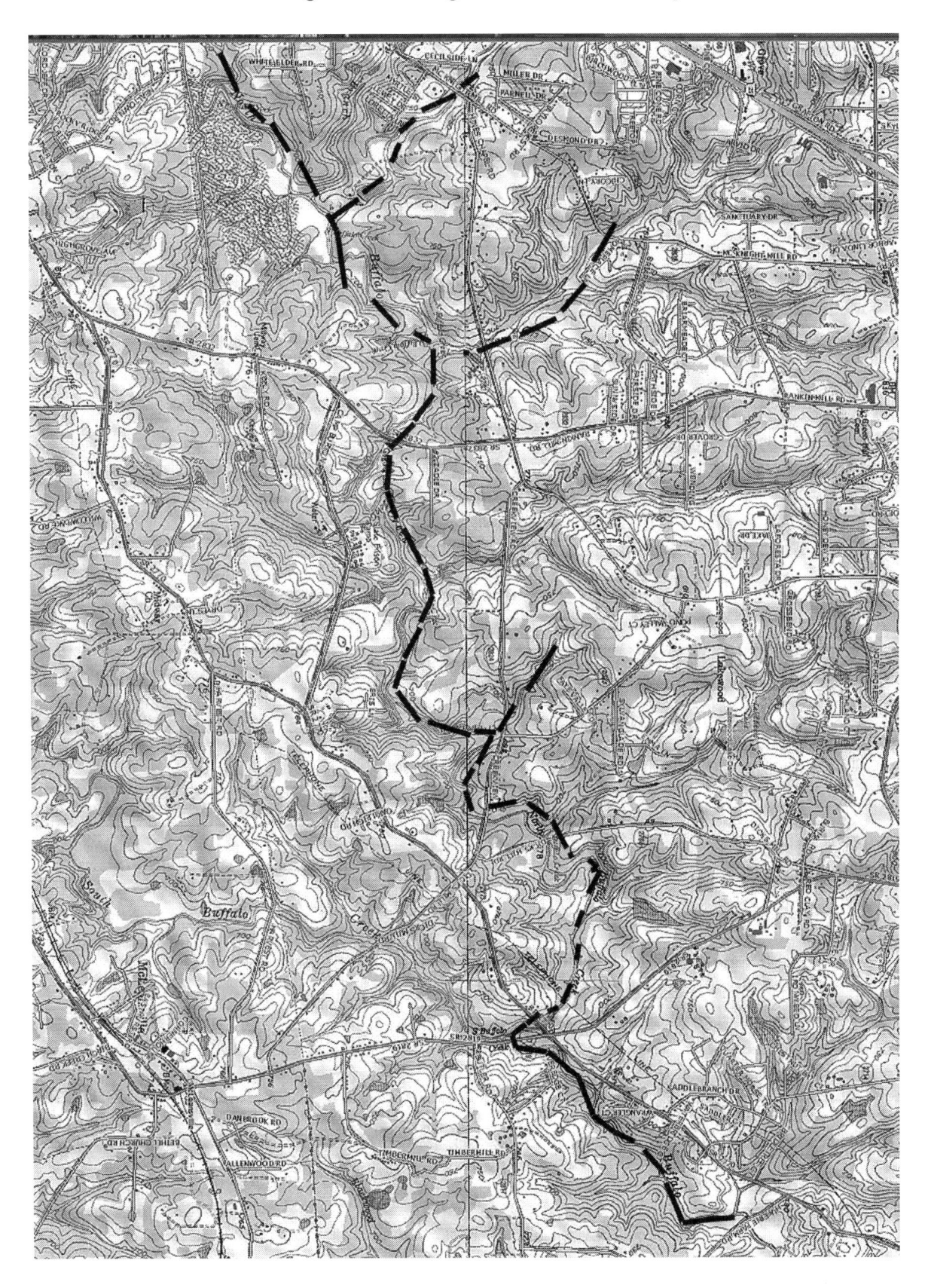

William Blackwood – Granville Grant – Haw River - 1754

William also purchased a grant for 640 acres of land on the waters of Brashears Creek, off the Reedy Fork, off of the Haw River. This too, was in Orange County during this early time. Today, this creek resides in the North-East corner of Guilford County. The Brashear family is well documented in this sector, and this was very close to the Revolutionary War battle site – Weitzel's Mill.

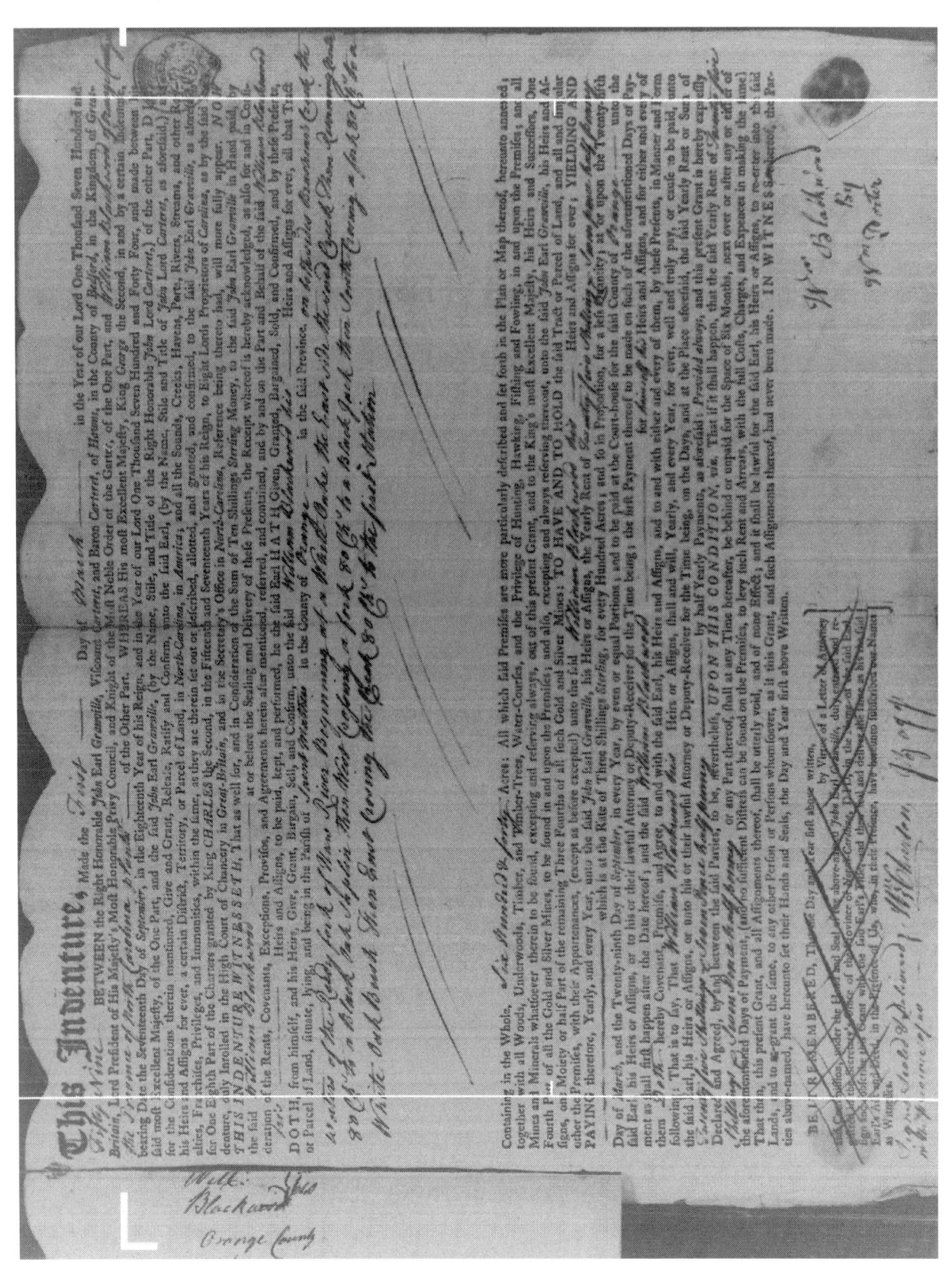

Here is the associated Plat.

N° Carolina
Orange County

Wm Blackwood
640 Acres

a scale of 50 Cha.ᵗ to an inch

This plan Represents a tract of Land Survey'd for William Blackwood on both sides Brashears Creek the waters of the Reedy fork of Haw-river Beginning at a white oak the East side the said Creek Then runing North 80 Cha.ᵗ to a Black oak Saplin; Then west Crosing a fork 80 Cha.ᵗ to a Black Jack; Then south Crosing a fork 80 Cha.ᵗ to a White oak Bush Then East Crosing the Creek 80 Cha.ᵗ to the first Station Containing Six hundred and forty Acres Survey'd the 11ᵗʰ day of November 1754

Sworn Cha } Rob.ᵗ Sam.ᵉˡ Brashear
Carriers   } Jesse Brashear

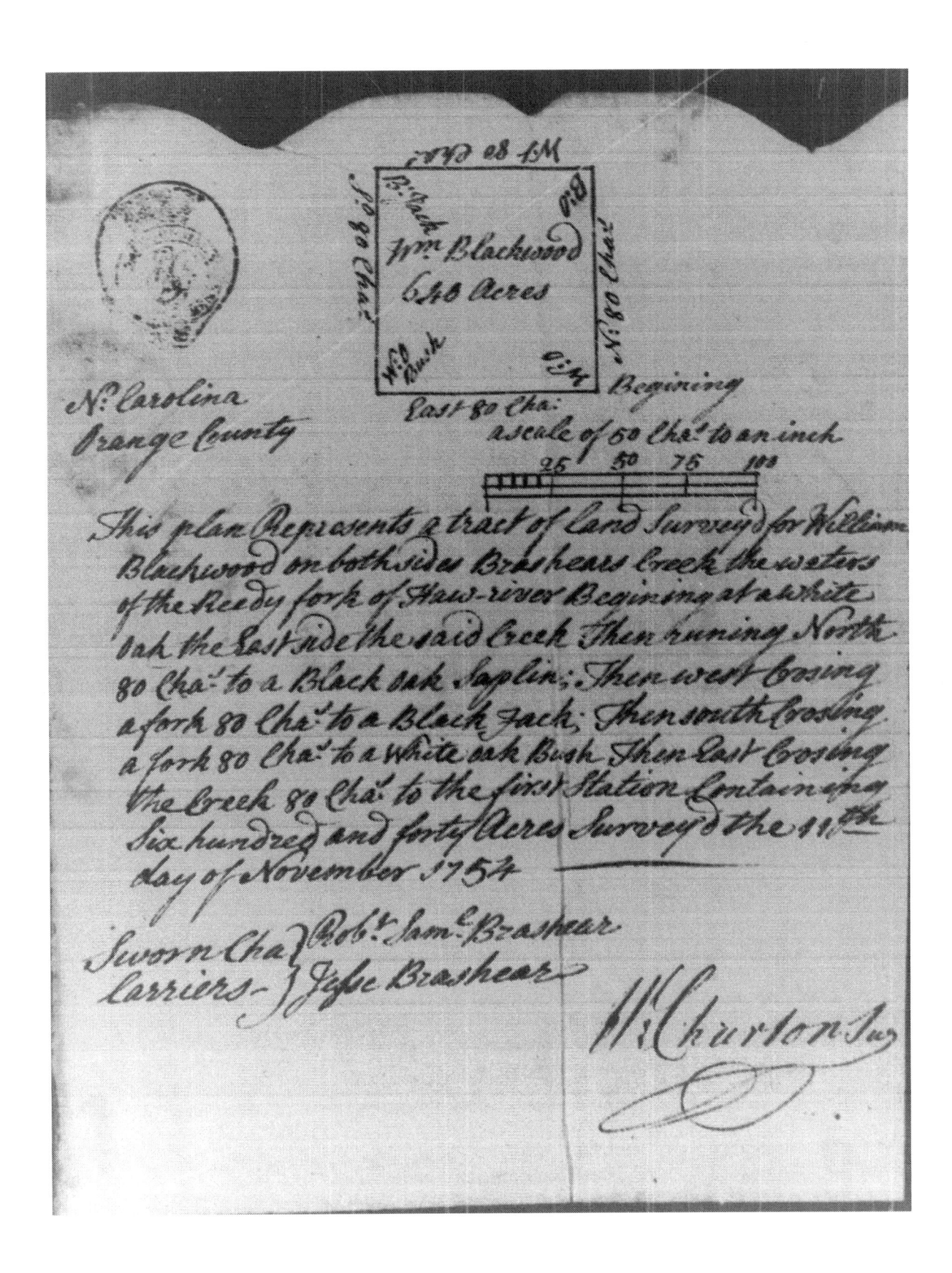

W. Churton Sur

Here is a map of the general area of Brashear Creek, that flows into Reedy Fork, as well as Buffalo Creek's intersection. Noted on this map is the location of the Revolutionary Battle – Weitzel's Mill in 1781.

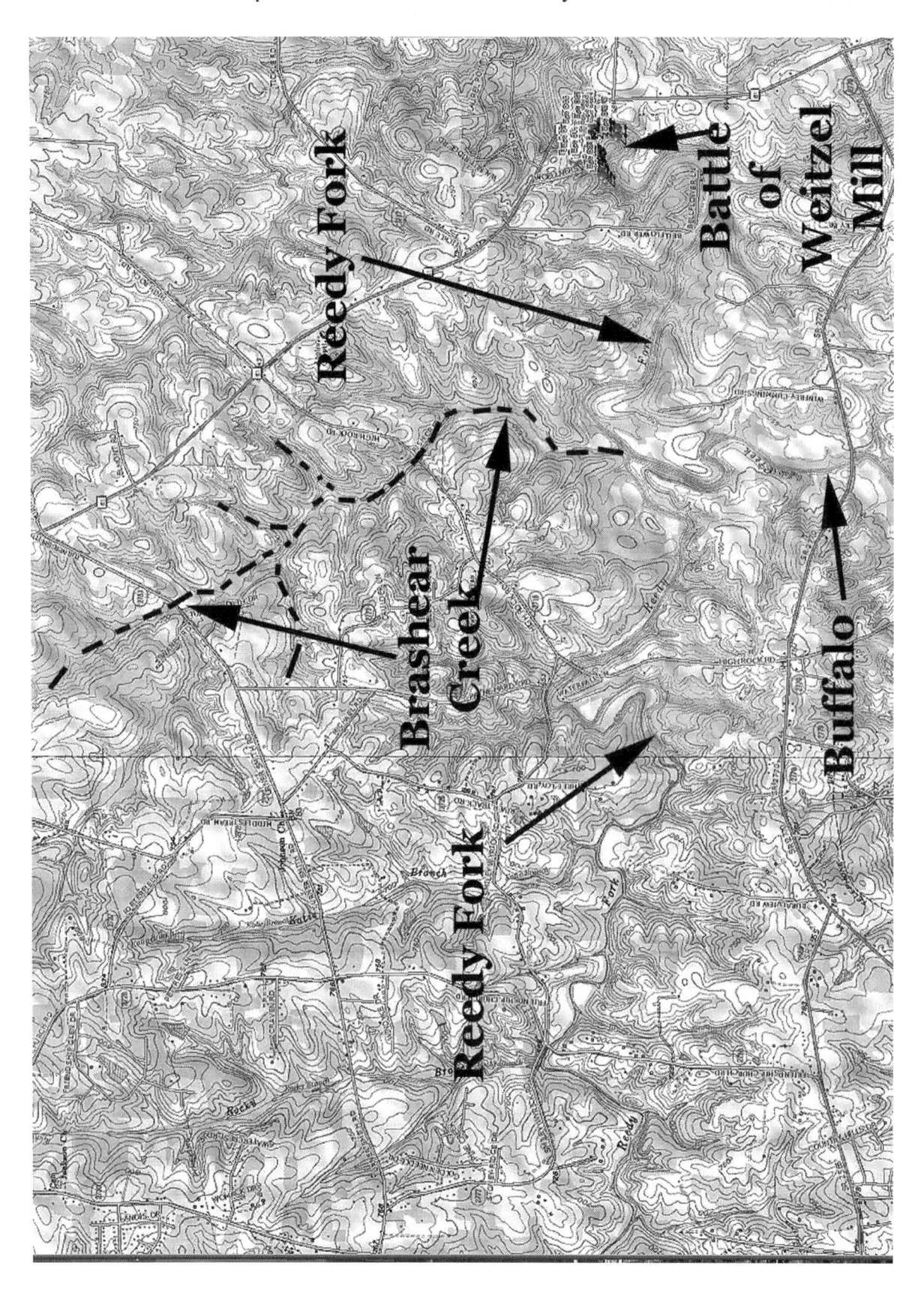

Charles Johnston – Land Grant

Here is a copy of Charles Johnston's land grant. Stories have this documented that Charles receives a grant of land from the King. This would allude to a Granville Land Grant. Charles Johnston (1725-1789) was certainly the proper age to have received a Granville Grant. However, he did not. Charles purchases a State Land Grant, as did his son, George (who I entitled George Sr.). Never the less, here is the grant, and it was really on Old Field Creek and NOT New Hope Creek proper. (Note: I searched the Granville entries, and NO Johnston is listed, nor Johnson, Johnstone – except one in Granville County.)

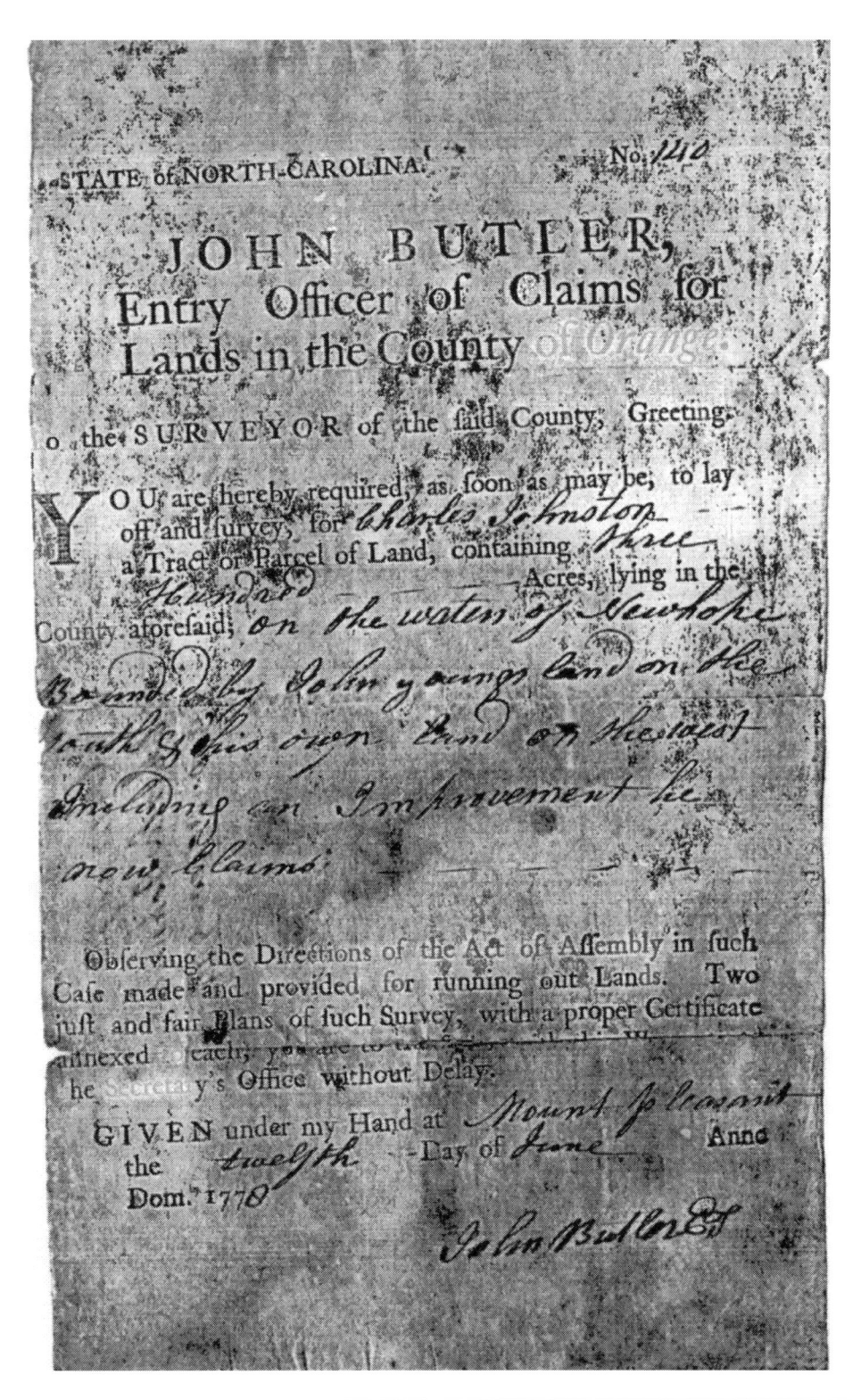

David Southern took the difficult to read document, and transcribed and drew the following plat.

State of North Carolina
to
Charles Johnston

13 March 1780

228 acres on Old Field Creek of New Hope

300 acres entered 12 June 1778

bounded on the north by John Young and on the west by his own land

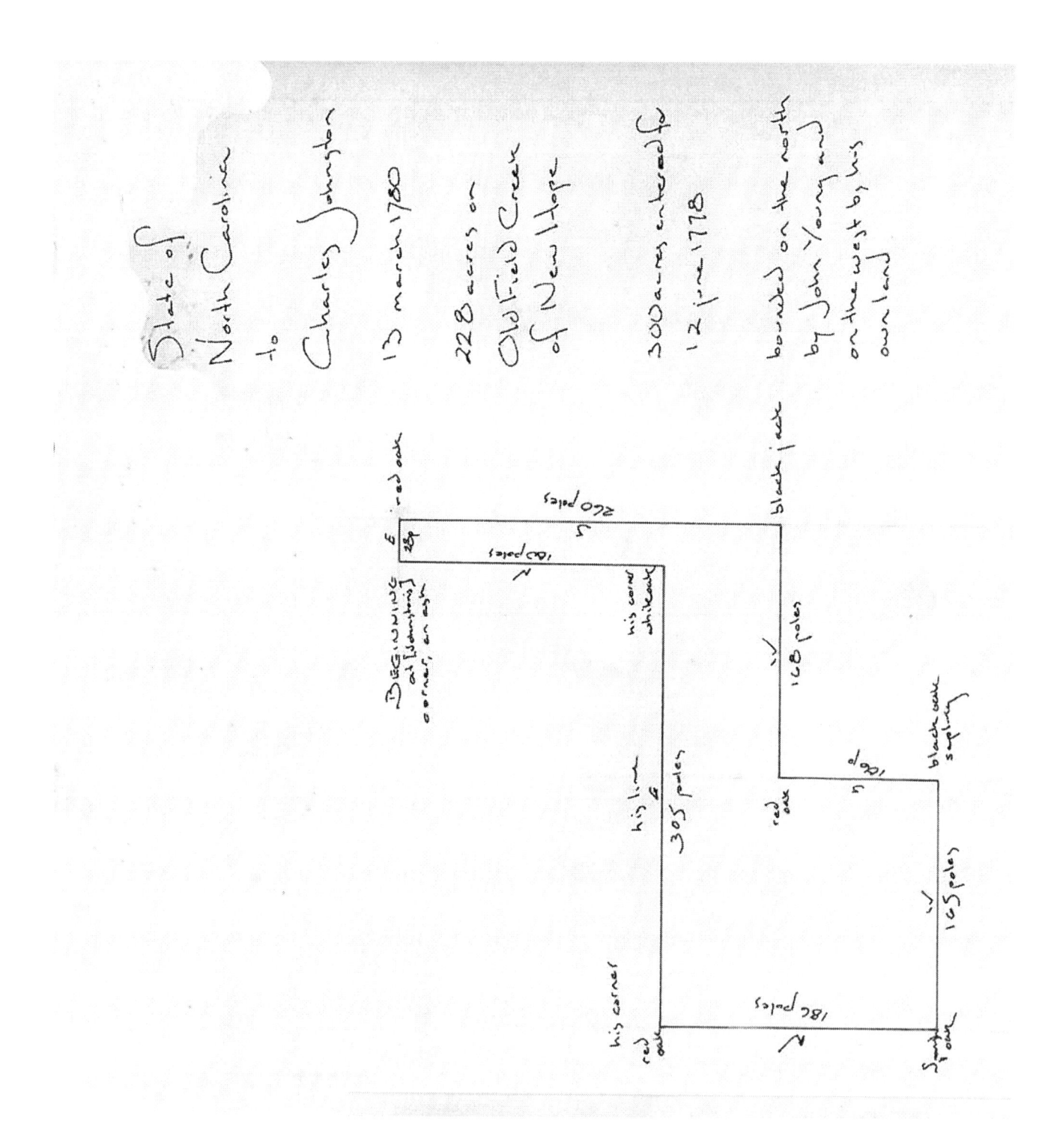

Here is the copy of the entry for this grant. It is also interesting to note that Charles acquired this grant towards the latter part of his life (he died in 1789).

> No. 1178
> County: Orange
> Name: Johnston Charles
> Acres: 288
> Grant No. 360
> Issued: 13 March 1780
> Warrant No. _____ Entry No. 140
> Entered 10" June, 1778
> Book No. 42 Page No. 16
> Location: On the waters of New Hope

Appendix A – Johnston Family Cemetery

The Johnston family cemetery was originally located at their homestead, off of (what is known today) Turkey Farm Road. It was moved to the New Hope Presbyterian Church off of SR #86. Here are images of their markers. Immediately below is a view of the Johnston Cemetery plot.

GEORGE W. JOHNSTON
1823 – 1828

MARY L. JOHNSTON
1835 – 1837

ELIZABETH JOHNSTON
1821 – 1822

MARY E. JOHNSTON
1831 – 1833

MARY JANE JOHNSTON
1820 – 1820

WILLIAM DUSKIN
1789 — 1869

MARY JOHNSTON
DUSKIN
1803 — 1870

TO
THE
MEMORY
OF
G.O. JOHNSTON
D.C.D DC.B 7th 1830
AGED. 65 Y.AS

MARY JOHNSTON
WIFE. OF
GEO. JOHNSTON
D.C.D APRIL.11.1810
AGED. 35 YRS.

Lydia Johnston
Born Sept. 14, 1797
Died
Oct. 14 1877

Charles W. Johnston
Died
Jan 27. 1855
E. 57 yrs. 2 ms.

IN MEMORY OF
GEORGE JOHNSTONE
A SCOTCHMAN
CAME TO AMERICA IN 1738
HIS WIFE
MARY WILSON JOHNSTONE

IN MEMORY OF
CHARLES W. JOHNSTONE
1725 — 1787
RECD. LAND GRANT BY
ROYAL CHARTER IN 1756
HIS WIFE
MARTHA JOHNSTONE

Above is another reference – "Recd. Land Grant by Royal Charter in 1756" – for Charles W. Johnstone.

JOHN C.
Son of
G.W. & L. JOHNSTON
DIED
Apl. 26. 1856.
Æ. 23 ys. 7 mos.
3 ds.

George Johnston (Sr.) wife – Mary Mulholland

Note that she died many years before George Sr., and George Sr., remarries.

MARY MULHOLLAND
JOHNSTONE
1775 — 1810

Appendix B – George Johnston Estate Papers

It will always remain a family disaster to fight over inheritance, but it appears to be a continuum in the history of life. George Johnston's life has just that issue, but from a different angle than usual. Typically the arguments over inheritance reside with siblings. But here it resided with his second wife.

These estate papers are an amazing and rare detailed look into the private life of the Johnston family, from friend's depositions. From these papers it was discovered more about the mill, but the real story comes from the estate division, and George's accident.

This is a sad story, and I'm sure one of many during this time, where people tended to be land rich and cash poor.

Charles Johnston Response – 1833

"…the answer of Charles Johnston to the petition of Clarisa Johnston….this defendant saving and reserving to himself the benefit of all just exception to the many errors and uncertainties in petition contained for answer thereof or to so much thereof as he is advised it is material for him to answer…that it is true …George Johnston died intestate in this year and that no administration has been taken out as it was generally understood and this deponent so states …to the best of his belief that he died entirely insolvent. He admits the intermarriage of petitioner with his said father and that the names of the children and heirs at law are correct as set forth – but denies that his said father died seized and possessed….real estate whatever within his knowledge and he more particularly denies that he this deponent is was or was at the death of his father in possession of any land which did not in good faith belong to him. He states that in the year 1819 he being the eldest son …gave him a deed bearing date the 5th of May of that year a tract of land containing six hundred and fourteen acre and three quarters…was duly issued the 31st July thereafter – that he took possession of said (cont)…"

"…land and placed on it including improvements and has been in continual occupation thereof….and he denies especially that said conveyance was made to him with the view of denying petitioner of her dower or for any other that the reason heretofore assigned - For he states that at that time his father was a man possessed of a large real estate and considerable personal property and continued to possess of his real estate until the 30th of October 1821 – when by deed he conveyed the balance of his land for his other children except the homestead place and tract adjoining containing 448 acres – which he reserved for himself and his wife the petitioner. Deponent denies that the conveyances made with a view to defeat or defraud petitioner of her dower – or if so that I knew it – for she stated that the conveyances were made with the knowledge an approbation of petitioner and that the homestead place and the tract adjoin were with the approbation retained as being sufficient for the old man and he during their joint heirs and that of the survivors. He further shows that at the time of the latter conveyance his father was as he believed free from debt or very nearly so – that he did not at that time he owed $50 in the world – further answering deponent states that in the year 1822 he became the endorser of Major Pleasant Henderson and also of Col Hugh Mulhollan in the State Bank at Raleigh for the amount of $_____ and also in the Cape Fear Bank at Hillsboro in the year 1823 for the said Pleasant Henderson for the sum of $130 and in the year _____ was sued by both banks and judgment was obtained against him for the amount of $_____ at the _____ term 1827 of (cont.)…."

"...*Orange County – and that executors or said judgment issued from the clerk's office...the land of the said George Johnston being the homestead tract and the tract adjoining that by him reserved for his own use and that of petitioner and that at the public sale made by Thomas D. Watt Sheriff of Orange County this deponent together with his brother George and Thomas and Gray Huckabee purchased the said his tract at the price of $160 – which was greatly under their value and fell so short of discharging the bank debt when upon it was agreed...that deponent should take the land himself and pay off the bank debt and that accordingly the said Sheriff Watt by deed having date the 25th Aug 1828 conveyed said land to this deponent and he avers that he repaid off and discharged said judgment so obtained by the Banks against his said father, That the same so paid was the full value of said two tracts that he discharged said judgment discounting his notes at Bank and he positively denies that his said purchase was made by collusion with his said father for the purpose of depriving petitioner of her dower but that he made it ??? with his own friends as any other purchase might have done....by deed bearing date the 31st of May 1825 purchased of George M. Johnston the tract of land so given him by his father at the price of $3500 – which was a full and fair compensation for the same and that by deed breading date the 17th Feb 1827 he purchased from his father for the sum of $80 seventeen acres of land – and that the price paid was full and fair one and he denies that either of these purchased were made with a view for depriving or defraud petitioner of her dower right. – F. Nash...*"

211

George M. Johnston Responds - 1834

"...*he admits that his late father George Johnston departed this life intestate in the year 1830 as stated in the petition that there had been no administration of his estate as he believes by this defendant and his children during his life by gifts of land and to this defendant among others, is also admitted – But this defendant by no reason admits or the contrary he expressly denies so far as he has any knowledge or belief, that to said conveyances of land were made by his said father with intent to deprive petitioner of her dower or with any fraudulent purpose whatever. He further states that the petitioner was the second wife of his father by whom he had children and that painful and unhappy dissensions' at times arose between his said father and wife during the later years of his life, but that there were long and frequent intervals of harmony between them. This defendant denies that as far as he had any knowledge or believe, that his said father was prevailed on by him this defendant or by any other person to alienate his affections from the petitioner or that he entertained any feelings of permanent hostility towards her although in moments of excitement there might have been mutual words of reproach between them. This defendant believes that the general current of his feelings toward her kind, and he well recollects that after the occurrence of those misfortunes which cause his said fathers (cont.)...*"

"…inharmony and when such of that cause which terminated his life, in a friendly and confidential conversation his said father ?????????????? the condition in which his wife would be left after his death in consequence of his involvements in ??? with deep feelings of ????. In regards to the conveyances of land to this defendant and his brothers and sisters stated in the petition, this defendant stated these to be the facts also far as they have come to his knowledge. That his brother Charles W. the eldest son, was married and which to live on a plantation previously owned by his father in the year 1819 or 1820, that he afterward was sold by his father that he had given that place to his brother Charles and had made him a deed for it and he also told this defendant about that time whether in the said conversation or not he cannot say, that he intended for him a tract of land which was afterward given to his brother Thomas. This was in answer to an inquiry by this defendant what lands were intended for him. This defendant further states that about the year 1821 his said father recovered a dangerous hurt from a fall and supposed his life was in danger. He accordingly sent for Col Hugh Mulhollan a friend to whom he was nearly connected and assist in making out a disposition of his affairs as he desired to take place after his death. Deeds were prepared by Col Mulhollan and executed by his said father and those children who had not before received gifts of land which said deed have been already produced to this court according to his said fathers direction Col Mulhollan at the same time prepared a will for him which he executed in which provision was made for the petitioner his wife by a reservation to her of this homestead place and 448 acres of land together with other property. This defendant solemnly avers that in all these transactions so far he known and believes that his said father acted under the belief that his life was soon to end and made this arrangement of his affairs with perfect honesty and (cont.)…"

"…and ease. The executors aforesaid who lived on the whole of this property and this defendant who lived and the time in Hillsborough upon a visit to his father found him in much distress on account of this situation. He said however that if he were ten years younger he could work through the debts, but being old an infirm there was no alternative but that his property should be sold. He also state to this defendant that as money was very scarce if the property were sold under the hammer he did not believe that it would pay the debts, but he did not wish to die indebted to any one, and if the property should not be sufficient to pay it he desired it of his sons as a special duty. That the whole should be made good by them if not paid out of the property. This defendant there agreed with his two brothers Charles W. and Thomas who were joined also by a brother-in-law Gray Huckabee to pay the debts according to his father's request and in order to indemnify themselves as far as they could to purchase his property if it did not sell for value. This defendant did not attend at the sales of stock to which took place at his father's residence but he attended at the sale of lands in Hillsborough when it was bid off by his brother Charles at the sum of $160 but with a distinct agreement that the whole debt should be paid that after the sales this defendant his brothers and brother-in-law aforesaid met at the house of his brother Charles and settled their respective liabilities. When after much conversation it was understood by this defendant that he would have to take the land himself together with the property which was ??? but it was afterwards agreed that his brother Charles should take the property and assume the whole of the dent and the sheriff was accordingly directed and make the conveyance to him. This defendant was entirely willing to be relived from taking it and conceives and believes that but for the determination of himself and brothers to paying the debts aforesaid the property would have failed to do it. In these transactions this defendant denies that he or so far as he knows or believes any other person had any intention or desire to injure the petitioner or in any way to molest her but what was done was in (cont.)…"

"...good faith and without intention whatever to defraud the claim of the petitioner's dower or in any wise to injure her or anything individual. And this defendant has no knowledge of any debts owed at that time by his said father to any amount. These transactions all took place in the presence of the petitioner so far as this defendant could understand were approved by her. He well recollects that in this division his said father gave to his brother Thomas the part of the land which he had before said he intended for this defendant and vice versa. That which had been intended for Thomas adjoined the homestead place and petitioner expressed her pleasure that this defendant was to have that instead of Thomas. He further states that after the whole division was made he well was read over in the hearing of petitioner and in answer to a question by his said father answering this defendant stated being in a dangerous state of health himself about the year 1825 he sold the lands as allotted to him and his aforesaid brother Charles W. executed a deed therefore in 1827. Further answering this defendant said that his said father survived the illness aforesaid, which was expected and determine his life and in or about the year 1822 being by his economy and prudence still free from debt he became endorser in the Banks of this State or loans of money made to the aforesaid Hugh Mulhollan and Maj Pleasant Henderson with both of whom, he was on terms of great intimacy. For the particular amounts of these loans this defendant refers to the evidence which he expects to obtain from the Banks and to the judgment and executor thereon, that the said Mulhollan and Henderson both failed in their estates without satisfying these debts to the Bank and suits were initiated, judgment renders and executions issued against all the defendants. His said father George Johnston owned at that time not only the lands reserved as aforesaid but some negro slaves, stock, furniture, etc amply sufficient to have supported himself and wife through life in comfort (cont.)..."

"*…respect alone to the agreed before state of his aged father and he very believes that his said father had no desire that the petitioner should be left destitute at his death….April 19th 1834…George M. Johnston….*"

Thomas Johnston Responds

"…This defendant answering…to the many errors etc. in said petition…that his father George Johnston intermarried with the petitioner according to his family record in the year 1813 [it appears being written in the top 22nd April – note that his wife died in 1810, the mother of these children] and as petitioner set forth in petitioner lived many years happily together and that in the year A.D. 1815 two years after their marriage defendants father as he said from consolation of the uncertainty of life his old age infirmity and affliction – and for the further consideration of dividing his property to his own satisfaction among his children himself and wife during his lifetime and of saving expenses of division of his lands in N.C. among his children himself and his wife and placing the papers in the hands of Col Hugh Mulhollan for safe keeping until called for which division was made in good faith to all parties under friendly feelings to all parties and without the least intention of fraud or depriving the petitioner of her dower. But on the contrary defendants father reserved the homestead place including the big barn, dwelling house, distillery and with another tract of land adjoining called the Burnt Cabin place in all about 450 or 70 acres together with stock, household and kitchen furniture etc negroes etc. for the special purpose and use of himself and wife – and defendant ….that his father did all of this business in the presence of petitioner…This defendants brother Charles W. Johnston entered into matrimony with his present wife sometime in the year 1819 and …settled and made many valuable improvements…. (cont.)…"

"…*In the fall of the year 1821 this defendants father and the petitioner still being together the defendants father got a very hard and dangerous fall from a high fence which as defendant understood nearly killed him – which dislocated his breast bone and caused it to protrude considerably and which occasioned a very bad cough, spitting of blood and excruciating pains almost unsupportable – defendant will recollect while he was waiting on his father which he left college to do in that when the cough would come on him he would after holler allowed and almost lose his breath. Defendants father fully believed that he would not survive the affliction he then was suffering and that he would not live very long and wished as he said to make some alterations and some of this conveyance and finally to arrange his business before his death and he the defendants father sent for Col Hugh Mulhollan his particular friend and ??? who did all of his business of that nature – who coming immediately the most distance of ?? miles having from his fledging became sensible of the dangers to all the rest of his children a deed for their respective allotments of land as before divided with this alteration that the tract of land this defendants father intended and allotted to defendant in 1815 gave to defendant (which alteration he made as he said for far 2 might sell the place or be more likely to do ??? then and thereby affect the value of the homestead place or the comfort of the families etc.) and which alteration the petitioner upbraided much satisfaction on account of saying (as defendant understood) that she preferred George's owing the tract adjoin the homestead place reservation to the defendants doing so and at the same time these deeds were delivered he executed a will, which defendant believes was place in the hands of Hugh Mulhollan for safe keeping in which he comprised the aforesaid reservation of land including the homestead place and the Burnt Cabin Tract adjoin both containing as (cont.)…*"

218

"…aforesaid 4 acres of land including the big barn…and kitchen furniture unto his wife also relinquishing to his wife all the right he claimed to two negroes name Landan and Annie and their increase which will also confirmed the aforesaid conveyances to his children as before mentioned and the reservation to his wife….made in good faith without any intention as defendant knows and believes to defraud the petitioner of her dower…and furthermore defendants father was at this time 1821 clear of debt or very nearly so and off all liability and the property thus conveyed perfectly clear of all encumbrances etc. The defendant further answers that his father survived the disease he expected would have terminated his life and by his industry, economy, and carried on his business as usual and thereby kept clear of debt nearly so on his own or family present ….in the year 1822 or 1823 or thereabouts the defendants father as he understood became security to Major Pleasant Henderson and Col Hugh Mulhollan ??? in the Bank of the State of NC at Raleigh and the Cape Fear Bank at Hillsborough in the sums of Pleasant Henderson and Col Mulhollan which notes defendant believes were unnerved until the year 1827 or near that time when the parties were sued for non-payment and judgment rendered and executions issued against all the defendants. His the defendant's father owned at that time 1827 or 8 – not only the lands reserved (cont.)…"

"...as aforesaid or near the amount – but stock, furniture, negro slaves amply sufficient to have supported himself and wife….and that he at that time lived with his wife as usual at the homestead place which he had reserved as aforesaid – and that they lived together harmoniously with the exception of occasional difference of opinion which sometime produced disagreement – which occurred during the latter year of his life but that there were long and frequent intervals of harmony between them and this defendant denies as far as he had any knowledge or believe that his said father was …to alienate his affections from the petitioner or to prejudice his mind to her inquiry…for the purpose of depriving her of her dower or for any other purpose whatever…and he recollects having had an ??? with his father about this time – after his property had been bound on by the sheriff to satisfy the executions he the sheriff sold the property to satisfy the same which executors were obtained against Col Hugh Mulhollan and Major Pleasant Henderson as principles and defendants father…and that his father was very much distressed in mind indeed and was fearful his property would not satisfy the debts and that he himself and wife would be reduced in their old days to bankruptcy and want he could not aver to his situation without lamenting and often weeping and remarked of he was younger and have the use of his limbs he would (cont.)…"

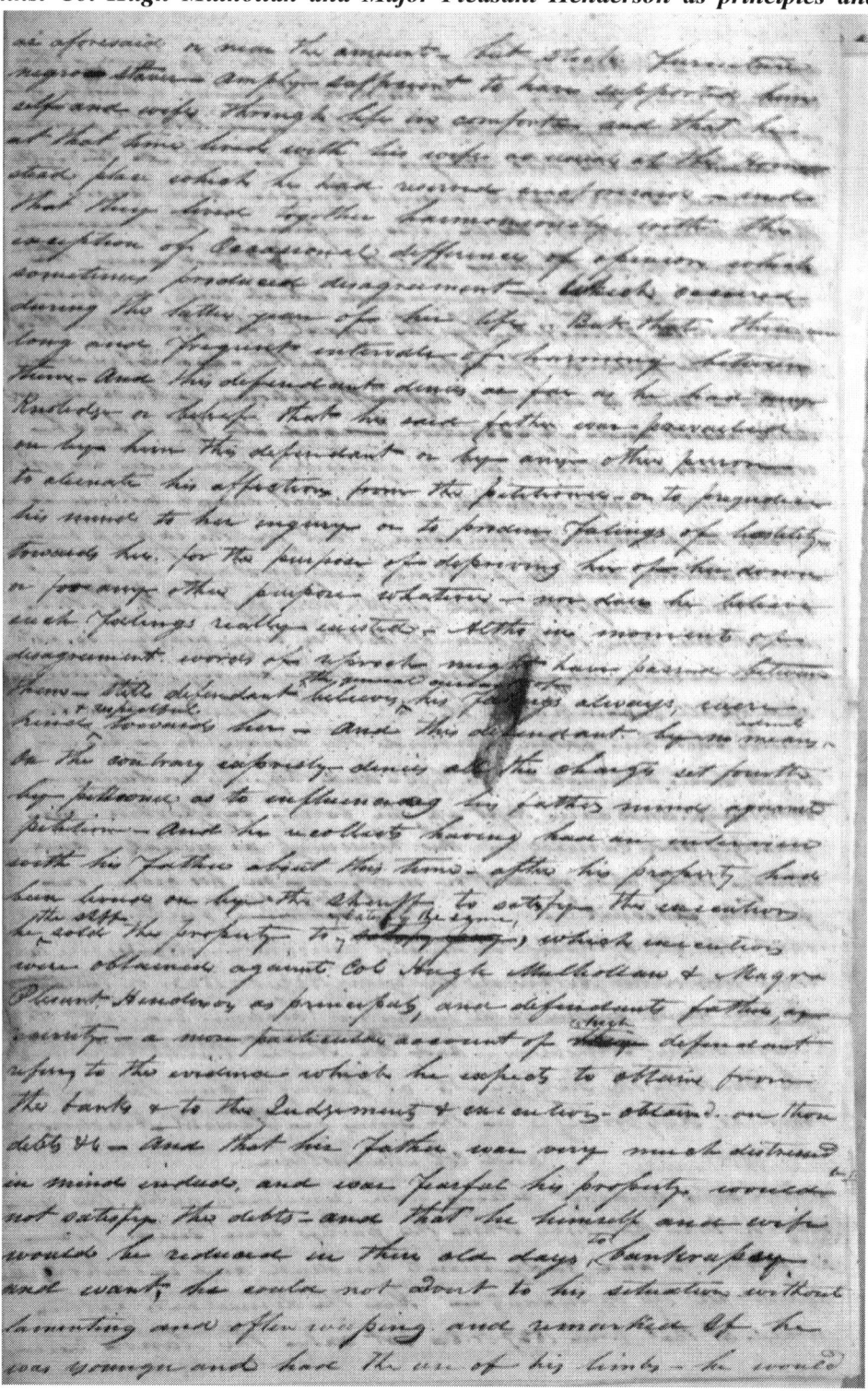

"…struggle through his indebtedness but being old and discharged and infirm he had not alternative but that his property should be sold…" – The remaining part of this page is almost an exact copy of the other brothers. I will add anything new, otherwise I will leave the transcript out. This page he explains the selling of the land "under hammer" and his brother Charles acquiring it.

"…the defendant further answers that after the sale and delivery of the property that his brother Charles W. Johnston proposed to his father to support him during his life (an also did this defendant) and said Charles defendant has understood offered the privilege and petitioner of living with him also but told him he could not consent to maintaining her family of your negroes – and she replied that she would not be supported from them etc and proposed as I understood she did do moving to said Charles plantation at which he lived before the sale of his father's property etc. and said defendants father took his son at his offer and offer etc. and lived and died on his premises etc. and did not as petitioner has said banish her from his security and the defendant further stated that his father extended to his wife little acts of kindness in dividing what means he had left him with her and that she often visited him especially when she had ??? need of any means he had which he gave according to his ability out of their things that were not taken from him and this defendant believes his father never did to the last hours of his life as petitioner has stated discarded her wholly from this affections nor banish her from his society and defendant state he visited his father on his death bed and saw and heard words of affection from him to her calling her his dear – and asking for some assistance from her the day before he died and requested as this defendant understood to try and get to heaven or to meet him in heaven as also he advised his children – this defendant admits his father departed this life in 1830 and was considered possessed of no property worth administering for he believes he had a deed for 500 acres of western lands which Col Hugh Mulhollan conveyed to him for the (cont.)…"

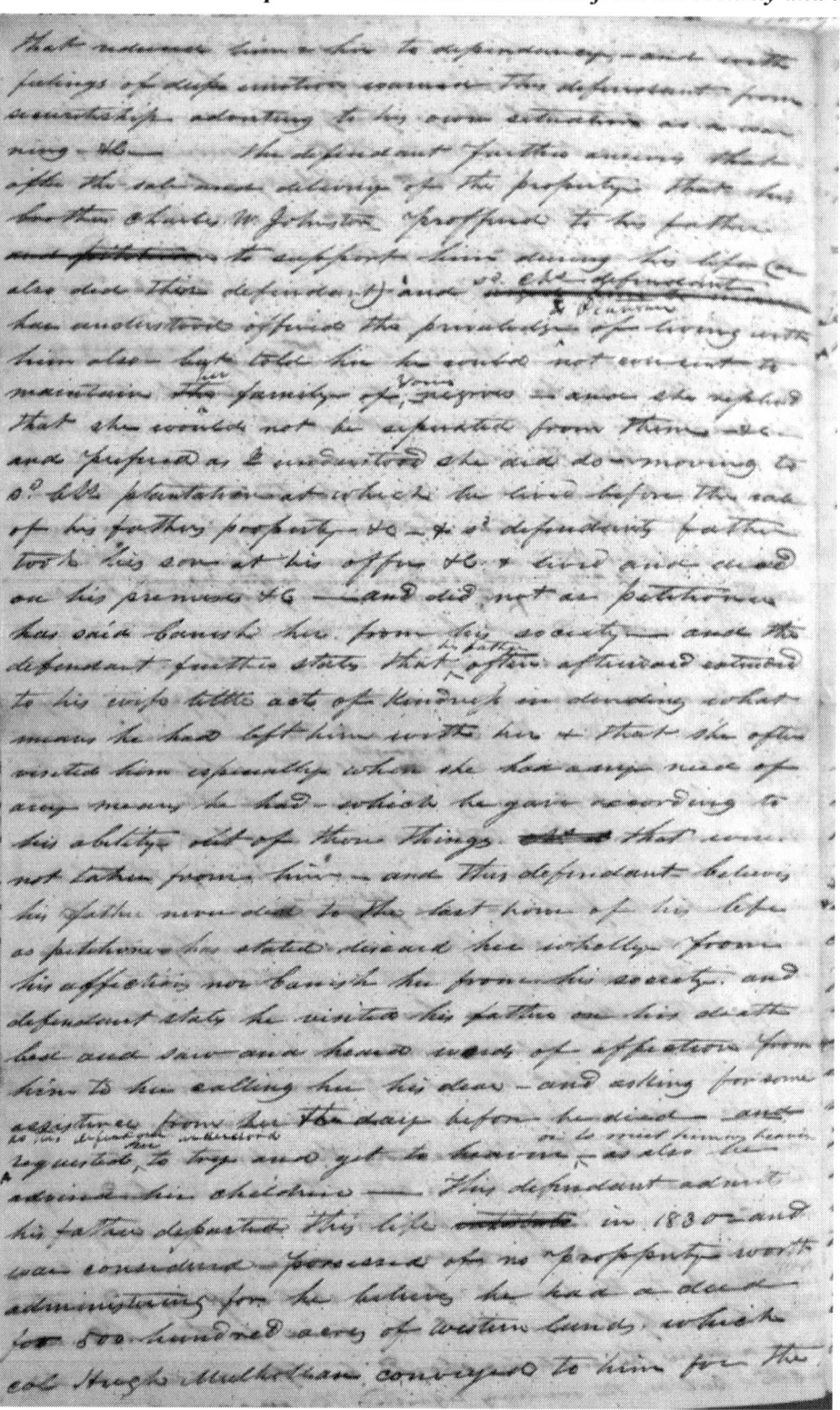

"...various considerations but defendant having often understood the land was not valuable and had often been sold for the taxes – did not consider it worth anything to him or not worth trouble himself about which deed is still with his father's old papers as he understands – and this defendant denying all fraud on his part and so far as he believes on the part of said deed and his brothers and sisters ..."

AT THE BOTTOM

"The defendant further answer that he entered into matrimony in the year 1823 with his present wife and in the year 1824 sold his land as conveyed in 1821 to his brother-in-law William Duskin in the year 1824 – and defendant having been informed by other defendants father that he intended dividing his western land lying in the county of Haywood in the state of Tennessee and on the waters of Hatchy River containing 2500 acres between all of his children reserving for himself and wife one childs part. This defendant having determined to move to Tennessee in 1824 – his father determined to have a division of said land and gave him ??? respective shares which he did as soon as he got Col Mulhollan to attend and in this conveyance he conveyed also the part Wm. Duskin and his wife Mary Drew – which I have part of the tract of land conveyed to me in 1821 for defendants father convened at same time each legated respective share and reserved to himself and wife an equal share among the children – all of which was done in good faith and without the least intention of fraud or depriving petitioner of her dower share as reserved as aforesaid to his brother George (cont.)..."

"...for such consideration as was satisfactory to both parties and in good faith and without any as defendant believes intention of fraud or of depriving her of her dower etc..."

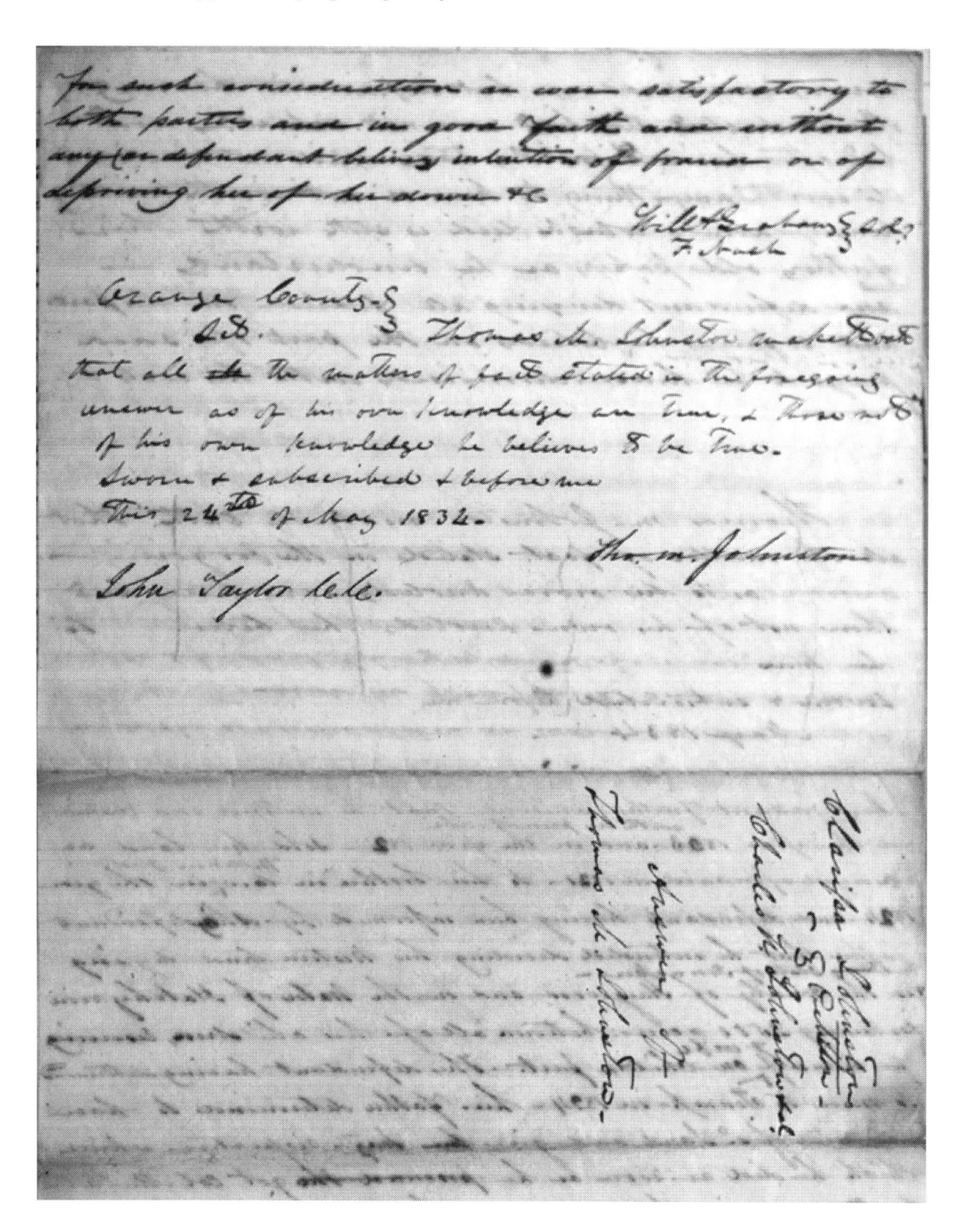

Deposition of Andrew Burns

"…*Question by Charles – Have you long been acquainted with my father? – I have. Q – What has been the conduct and character of my father from your first acquaintance with him until his death? – He was always esteemed as an honest and upright character. Q – What do you know of the division of my father's made of his land amongst his children and did he reserve a portion for himself and wife?* – That on a visit with your father the time not recollected, your father told me that he had divided his lands amongst his children that deeds of conveyance had been written, and that he had signed them, but had not as yet given them over to his children and that he had also reserved a portion of his home tract to himself and wife stating that in this reservation the new barn, old store house, and corn crib was reserved and a part of the garden and spring being made a corner for the purpose as he said, that his son George should not be deprived of the use of water – as he expected him to settle at or near the new store house. *Q – Did he state anything to you about any other reservation?* – That he had reserved a lot of western lands for himself and wife. (cont.)…"

"…Q – *Do you know what was the cause of my father taken up his meadow with me after the sale of his property?* – Your father told me he resided with your, on account of his age and infirmities that his wife was but a woman, that he required frequent lifting about and steadying and that there was no person more suitable to perform these things than Charles…Andrew Burns.

Deposition of Alexander Gattis

"…*What do you know about the division of lands my father made amongst his children and of the reservation he made for himself and wife?* – On a visit to your fathers shortly after the transaction as he said, I was informed by him that he had divided his lands amongst his children and that he had reserved for himself and wife the home plantation and the barn, cabin tract making inclusive upwards of four hundred acres. Q – *From the knowledge of my father's lands and the division he made amongst his children, was the reservation he made for himself and wife as valuable as any of those he allotted to his children?* – I think a great deal more so, as it included the principle buildings and orchard and the principle part of the meadows. Q – *If this reservation was so valuable why did it not sell for more money?* – I do not know if I must give an opinion it was a sheriff stale and no one could be compelled to bid. Q – *What was the state of my father's health when this conversation took place about the division of land?* - His health was bad, he had gotten a fall, that materially injured him during the remainder of his life. Q- *Did prudence require from the then state of his health, that some arrangement of his property should be made?* – I think it did. Q- *Was the conversations frequent and did he ever manifest any disposition to exclude his wife from this plans?* - Our conversations were frequent, and she was always included in his plans with himself. Q – *Was this reservation so said to be made sufficient to sustain them in this then character?*(cont.)…"

"…character? – I think it was amply sufficient. Q – <u>Was not this property afterwards sold for currency debt?</u> – I think it was. I saw the sheriff advertisement stating to satisfy executors ??? C. May, Henderson, Col Hugh Mulhollan and Geo Johnston for which Geo Johnston said he was seventy. Q – <u>Was it in my father's person from his age and infirmities ???the sale of his property?</u> – I think it was not, as he told me after I had saw the advertisement and asked him if it would come to a sale – that it would not be in his power to prevent it that he had not the money and that his infirmities prevented him from making sufficient expectations to get it. Q – <u>From your knowledge of my father and of the whole transaction, do you believe he had any desire to deprive his wife of her life estate in his property?</u> – I have no such knowledge and believe it was his misfortune. Q – <u>Did not this division of his land take place long before there was any intimation of the sale of his property by the sheriff – and did he not take up his residence with me after the sale of his property by the sheriff?</u> – The division of the land took place long before and he took up his residence with your after the sale of his property by the sheriff. Q – <u>Is it the fact that my father ??? his affections from his wife and banished her from his society?</u> – Not to my knowledge. Q – <u>Do you know the reason why I am not living where I am or the reason why my husband and myself live apart when he died and for sometime before?</u> – I know no reason. Q – <u>Do you know that I was the cause of the above transaction?</u> – I do not. Q – <u>Did my father ever make any conveyance of any other property?</u> – Not to my knowledge. Q – <u>Did he ever manifest any partiality towards me as ??? his property, above his other children?</u> No. Q - <u>Do you think that it was my power to have paid the said security debts without the use of the property that was sold by the sheriff?</u> – I think not. Q – <u>Did not my father aid and assist the petitioner</u> (cont.)…"

"...*to the almost of his resources until his death?* – My impression at present is that he did. – Alexander Gattis."

Deposition of Archibald Brockwell

"…*That some time in the year 1826 I went to Mr. Johnston, he was not at the house but at the spring. I went to the spring and found him easting a piece of bread ??? a conversation took place between us in which he told me he had divided his lands amongst his children, and reserved for himself and wife a part of his home place – showed me the lines running through the garden to the spring where he said he had made a corner, so that his son George should not be prevented from the use of water, he said he knew not how long he should live and his wife was sometimes contrary. His design was that one family should not have in their power to deprive the other from the use of water. Q – Do you no know from circumstances that the petitioner had declared her right to this separation so described which was never relinquished until the sale of the property? – I do from this circumstance, I was at your fathers one morning (being hired to work) I found Mr. and Mrs. Johnston at cross questions, in their course of their sparring – Mrs. Johnston said she would go that day and sell her right to that land. Mr. Johnston observed that she could not sell the land while he lived. Mrs. Johnston then remarked that she wished his head then six feet under the clods, as far beneath as it was then above, so that she might lay down Mistress and rise up Master. Q – Do you know any cause why I bought 17 ½ acres of land of my father over the creek? – I heard your father say that the reason he sold you 17 ½ acres over the creek was to preserve your mills, the situation of land being such that he owner of the land could by a canal drain (cont.)*…"

"…your mill pond at pleasure. Q – Was it not the rumor of the neighborhood that after the death of my father she would sell the aforesaid land for the aforesaid purpose? – It was the rumor in the neighborhood. Q – Did you ever hear any conversation with my father respecting the aforesaid state of his property to the sheriff? – I was in the habit of going once a week to ??? Mr. Johnston I think it was in the year 1828 whilst at his house I told your father what little property that had been sold for debt, will he said Archie I heard of it but it was out of my power to help it for I am in the same situation myself unless Col Mulhollan and May Henderson should come forward and ?ltion me, my property will go the same way. But if he could work fifteen years of his life, he thought he might get through with it, but with his present infirmities there was no chance for him. This communication was made with much failing stating at the same time that he did not know whether any of his children at the time were able to buy the property and was afraid that himself and wife would be left without a home in their old age. Q – Who was the purchaser of the property at the sheriff's sale? – Thomas George, Charles Johnston, and Gray Huckabee. Q – Did you hear any proposition made by me after sale of the property to my father and stepmother? – Whilst I was at your fathers you came one evening and told him that you had taken the whole debt on yourself and would keep the property and that he need not be uneasy for there was a home for him his life time and your mother also, provided you will stay and live in (cont.)…"

"...peace. But that you could not raise her negroes without an interest in them and would not. She then replied curse me Charles if I care, for I think as much of my negroes as I do of you, your father or any of your and when they go I will go also, for John Minor has land enough for me and my negroes my live time. Charles then walked to the door apparently hurt in his feelings and his father hobbled after him, and said Charles this is not your mother, but she is my wife, cannot your provide for her as long as I live? Charles then observed you have heard the proposition I have made…." Archibald Brockwell.

Deposition of Daniel Booker

"…*Store House on Charles W. Johnston's plantation on the 8th July 1834…Q – <u>What do your know Mr. Booker concerning the disposition that my father made of his property and the reservation he made for himself and Clarisa Johnston the present petitioner?</u> – I think it was in the month of Feb 1826 that I went to the house of Mr. George Johnston and after spending a day or so with him and his family he told me in conversation that he had divided his land between his children and after giving all a portion he had reserved about 260 or 270 acres for himself and wife. He was particular to show a part of the boundary line of this reservation – that it divided a two acre garden and cornered in the center of the spring stating at the same time that as his wife at times was disposed to be contrary and contentious, he had thought it best to make the right of the spring equal with his son George, (to whom he had given an adjoining tract of land) (cont.)…*"

"…land so that each (that is his wife, and George) might have equal privilege to the water, as it was the only good water near to the settlement on said lot. Q – *Did this reservation contain any valuable improvements?* – It contained the new barn, and home mill distillery all the meadows, together with the dwelling house. Q – *Was this reservation as valuable as any other lot given to his children?* – I think that at that time the most valuable. Q – *Were you acquainted with my father and his character – and was the reservation sufficient to sustain him in that character?* – His character was that of an honest and upright man that he made ample provision for his family and I think the reservation so made was amply sufficient to sustain him in that character. Q – *Was there any other reservation of land besides this you have detailed?* – There was, he said, another tract of land he called the Burnt Cabin tract, but it was not large enough for my purposes as I informed old Mr. Johnston I wanted to purchase land in this neighborhood ….Daniel Booker.

Deposition of Joseph Kirkland

"…question by Charles W. Johnston as follows – *What do you know respecting a division of my father's land* – A. - …that he had dividing his lands amongst his children and that he had reserved a portion for himself and wife and that for plan of accident he had made a corner in the center of the spring – and that he had reserved a part of the garden (cont.)…"

"...*Question by Charles – from what your know of the reservation alluded to to wit supply sufficient to sustain them or not?* – I think that it was amply sufficient to sustain them in their then character. This deponent further states that ??? all the conversations that he ever had with old Mr. Johnston which was very frequent of an unrestrained and ??? character that he Mr. Johnston was very anxious expressed anything like a disaster to deprive his wife from the enjoyment of an ample sustenance, that she was always included in the plan of his domestic arrangements of himself – her name always being mentioned with his when on the subject of the reservation. *Q- Was he in debt at the time when he made or when this conversation took place on the subject of this reservation?* – I think not. He Mr. Johnston was a man that always kept clean of debt so far as I know, and if he had been in debt I think he would have told me, for we were intimately and our conversation frequent. *Q - Do you not know from the fact that my father received a very dangerous fall from a fence that his life was in despaired of – and from his age and infirmities, that it was necessary for him to make a distribution of his property at this time he did so ?* – I think that it was, as his life was despaired of...Joseph Kirkland..."

Deposition of Thomas D. Watt

"…Q – Have you any knowledge of my father's dividing his lands amongst his children and reserving for himself and wife a portion of the same? – I have that in frequent conversations with Mr. Johnston long before there was any intimation of any danger from any Bank of his being security for Maj. Henderson and Col Mulhollan, Mr. Johnston told him that he had allotted his lands amongst his children and had reserved for himself and wife his home lace and that these conversations took place in the years 1823, 1824 or 1825 and that the conversations might have occurred in all of these years – as he frequently called on Mr. Johnston in his travels through the county. Q – Was not this property so said to be reserved by my father sold by you at Sheriff for security debts? – That is was. Q – Was any part of my father's property sold by you for any debts but for security debts? – I think not. Q – Do you believe that it was in my father's power to prevent the sale of his property or his ?? resources? – He told me it was not and from what he told me think not – he manifested much failing on account of his situation, shed tears, and said it was hard that he should be deprived of a home in his old days. Q – Did you or sheriff sell all the aforesaid reservations of lands and personal property that my father then possessed and what was the conduct of the petitioner on the day of the sale? – I did – that on the day of the sale of the personal property she the petitioner was active in showing me articles or items of property for sale particularly as to the household and kitchen furniture – and on the day the land and negroes went to be sold at the court house in Hillsboro after exposing the land for sale, according (cont.)…"

"...to persons instruct from Wm. H. Haywood the attorney for the State Bank, he informed him that the land was then under the hammer, and was about to be ??? and that the children of George Johnston were unable to purchase it without Bank accommodating as they stated to me – and William H. Haywood then asked me whether the children of Geo Johnston could secure the debt to the Bank, and he W. H. Haywood came out of the Court House and publicly declared that the Bank or he as agent of the Bank would purchase the land as the debts were not secured to the Bank – which was considered by me as sheriff as a bid for the lands to the amount of the bank debts. I as sheriff then vouched that the children of Geo Johnston would secure the debts, the property being still expounded for sale, and after publicly and fairly expounding the lands for some length of time it was bid off by Charles W. Johnston one of the defendants. There being some other person who also bid for the lands besides the said Charles. Q – <u>Was not the whole transaction conducted with fairness and publicity?</u> – It was as much so as any I ever made in my life and to my knowledge there was nothing like fraud manifested from beginning to end. The deponent further states that had the property been forced into market his impression was that without Bank accommodations it would not brought anything like the Bank debts....Thomas D. Watts.

Deposition of William Duskin

The information in this series of papers contain more of the same story. I will include only new information for this account. The beginning part of this letter discusses the same issue as Thomas Johnston had mentioned in selling land to Duskin.

"...he now recollects that at May Term 1828 judgments were attained and for which executions issued…Mulhollan…Henderson for their debts due the State and Cape Fear Banks…was bound or security in common with Samuel Morgan as security for Maj Henderson…Thomas D. Watts sheriff of Orange County and sold by him…this defendant further declares that until the knowledge of the failure of said Henderson and Mulhollan became manifest that there was no appearance of alarm or disquiet by said George Johnston or petitioner…about this time had frequent interviews and conversations with his said father-in-law and that almost on every occasion that he was present with him he appeared to be dissatisfied and lamented the apprehension of his becoming dependant fearing that it would take all his property to pay… (cont.)…"

Nothing new being stated here.

"…destitute of a home and that this destitution was by no means intentionally as set forth in the petition premeditated but was occasioned by circumstances entirely beyond the control of the said George Johnston and defendant further declares that the said Charles W. Johnston moved to the homestead place his father being in a helpless situation and offered to support and take care of his father during his life and has always understood and believes that the said Charles proffered [preferred ?] also to support and take care of the petitioner if she would stay in peace but that the said Charles could not support and raise the negroes of the petitioner without an interest in them to this proposition defendant has always understood the petitioner violently objected to and knows that she abandoned the society of her husband the said George Johnston and took up her said residence on that lot of land conveyed to the said Charles W. Johnston. Defendant declares as far as he knows and believes that at this time the petitioner became the most hostile and notwithstanding the said Geo Johnston manifested feelings of friendship and tenderness to said petitioner in giving her his last remains of property and consulting for her comfort in every particular that he could possibly affect to command this defendant further declares the petitioner at times visited her husband and defendant has frequently observed a manifestation of affection and kindness on the part of said George Johnston to the petitioner – and defendant further declares that to the last apparent sensible moments of his said father-in-laws life he manifested tokens of affectionate kindness to the petitioner and defendant verily believes that his father-in-law had no desire or intention that the petitioner should be left destitute at his death…"

Appendix C – Charles W. Johnston Estate Papers

This estate filing was not as controversial as Charles had to face with his dad. The main reason it is included is the super plats included in this collection. They are very helpful with the transition of this very large estate of George Johnston Sr. to the 21st century.

Total content of all the Lots   675 acres

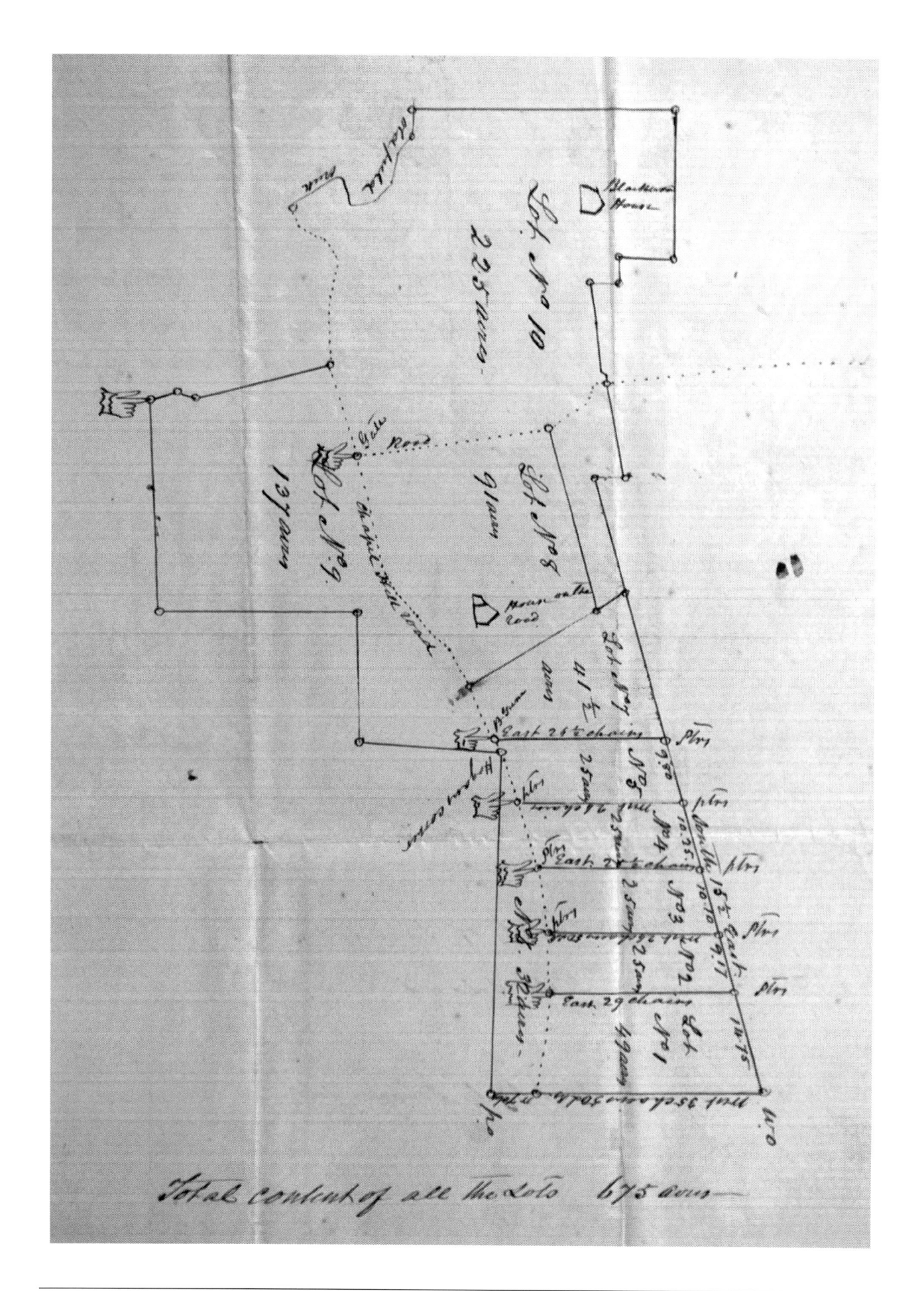

State of North Carolina } County Court
Orange County } February Term 1855

To the Worshipful the Justices of the Court of Pleas and Quarter Sessions for the County of Orange

The Petition of John C. Johnston, Thomas Johnston, Daniel W. Kerr & Martha his wife, Paschal P. Burt and Moriah his wife, George W. Jones and Dana his wife and Margaret L. Johnston a minor who sues by her Guardian said Jones

Respectfully sheweth unto your Worships that Charles W Johnston late of the County of Orange departed this life on the 27th day of January, at his residence in said County having first made his last Will & Testament duly executed to pass both his real and personal estate which was duly proved at the present Term of Orange County Court and all the executors therein named having released their right to qualify as such Letters of administration were granted with the Will annexed to your Petitioner George W. Jones who has accepted the said Office. Your Petitioners shew that the said Will among other dispositions therein contained left all his Slaves with the exception of such as he had by the Will given for life to his wife to be equally divided among your Petitioners John C. Johnston Thomas Johnston Martha married to Daniel W Kerr, Moriah married to Paschal P. Burt, Dana married to George W Jones and Margaret L. Johnston and including such Slaves also as he had previously put into possession of his married daughters they to retain such at valuation in the division if they chose to do so.

And your Petitioners shew that the said negroes are not necessary for the payment of the debts and expenses of the estate and the administrator has assented to the legacy of the same to your Petitioners, whereby they have become tenants in common of them; and to the end that they may be divided so that each one of the legatees may hold his or her share of the Slaves in severalty: May it please your Worships to appoint three Commissioners who shall divide the said Slaves among them according to Law.

J. W. Norwood
Atto for Petitioners

This Case coming on to be heard upon the Petition and the whole matter having been considered by the Court it is ordered that Thomas Hogan, James C. Surrontine and James N. Patterson be appointed Commissioners to divide and allot the Slaves mentioned and described in the Petition among the Petitioners after having first been duly sworn under their hands and Seals and Report to the next Term of this Court. The said division to be made according to the Will of said Charles W. Johnston as set forth in this petition. The Clerk of the Court will issue to said Commissioners a copy of the Petition and also of the Will with this Commission.

In the name of God Amen! I Charles W. Johnston being of sound and disposing mind and memory do make and publish this to be my last Will and Testament revoking all others.

Item 1st. I desire all my just debts to be paid.

Item 2nd. I give to my beloved wife Lydia during her natural life, time or widowhood my Homestead plantation including my Mill and that part of the burnt Cabin tract lying west of a line beginning at Mr. Duckin's South West corner and running South to Stie Kerras line and excluding about twenty five Acres known as the Moccasin Meadow said Homestead supposed to contain about one Thousand Acres. The following Slaves viz: Primus and his wife Charity, Madison and his wife Mary and their child, David & his wife Phoebe and their child and Matthew. Four Mules her choice — ten head of Cattle her choice, my Carriage & Carriage horses. 50 head of Sheep her choice my best Waggon and waggon gear — twenty five hogs her choice all such farming utensils as she may select as necessary to carry on her farm. All my household and Kitchen furniture.

Item 3rd. I give to my son Charles W. Johnston on the death of his Mother all the property both real and personal which by my Item 2nd. I have willed to my wife Lydia, my watch a horse worth one hundred dollars and a good saddle & bridle.

Item 4th. I give to my Son John C. Johnston my road Plantation containing seven hundred acres and the Moccasin Meadow containing about twenty five acres, and the Blackwood tract containing about seventy five acres my horse Jim my saddle & bridle

Item 5th I give to my son Thomas the tract of land I bought of Mr. Duskins and that part of the Burnt Cabin tract lying East of a line beginning at Mr. Duskins' South West corner and running South to Hortt Timms line, one horse with one hundred dollars and a good saddle and bridle

Item 6th I give to my sons John C. Johnston and Thomas Johnston and my daughters Martha S. Kerr Moriah P. Burt Dena C. Jones and Margaret L. Johnston all my slaves now living to be equally divided between them, and as I have advanced to my daughters married daughters some slaves it is my desire that all such slaves now living shall be considered a portion of my estate and to be valued with the other slaves in the division but my said married daughters are to have the privilege of holding the slaves now in their possession as a part of their distributive share in said slaves

Item 7th I desire my stock in the North Carolina Central Rail Road to be equally divided among my wife and children

Item 8th I give my negro girl Rachael to my wife Lydia during her life time her and her increase if any to be equally divided among all my children at her death —

Item 9th I desire my personal estate not otherwise disposed of in this Will to be sold by my Executors and equally divided among all my children

Item 10th I appoint David W Kerr guardian for my son's Thomas and Charles

I nominate and appoint my son John and my sons in law David W Kerr Rosebud P Burt and George W Jones Executors of this my last Will and Testament upon the condition that they will settle the Estate without charge for their services as Executors and if they refuse to act without compensation I nominate and appoint my friend John U Kirkland of Hillsbrough my Executor

In Testimony whereof I have hereunto set my hand and

State of North Carolina }
Orange County } Court of Pleas & Quarter Sessions
                  February Term 1855

John C. Johnston & others }
        Exparte   } Petition to divide Slaves

In pursuance to the annexed Commission appointing the undersigned Commissioners at February Term 1855, to divide and allott the Slaves mentioned and described in the petition among the petitioners according to the Will of Charles W. Johnston dec'd. the undersigned after having been duly sworn according to law have proceeded to divide the Slaves as nearly coequally as possible, and allott to each of the petitioners their share in severalty as follows. To Wit. To Miss Margaret C. Johnston Lot No. 1. the Slaves Emaline, Jack, Buck, Horace, Anthony & Anna.— To Thomas W. Johnston Lot No. 2. the Slaves Kerabe, Ellen, Martin, Bob, Virgil, Dinah, & Jane;— To John C. Johnston Lot No. 3. the Slaves Abner, Patsey, Hanny, Lin, Dennis, Julia & Caroline;— To David W. Kerr Lot No. 4. the Slaves Piety, Wilson, David, Nelson, Tabitha, & Lucy;— To Paschal B. Burt Lot No. 5. the Slaves Mahala, Ben, Alexander, Simon, Hannah & child Lewis;— To George W. Jones Lot No. 6. the Slaves Mariah and child Sizzy, Sam, Henry, Solomon & Sarah; and that Lot No. 4. David W. Kerr pay to Lot No. 2 Thomas W. Johnston Twenty five Dollars.— That Lot No. 5 Paschal B. Burt pay to Lot No. 2. Thomas W. Johnston Twenty five Dollars;— That Lot No. 6. George W. Jones pay to Lot No. 3 John C. Johnston Twenty five Dollars—

State of North Carolina
Orange County

This Plat represents a part of the Lands of John C. Johnston dec'd. Bounded as follows. Beginning at a stake on the Chapel Hill road at a Gate running thence with the road North 80½ degrees East 29 chains 70 Links to a stake on the south side of said road, thence South 15½ degrees East 27 chains 90 Links to pointers on the west side of the new road, thence North 58¼ degrees East 5 Chains to pointers, thence North 15½ degrees West 18 chains 35 Links to a stake, thence East 4 chains 75 Links to a stake, thence South 11 degrees West 14 chains 60 Links to a rock in the Lane on the East side of the Morasin meadow, thence North 50 L's to an Apple tree, thence North 57 West 1¼ chain to a stake, thence North 21¼ degrees West 1 Chain 90 Links to a Mulberry, thence North 2½ degrees West 6½ chains to a sweet Gum, thence North 12 degrees West 5 Chains to a stake on the line of the Blackwood tract, thence East with the same 4 ch. 50 L's to a stake, thence North 3¾ chains to a stake, thence East 8 chains 25 Links to a stake, thence North 2 ch, 75 Links to a Black Gum, Robson's Corner, thence West 40 chains to a stake on the West bank of the Old field Creek on Pruden's Old line, thence his line south 4 ch, 75 Links to a stake on the Bank of the Creek, thence up the creek to the Chapell Hill road & South ward with the road to the beginning, Containing by Survey 225 acres.

Surveyd April 10th 1857.

H. W. Jassey S.O.
Charles Johnston / Ch. Car.

Lot. No 10
225 acres

Lot No 10

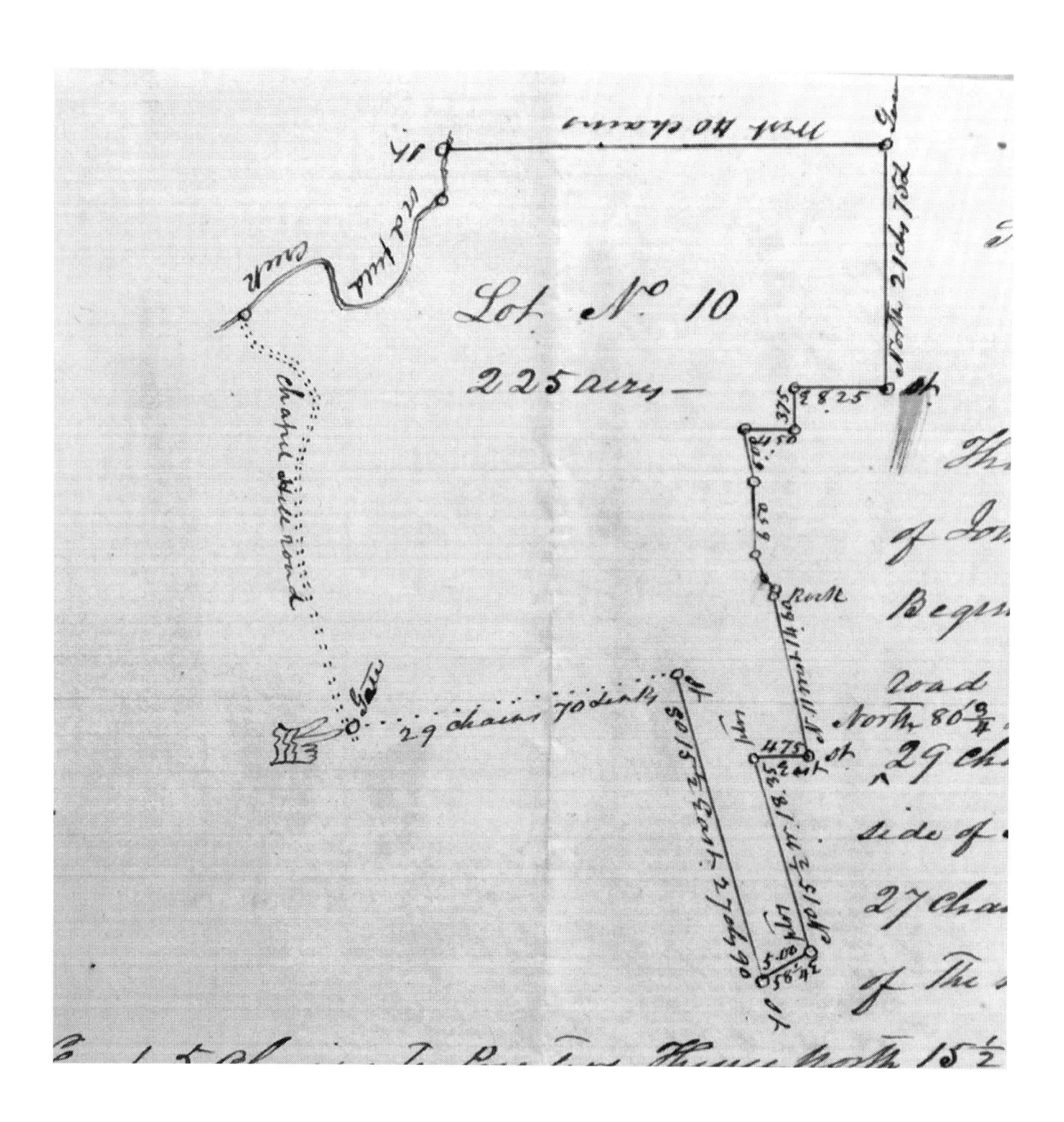

225 acres

chapel hill road

29 chains 70 links

State of North Carolina
Orange County

This Plat represents Lot N° 6 of
the Lands of John C Johnston Dec'd Lying between N.I. Hogans
Line & the Chapel line and Bounded as follows. Beginning
at Bunters on the East side of the road & Hogans corner
running thence South with his line to his corner containing
South in all 51 chains 75 links to a post oak. Thence East
7 chains to the center of the road. Thence North west with the
road to the beginning containing by survey 32 acres —

H.P. Sennett
Charles Johnston   G Anderson

State of North Carolina
Orange County

This Plat represents Lot No 7.
of the Lands of J. C. Stanton dec'd. Bounded
on the west by the Chapel Hill road, Beginning
at a Black Gum on the East side of the Chapel Hill road 18 chs
Northward from R. I. Hogan's corner on the road, running thence East 26 chs
50 links to Pinter's, thence North 13½ degrees west 23 chains to Pinter's, thence
South 38½ West 28 chains 35 links to a stake in the road at the corner of a field
thence Southward with the Chapel Hill road to the beginning Containing by survey
41½ acres Surveyed 11th April 1857 —
A. N. Parnes &
Charles Stanton } Chain carriers

J. M. Link Surveyor

State of North Carolina
Orange County

This plat represents Lot No 8 of the lands of John C. Johnston dec'd. in the city [?]
The six boundaries thereof C.W. Johnston dec'd.
Bounded as follows. Beginning at a stake in the Chapel Hill road, at a late survey, thence with the road North 80¾ East 29 chs. 70 links to a stake a corner of Lot No 10.

Thence South 15½ degrees East, 27 chains 90 links to pointers, on the west side of the new road. Thence South 58½ West 23 chs. 35 links to a stake in the centre of the Chapel Hill road. Thence northward with the chapel Hill road to the beginning, Containing by Survey 91 acres — Surveyed 9th [?] 1857.

H. W. Farrar }
Charles Johnston } S. Hogan S. O. Surveyor

Scale 20 chains to an inch

North 80 3 East 29 chs 70 lk
South 15½ East 27.90 pointers
Lot No 8.
91 acres
Chapel Hill road
South 58½ West 23 chs 35 lk

Scale 20 chains to an Inch

This Plat represents a part of the Lands of John C. Johnston dec'd being Lot No 9 as laid out lying West of the Chapel Hill road adjoining Wm J. Hogan & Prof. Shipp. Bounded as follows Beginning at a stake on Hogans line, where a road crosses Old field creek, Shipps corner running thence Shipps line North 77 degrees East 3 ch. 90 links to a White Oak, thence his line South 72½ degrees East 3 chains 70 links to pointers, thence North 74 degrees East 20 4/ chains to a stake in the centre of the Chapel Hill road thence Southward with the road to pointers W J Hogan's corner, thence his line North 85 degrees West 22 chains to a stake, thence North 79½ chains to a White Oak, thence West Hogan's line 29 ch. 50 lks. to pointers his corner thence his line North 29 chains 70 links to the Beginning Containing by survey 137 acres —

A. H. James &
Charles Johnston / C. h. Cor.

J. M. Link Sur.

References and Notes

What was NOT found:

- The NC Archives did not have any Johnston/Johnson family papers in personal collections related to the Orange Co. family. Same goes for Robson/Robeson.

- Orange Co., Deed Office – I was hoping to find plats. I saw a number of references to the land being divided up in 1916 and that each lot was surveyed. I searched the Plat Book and looked for anything that was related. I found a few items and are included here.

- The Southern Historical Collection (UNC) – had some 186x letters from Thomas Johnston from his Alabama home, and from the catalog it looked as the topics were related to life in AL. Nothing on the Robson/Robeson family for this area. I looked into Blackwood and didn't find anything that was old enough.

- I re-reviewed the Orange Co., Court Minutes looking for Robson/Robeson and Nothing. I re-reviewed the records for Johnston. Nothing new, and mostly court attendance. I also looked for Johnston's petition for his saw mill and did not locate anything in 1819 to 1821 minutes. This was the actual book, not copies/transcripts.

- I did NOT find anything with Orange Co., Bridge Records that list specifics on a bridge by Johnston's mill. There is a reference to his mill in an 1809 petition for a road. But the description of the route (the road was to follow) was too general to locate where it was running.

- I read the Hillsborough Recorder newspapers for the 1820 year and then browsed them during the law suite time frame. Nothing was found. However, I did find the "Legal Notice" on Edward Robson on the microfilm.

- I re-reviewed the court records on microfilm and did not find any other William Robson or George Johnston (SR or JR) listed. I looked in 1819, 1820, 1823, and 1825.

- Orange County Marriage records and bonds did not show William and Ann Robson's marriage. I only found one female of the three listed in the 1840 census in marriage records. By 1860 there weren't any more females at home, and 1850 remains a mystery.

References

- *Civil War M230 roll 34* – for Milton B. Robson
- *The Millers, Millwright's and Engineers Guide* – Henry Pallett (1866)
- *Rudimentary Treatise on the Power of Water* – Joseph Glynn F.R.S. (1853)
- *Water Rights Determination – From an engineering Standpoint* – Whitmam (1918)
- *The Young Mill-Wright and Miller's Guide* – Oliver Evans (1860)
- *Construction of Mill Dams and Millwright and Mechanic* – Leffel (1881)
- *Treatise on Mills and Millworks – Construction and arrangement of Mills* – Fairbairn (1871)
- *The Practical American Millwright and Miller* – Craik (1870)
- *Death and Marriage Records in the Hillsborough Recorder* – Shirley Jones Mallard
- *Orange County Deed Records*
- *Historical Overview of Road, Bridges, Ferry and Mills* – Stewart Dunaway
- *Orange County, N.C. - Mill Petitions* – Stewart Dunaway
- *Orange County Road Records – V1, V2, V3* – Stewart Dunaway
- *Orange County Bridge Records* – Stewart Dunaway
- *Freedmen's Marriage Records* – (Negro Cohabitation Certificates) – Shirley Jones Mallard
- *Abstracts from Newspapers of Edenton, Fayetteville, Hillsborough (1785-1800)* – Raymond Parker Fouts (nothing listed for Robson)
- *The Complete History of Thomas Burke* – (ISBN 978-1-4357-1925-5) Stewart E. Dunaway

Index

Adams 92
Agnew 157
Alabama 12, 251
allegiance 97
Allen 13, 113, 114, 157, 159, 169, 185
Allen line 159
Allens. 113, 157, 158, 159, 160, 169
Andrews 63, 168
Annie 219
apple tree 167
Ash 119, 162, 163, 164, 166
Atkins 95
Babs branch . 20, 120, 161, 162, 166
Babs Branch114, 119, 121, 122, 161, 162, 163, 165, 166, 167, 169
back water 88, 89, 91, 97
Backwood 86
Bank of the State of NC 219
Barbee 156, 158, 160
beach 91
Bevill 94, 156
Bevills 161
black gum 167
Blacknall 13, 113, 164, 169
Blackwood ... 7, 8, 9, 10, 13, 63, 73, 74, 85, 87, 88, 90, 91, 92, 97, 99, 100, 129, 141, 155, 157, 158, 159, 160, 161, 162, 163, 164, 165, 167, 168, 171, 192, 195, 198, 251
Blackwood's 157, 168
Blackwoods 158, 160, 161, 164, 165, 168
blood 218
Bolands Creek 159, 160
Bolins Creek 159

Bollings Creek 163
bolting cloth 21
Booth 130, 156, 158, 166
Booth Creek 156
Boothe 95, 156
Booths 158, 166
Borlins Creek 166
Borough 160, 161, 163
Boroughs73, 159, 160, 161, 165
Borrough 166
Borroughs 160, 163, 166
Bowers 90, 92, 100
Brashear Creek 200
Brashears Creek 198
breast bone 218
bricks 51
bridge22, 45, 57, 130, 167, 181, 183, 189, 251
British 97
Brockwell ... 87, 90, 92, 99, 100, 228, 230
Buffalo Creek 157, 195, 197, 200
Buffalo Creek's 200
Burch 156, 160, 161
Burch's 160
Burch's line 161
Burchs 161
Burke 7, 12, 99, 252
Burn 164, 165
Burns .. 159, 161, 163, 164, 165, 225, 226
Burnt Cabin . 163, 217, 218, 232
Buroughs 161, 162, 164
Burrough 162
Burroughs ... 62, 63, 73, 74, 155, 159, 160, 161, 162, 164, 165, 167, 168
Burt 167

Burton 63, 166
Cabbin's Old Field 156
Cabe 7, 105, 162, 164
Cabe Mill 105, 162
Cain 164
Caldwell 105, 162
Cape Fear Bank 210, 219
Carden 113, 169
Carden's 166
Carter 88, 89, 91, 160
Caswell .. 61, 63, 129, 141, 146, 157, 192, 194
Caswell County 61, 63
Cedar Fork 160
Chapel Hill 9, 156, 163, 165, 166, 167
Chapel Hill road 167
Chapel Hill Road 165
Chapel Road 160
chimney . 47, 51, 52, 57, 58, 59, 72
Civil War 108
Clarks 168
Cobb 159
Colby 157
Cole 113, 165, 169
Coles 169
Coman 9
concrete bridge road 189
Connally 159
Copley 87, 90, 92, 99, 165
Copley's old Mill seat 165
corn crib 225
Couch 13, 95, 113, 162, 163, 166, 167, 168, 169
Couch, ... 95, 163
Couch's 162, 166, 167
cough 218

253

country road 168
county road 112, 167
Courtney...13, 78, 80, 158, 159, 160, 186, 189
Courtney line 160
Courtney's line 158, 159
cowford 99
Cox 157
Craig) 165
Craigs 161
dam 87, 88, 89, 91
Dickson .13, 110, 111, 113, 169
dislocated 218
dogwood 91, 157, 158, 162, 163, 166, 167, 169
Dry Creek 156
Duke .6, 13, 14, 22, 45, 66, 110, 112, 113, 115, 121, 126, 127, 169
Duke Forest 14, 22
Durham .14, 112, 166, 168, 169
Durham road 168
Durham Road 168
Duskin 7, 155, 161, 162, 163, 164, 165, 166, 167, 172, 223, 236
elevation 89
Elizabeth 13, 162, 163, 165
England 61
Eno River 105, 162
Erwin Cotton Mill Corp .13, 14, 112, 113
Erwin Cotton Mill Corp. 112
fence 48, 55, 110, 113, 161, 162, 165, 169
Fiber Industries 9
First Creek 164
fixtures 110, 166, 167
Flintoff 61, 163, 164, 165
flour 21
flouring mill 21
ford 87, 88, 90

forks 157
foundation 23, 24, 25, 27, 29, 30, 32, 33, 48, 49, 51, 87
fraud 217, 223, 224, 235
Freeland 156, 158, 161, 164, 167, 170
Freelands 156, 165, 167, 168
Gappins 88, 89, 91
garden 161, 162, 225, 228, 231, 232
gate 165, 167, 169
Gattis 94, 161, 226, 228
George's Mill tract 159
Gov. Burkes 7
Gov. Thomas Burke 7, 12, 13
Graham 166
Granville 129, 141, 157
Granville Grant .. 157, 171, 195, 198, 201
Granville Land Grant .. 192, 194
Green Hill 8, 9, 129
Greene 10
grist mill. 21, 27, 105, 160, 162, 167
Guilford County 195, 198
gum 157, 160, 161, 162, 163, 164, 165, 166, 167, 168
Hall's corner 160
Hatchee River 105, 163
Hatchy River 223
Haw River 195, 198
Hawfield 8
Hawfields 7, 160
Hawks 90
Haywood 105, 163, 223, 235
Haywood County 105, 163
Henderson 64, 95, 159, 210, 215, 219, 220, 227, 229, 234, 236
Henderson's 159
Hephen's corner 165
Hightower 159

Hill 112
Hillsboro Road 158, 167, 168
Hillsborough 12, 14, 62, 110, 155, 165, 214, 219, 251, 252
Hillsborough Road 165
Hogan .61, 62, 63, 64, 149, 156, 161, 164, 165, 166, 167, 168, 170
Hogan's Bottom 149
Honeycutt 9
Hopkins 159
Huckabee..7, 12, 105, 108, 162, 163, 165, 211, 214, 229
Hutchins 95
iron 90
Jenkins.162, 164, 165, 166, 167
Johnston ...6, 13, 14, 16, 81, 87, 88, 89, 90, 92, 94, 97, 100, 110, 113
Johnston Mill6, 14, 16, 78, 128, 129, 170
Johnston Trust 154, 170
Kerr 167
King7, 108, 158, 162, 163, 164, 165, 166, 167, 201
Kirklands 167, 168
Land Conservatory ..6, 129, 170
Landan 219
Lawrence Drive 9
Leigh 95
Lessley 158
Lewis 95, 112
Lloyd 167
Lloyds 168
Lockharts 169
log cabin 8, 9
Long 160
Lower Mill Tract 110, 165
Lower Robson Mill Tract 113
Major Trice 169
malicious 97
Marcom 95

254

Markham 95

Marshall's Spring 168

Marshells spring branch 168

Mason Spring Branch 169

Mason's Spring 160, 165

Masons Spring 61, 114, 166, 167, 169

McAdams Creek 160

McCain 61, 62, 63

McCaulay 87

McCauley . 90, 92, 99, 155, 159

McLellan 158

McNair 8, 155, 157, 158

Mebane's 159

merchant . 13, 21, 105, 160, 162

merchant mill 13, 21, 160

Merchant Mill 14

Mill Creek 159

mill dam 81, 110, 162, 166

mill pond .. 6, 31, 35, 36, 38, 39, 41, 110, 113, 114, 130, 144, 146, 160, 163, 165, 166, 167, 169

mill race . 17, 27, 31, 32, 33, 36, 37, 39, 41, 76, 113, 124, 130, 134, 140, 143, 144, 145, 169

mill seat ... 6, 15, 44, 82, 83, 88, 89, 90, 92, 93, 110

mill yard 88

millerons 99

millseat 99

millstone 39

millwright 39, 87, 88

Millwrights 91

Millwrights and Engineers Guide 40

millyard 88

Minor 230

Moccosin Meadow 167

Moore 7, 160

Morgan 158, 159, 160, 164, 236

Morgan's 160

mouth ...38, 113, 114, 122, 160, 162, 163, 164, 165, 169

mulatto 62, 63, 69

Mulhollan ... 155, 210, 213, 215, 217, 218, 219, 220, 222, 223, 227, 229, 234, 236

Mulholland 7, 155, 163

Mulhollans 155

Mullholland 92

Murdock's Mill 160

National Bank 163

negroes 217, 219, 222, 230, 234, 238

Nelson 105, 162

Nevill's 159

Nevill's Mill 159

New Durham Road 169

New Hope 21, 82, 83, 87, 93, 94

New Hope Church 9

New Hope Creek 1, 6, 8, 13, 14, 17, 22, 24, 29, 31, 37, 57, 59, 61, 75, 76, 77, 78, 81, 82, 93, 94, 99, 110, 113, 114, 116, 125, 142, 146, 149, 153, 157, 163, 164, 165, 167, 169, 183, 185, 186, 189, 190, 201

Old Field Creek .. 129, 130, 131, 132, 140, 141, 145, 146, 153, 157, 158, 161, 164, 167, 168, 179, 201

old mill seat 165

old road ... 47, 77, 160, 162, 168

old roadbed .. 47, 49, 57, 60, 189

Orange County .7, 8, 12, 14, 19, 21, 62, 64, 73, 81, 95, 110, 111, 115, 154, 155, 156, 157, 160, 195, 198, 251, 252

Ordinary 57, 58

Pallett 40

Patterson 105, 156, 158, 159, 160, 161, 162, 164, 165, 166

Patterson's Mill 166

Pattersons 158, 162, 164

Pendergrass 63, 166

Perkins 168

Perry Co 12

persimmon 161, 162

Peterson 158

Phills Creek 64

pocket watch 7, 12, 13

pond 83, 93

Ponns creek 161

Ponns Creek 158, 161

poplar 89, 90, 92, 100

public mill road 166

race ... 25, 31, 32, 33, 34, 35, 36, 37, 38, 39, 40, 41, 77, 89, 110, 130, 140, 142, 144, 145, 146, 165, 167, 169

raceway .. 25, 28, 31, 39, 41, 42, 77, 78, 189, 190, 191

Rail Road 167

Raleigh 6, 9, 210, 219

Red House 8

Redmond Place 112

Reedy Fork 195, 198, 200

Reeves 95

Restoration Specialist 9

Revolutionary 10, 12, 61, 81, 97

Revolutionary War ... 10, 61, 81, 97

Rhoads 159

Robson ... 1, 2, 6, 13, 14, 15, 18, 21, 46, 47, 48, 61, 62, 63, 64, 65, 66, 67, 68, 69, 71, 72, 73, 76, 80, 81, 82, 84, 86, 87, 88, 89, 90, 91, 92, 93, 94, 95, 97, 100, 103, 104, 105, 108, 109, 110, 112, 113, 114, 117, 118, 119, 122, 125, 127, 130, 146, 160, 161, 162, 163, 164, 165, 166, 167, 169, 172, 251, 252

Robson Homestead Place ... 166

Robson Mill 14, 18, 91, 112, 113

Robson Mill pond 162

Robson's Mill 6, 91

rock pile 110, 165, 166, 167

255

rock-dam 40
Royal Oak 61
Ruffin 10, 81, 90, 92, 97, 99
sassafras 157, 160
saw mill .. 13, 73, 74, 76, 77, 78, 87, 89, 90, 91, 92, 100, 130, 158, 159, 251
Sharp 13, 110
Shelton 63
Shepard 95
sheriff 83, 94, 163, 166
Sheriff . 155, 163, 165, 211, 234
Sloan 7
Spanish oak 110, 113, 163, 164, 166, 169
Spanish Oak 105, 162
spring 61, 112, 113, 114, 116, 125, 159, 161, 162, 165, 167, 169, 225, 228, 231, 232
spring branch 61, 113, 114, 161, 162, 165, 167, 169
Squire Robson 62, 69
St. Mathews 157
State Land Grant 201
stone pile 161, 162, 164, 165, 166
Stone pile 165
Stoney Creek 156

Store House 231
Strain 157
Strains 161
Strayhorns 159, 160, 163
stream 83, 91, 93
Stroud 157
Strouds 168
Superior Court 90, 95, 100
Tate 13, 110, 111, 129, 165, 167, 169
Tavern 58
Tennessee 100, 105, 223
till hammer 81, 82
tilt hammer 93
Timman 113
Trice ... 113, 156, 161, 164, 165, 169
Trice's 163
Trices 164
Turkey Farm Road 6, 16, 76, 78, 128, 129, 132, 134, 150, 152, 154, 156, 181, 183
Turrentine 165
UNC library 99
University Rd 168
University Road 167, 168
Upper Mill 113

Vickers 165
violently 238
volume 39
Walkers 168
Walson's 165
Watt 211, 234
Watts 163, 235, 236
Weaver 168
Webb 99, 113, 166, 167, 170
Weitzel's Mill 198
Whitfield road 8
Whitteds 168
Wilkens 169
Wilkins 169
Wood 88
Wooden Bridge Road 22, 47, 48, 57, 60, 72
Woods 89, 92
Yeargain's 159
Yeargans 160, 168
Young 13, 39, 114, 157, 158, 160
Youngs 157, 158
Zacheus 160
Zachias 163

Made in the USA
Lexington, KY
21 May 2014